HERE COMES...
DAREDEVIL

DAREDEVIL BY MARK WAID VOL. 1. Contains material originally published in magazine form as DAREDEVIL #1-6. First printing 2012. Hardcover ISBN# 978-0-7851-5237-8. Softcover ISBN# 978-0-7851-5238-5. Published by MARVEL WORLDWIDE, INC., a subsidiary of MARVEL ENTERTAINMENT, LLC. OFFICE OF PUBLICATION: 135 West 50th Street, New York, NY 10020. Copyright © 2011 and 2012 Marvel Characters, Inc. All rights reserved. Hardcover: $19.99 per copy in the U.S. and $21.99 in Canada (GST #R127032852). Softcover: $15.99 per copy in the U.S. and $17.99 in Canada (GST #R127032852). Canadian Agreement #40668537. All characters featured in this issue and the distinctive names and likenesses thereof, and all related indicia are trademarks of Marvel Characters, Inc. No similarity between any of the names, characters, persons, and/or institutions in this magazine with those of any living or dead person or institution is intended, and any such similarity which may exist is purely coincidental. **Printed in the U.S.A.** ALAN FINE, EVP - Office of the President, Marvel Worldwide, Inc. and EVP & CMO Marvel Characters B.V.; DAN BUCKLEY, Publisher & President - Print, Animation & Digital Divisions; JOE QUESADA, Chief Creative Officer; DAVID BOGART, SVP of Business Affairs & Talent Management; TOM BREVOORT, SVP of Publishing; C.B. CEBULSKI, SVP of Creator & Content Development; DAVID GABRIEL, SVP of Publishing Sales & Circulation; MICHAEL PASCIULLO, SVP of Brand Planning & Communications; JIM O'KEEFE, VP of Operations & Logistics; DAN CARR, Executive Director of Publishing Technology; SUSAN CRESPI, Editorial Operations Manager; ALEX MORALES, Publishing Operations Manager; STAN LEE, Chairman Emeritus. For information regarding advertising in Marvel Comics or on Marvel.com, please contact John Dokes, SVP Integrated Sales and Marketing, at jdokes@marvel.com. For Marvel subscription inquiries, please call 800-217-9158. **Manufactured between 12/12/2011 and 1/9/2012 (hardcover), and 12/12/2011 and 7/9/2012 (softcover), by R.R. DONNELLEY, INC., SALEM, VA, USA.**

10 9 8 7 6 5 4 3 2 1

WRITER
MARK WAID

ISSUES #1-3
PENCILER
PAOLO RIVERA
INKER
JOE RIVERA
COLOR ARTIST
JAVIER RODRIGUEZ

ISSUES #4-6 AND ISSUE #1 BACKUP STORY
ARTIST
MARCOS MARTIN
COLOR ARTISTS
MUNTSA VICENTE
JAVIER RODRIGUEZ (ISSUE #5)

LETTERER
VC'S JOE CARAMAGNA
ASSISTANT EDITOR
ELLIE PYLE
EDITOR
STEPHEN WACKER

COLLECTION EDITOR & DESIGN
CORY LEVINE
ASSISTANT EDITORS
ALEX STARBUCK
NELSON RIBEIRO
EDITORS, SPECIAL PROJECTS
JENNIFER GRÜNWALD
MARK D. BEAZLEY
SENIOR EDITOR, SPECIAL PROJECTS
JEFF YOUNGQUIST
SENIOR VICE PRESIDENT OF SALES
DAVID GABRIEL
SVP OF BRAND PLANNING & COMMUNICATIONS
MICHAEL PASCIULLO

EDITOR IN CHIEF
AXEL ALONSO
CHIEF CREATIVE OFFICER
JOE QUESADA
PUBLISHER
DAN BUCKLEY
EXECUTIVE PRODUCER
ALAN FINE

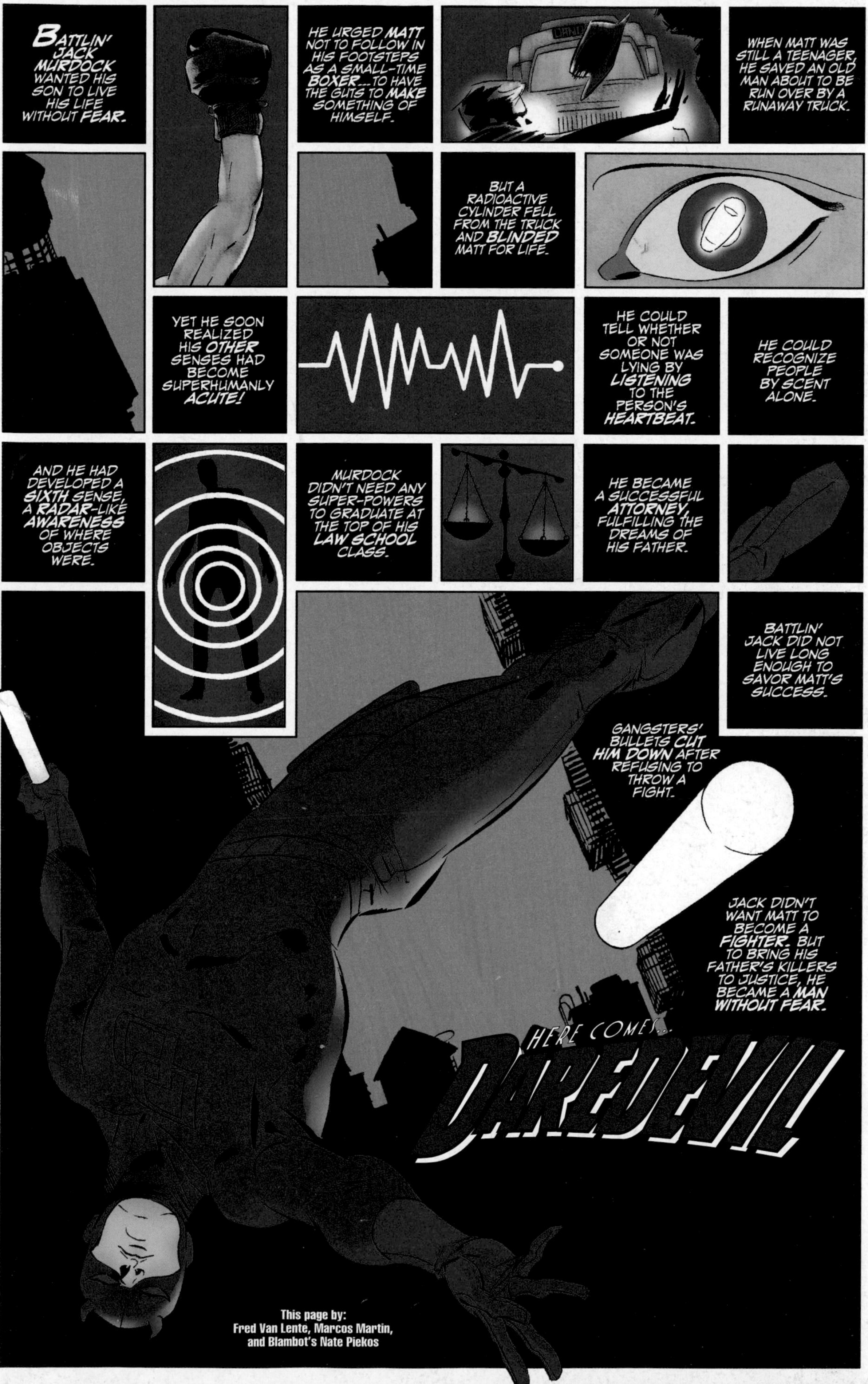
BATTLIN' JACK MURDOCK WANTED HIS SON TO LIVE HIS LIFE WITHOUT FEAR.
HE URGED MATT NOT TO FOLLOW IN HIS FOOTSTEPS AS A SMALL-TIME BOXER... TO HAVE THE GUTS TO MAKE SOMETHING OF HIMSELF.
WHEN MATT WAS STILL A TEENAGER, HE SAVED AN OLD MAN ABOUT TO BE RUN OVER BY A RUNAWAY TRUCK.
BUT A RADIOACTIVE CYLINDER FELL FROM THE TRUCK AND BLINDED MATT FOR LIFE.
YET HE SOON REALIZED HIS OTHER SENSES HAD BECOME SUPERHUMANLY ACUTE!
HE COULD TELL WHETHER OR NOT SOMEONE WAS LYING BY LISTENING TO THE PERSON'S HEARTBEAT.
HE COULD RECOGNIZE PEOPLE BY SCENT ALONE.
AND HE HAD DEVELOPED A SIXTH SENSE, A RADAR-LIKE AWARENESS OF WHERE OBJECTS WERE.
MURDOCK DIDN'T NEED ANY SUPER-POWERS TO GRADUATE AT THE TOP OF HIS LAW SCHOOL CLASS.
HE BECAME A SUCCESSFUL ATTORNEY, FULFILLING THE DREAMS OF HIS FATHER.
BATTLIN' JACK DID NOT LIVE LONG ENOUGH TO SAVOR MATT'S SUCCESS.
GANGSTERS' BULLETS CUT HIM DOWN AFTER REFUSING TO THROW A FIGHT.
JACK DIDN'T WANT MATT TO BECOME A FIGHTER. BUT TO BRING HIS FATHER'S KILLERS TO JUSTICE, HE BECAME A MAN WITHOUT FEAR.
HERE COMES...
DAREDEVIL!
This page by:
Fred Van Lente, Marcos Martin,
and Blambot's Nate Piekos

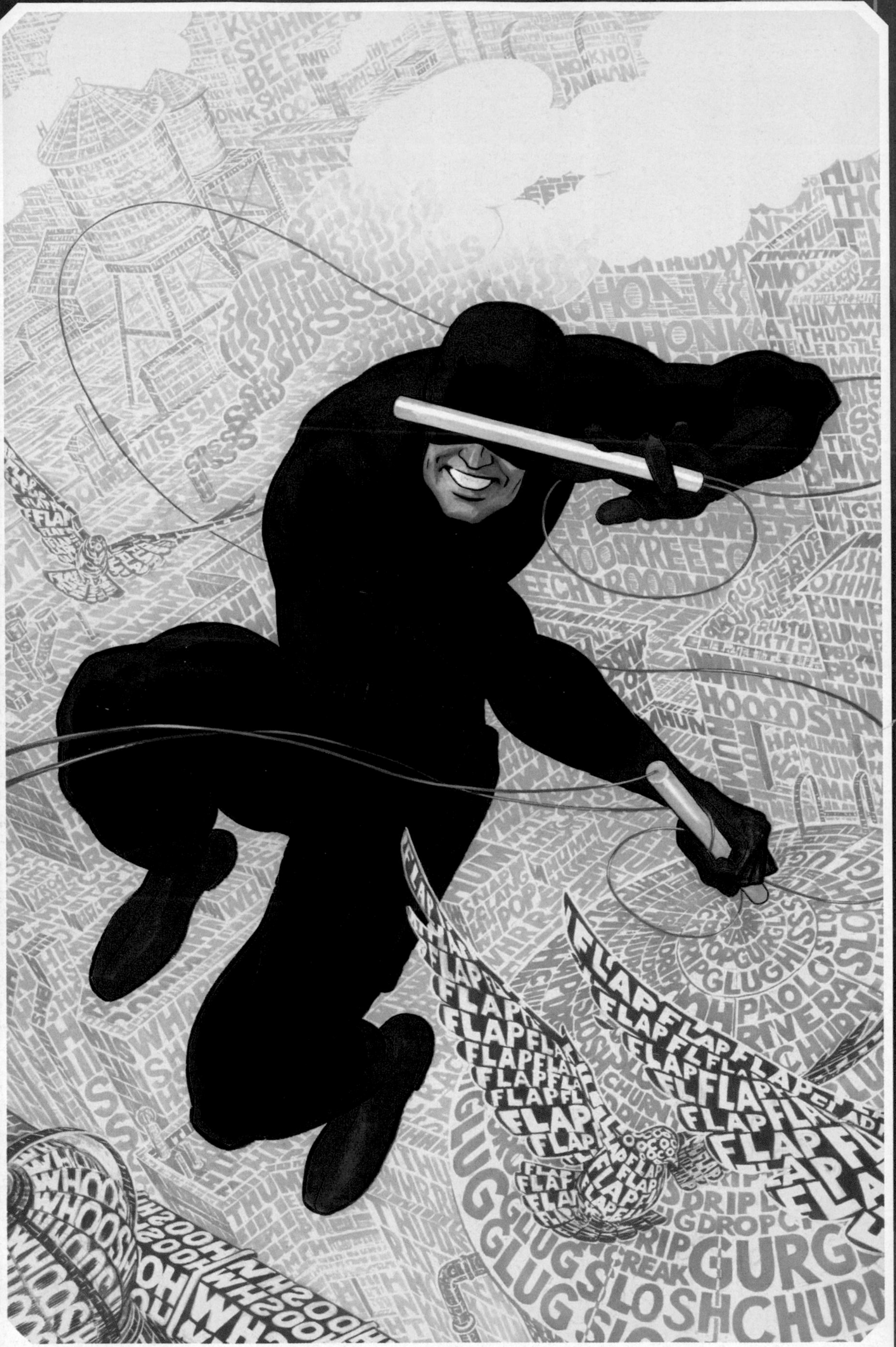
HONK
FLAP
WHOOSH
DRIP
DROP
CREAK
GURG
GLUG
SLOSH
CHURN
PAOLO RIVERA

ONE

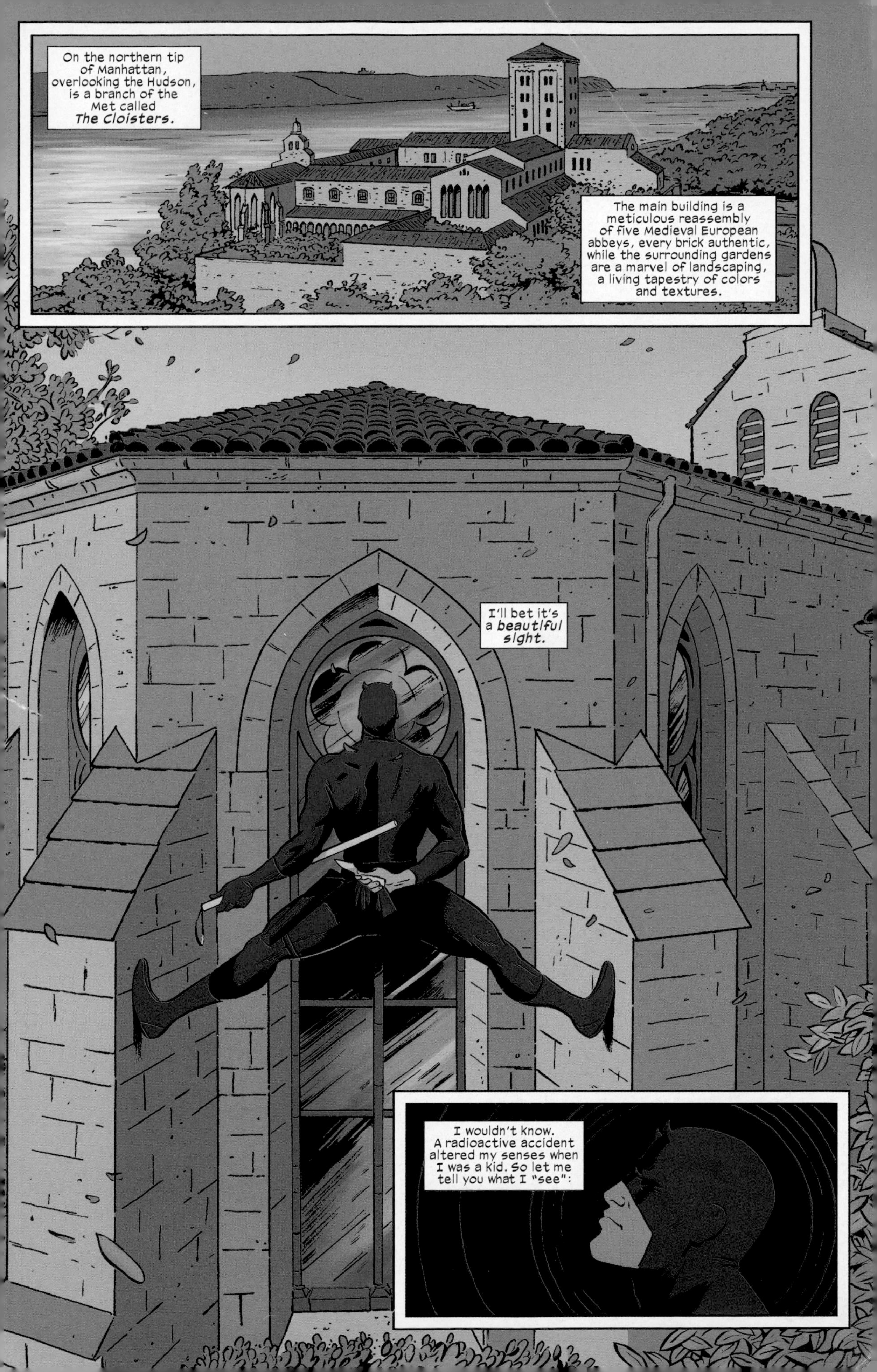
On the northern tip of Manhattan, overlooking the Hudson, is a branch of the Met called *The Cloisters.*
The main building is a meticulous reassembly of five Medieval European abbeys, every brick authentic, while the surrounding gardens are a marvel of landscaping, a living tapestry of colors and textures.
I'll bet it's a *beautiful sight.*
I wouldn't know. A radioactive accident altered my senses when I was a kid. So let me tell you what I "see":

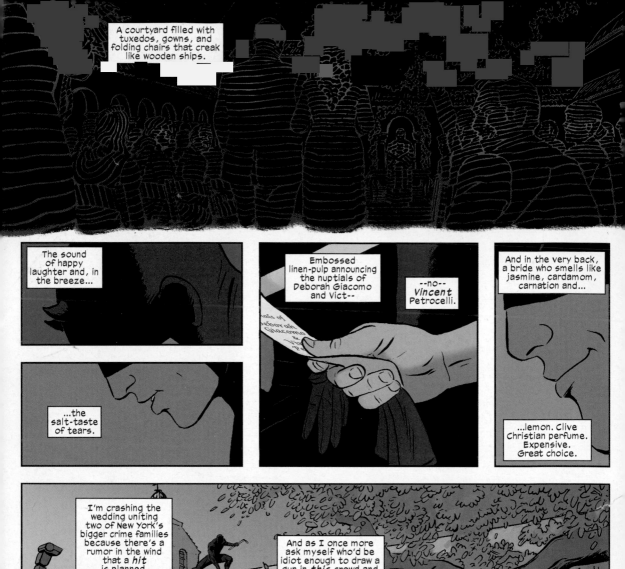

A courtyard filled with tuxedos, gowns, and folding chairs that creak like wooden ships.

The sound of happy laughter and, in the breeze...

...the salt-taste of tears.

Embossed linen-pulp announcing the nuptials of Deborah Giacomo and Vict-- --no-- *Vincent* Petrocelli.

And in the very back, a bride who smells like jasmine, cardamom, carnation and...

...lemon. Clive Christian perfume. Expensive. Great choice.

I'm crashing the wedding uniting two of New York's bigger crime families because there's a rumor in the wind that a *hit* is planned.

And as I once more ask myself who'd be idiot enough to draw a gun in *this* crowd and hope to walk away...

...there's an almost-imperceptible shift to the echo of the organ music...

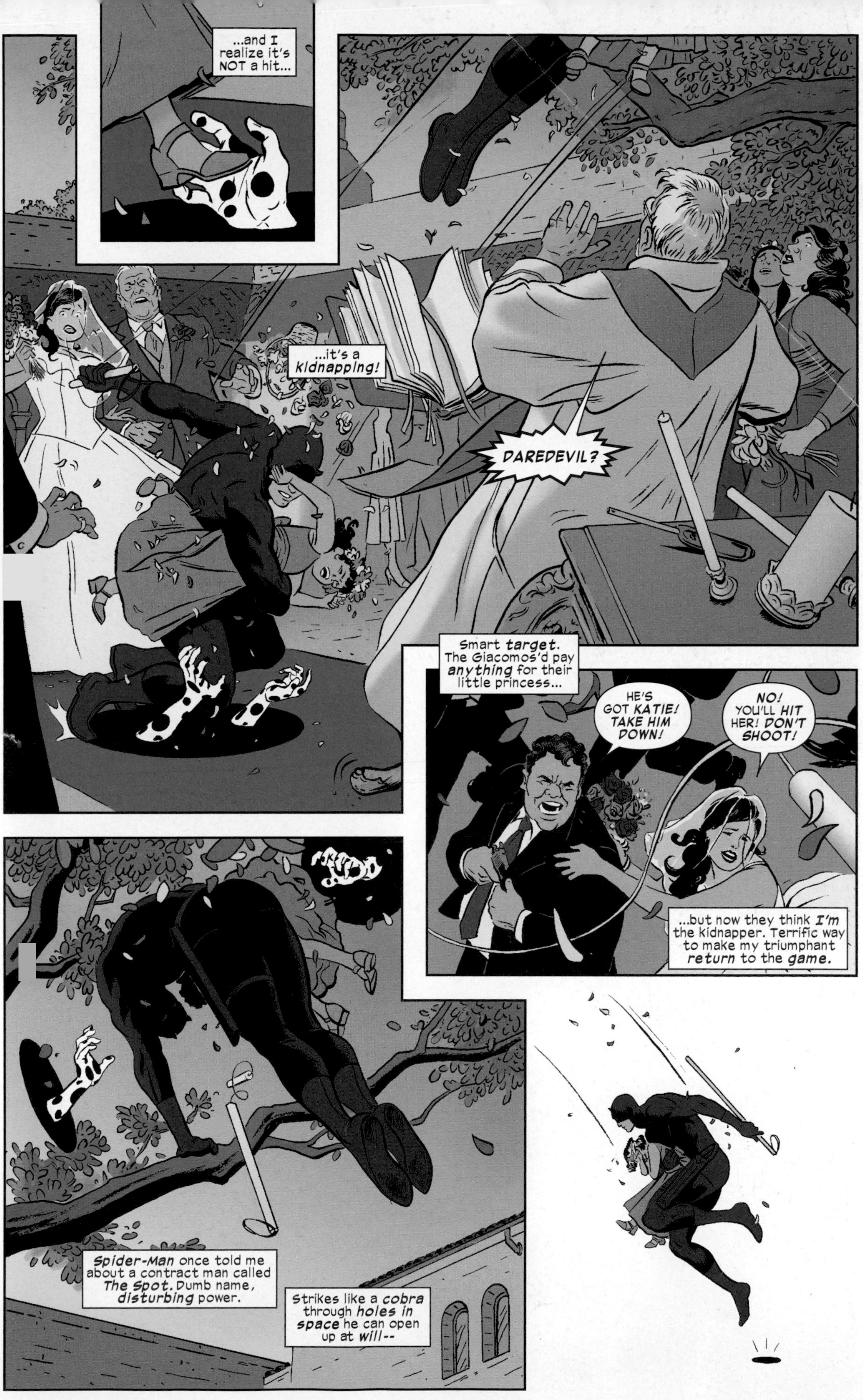
...and I realize it's NOT a hit...
...it's a kidnapping!
DAREDEVIL?
Smart target. The Giacomos'd pay anything for their little princess...
HE'S GOT KATIE! TAKE HIM DOWN!
NO! YOU'LL HIT HER! DON'T SHOOT!
...but now they think I'm the kidnapper. Terrific way to make my triumphant return to the game.
Spider-Man once told me about a contract man called The Spot. Dumb name, disturbing power.
Strikes like a cobra through holes in space he can open up at will--

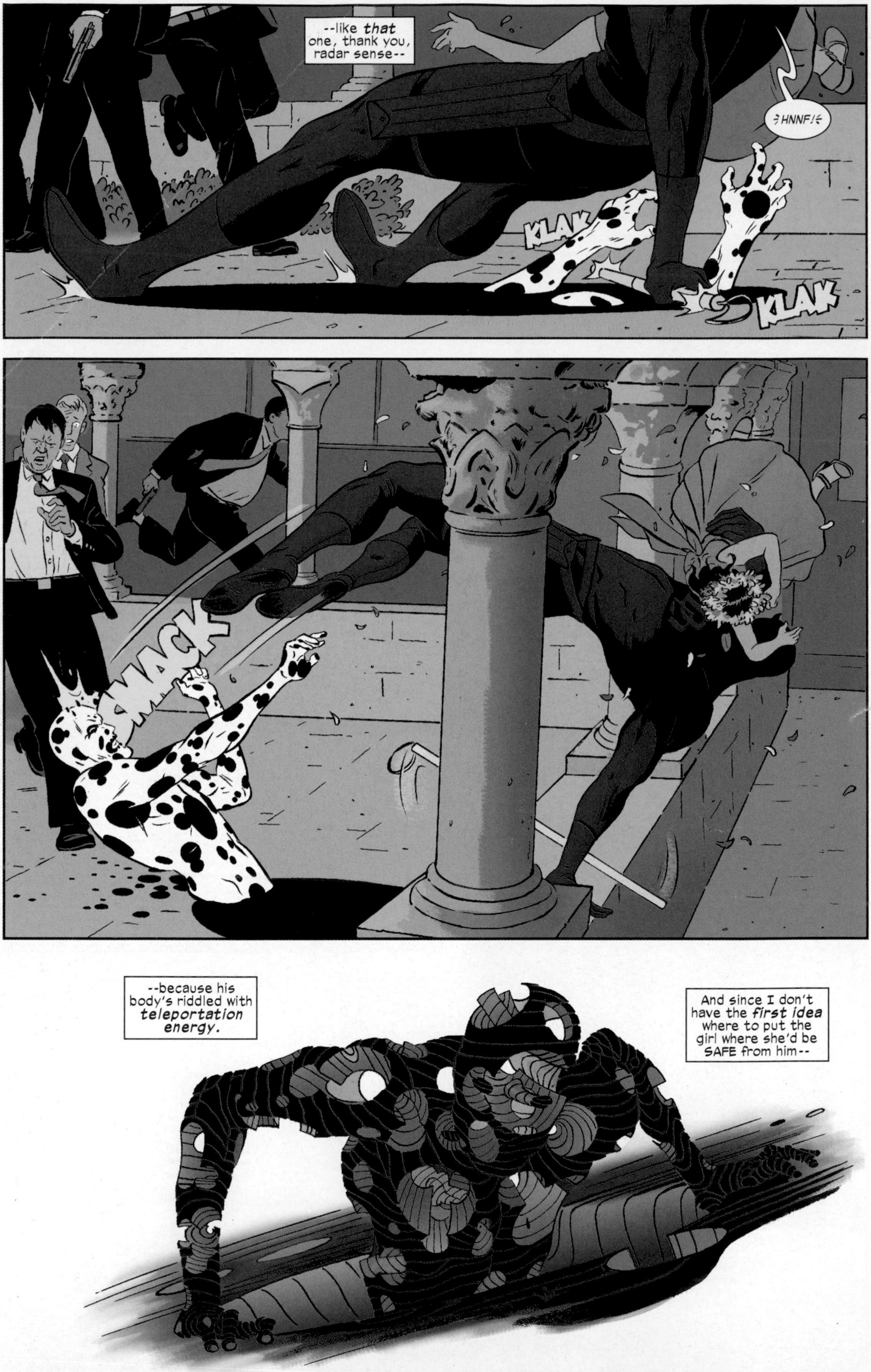
--like *that* one, thank you, radar sense--
HNNF!
KLAK
KLAK
WHACK
--because his body's riddled with *teleportation energy.*
And since I don't have the *first idea* where to put the girl where she'd be SAFE from him--

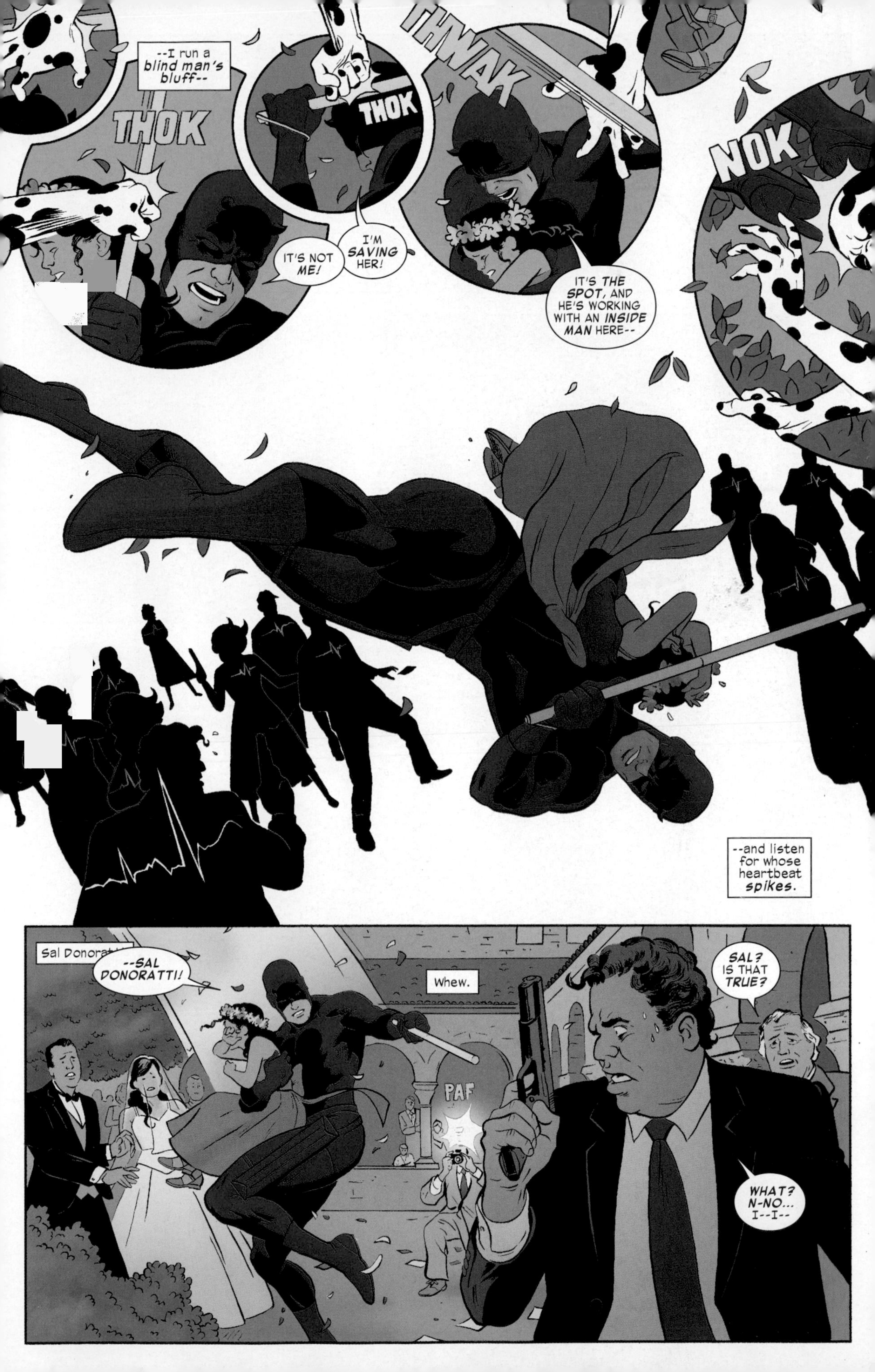
--I run a blind man's bluff--
THOK
IT'S NOT ME!
I'M SAVING HER!
THOK
THWAK
IT'S THE SPOT, AND HE'S WORKING WITH AN INSIDE MAN HERE--
NOK
--and listen for whose heartbeat spikes.
Sal Donorat
--SAL DONORATTI!
Whew.
SAL? IS THAT TRUE?
PAF
WHAT? N-NO... I--I--

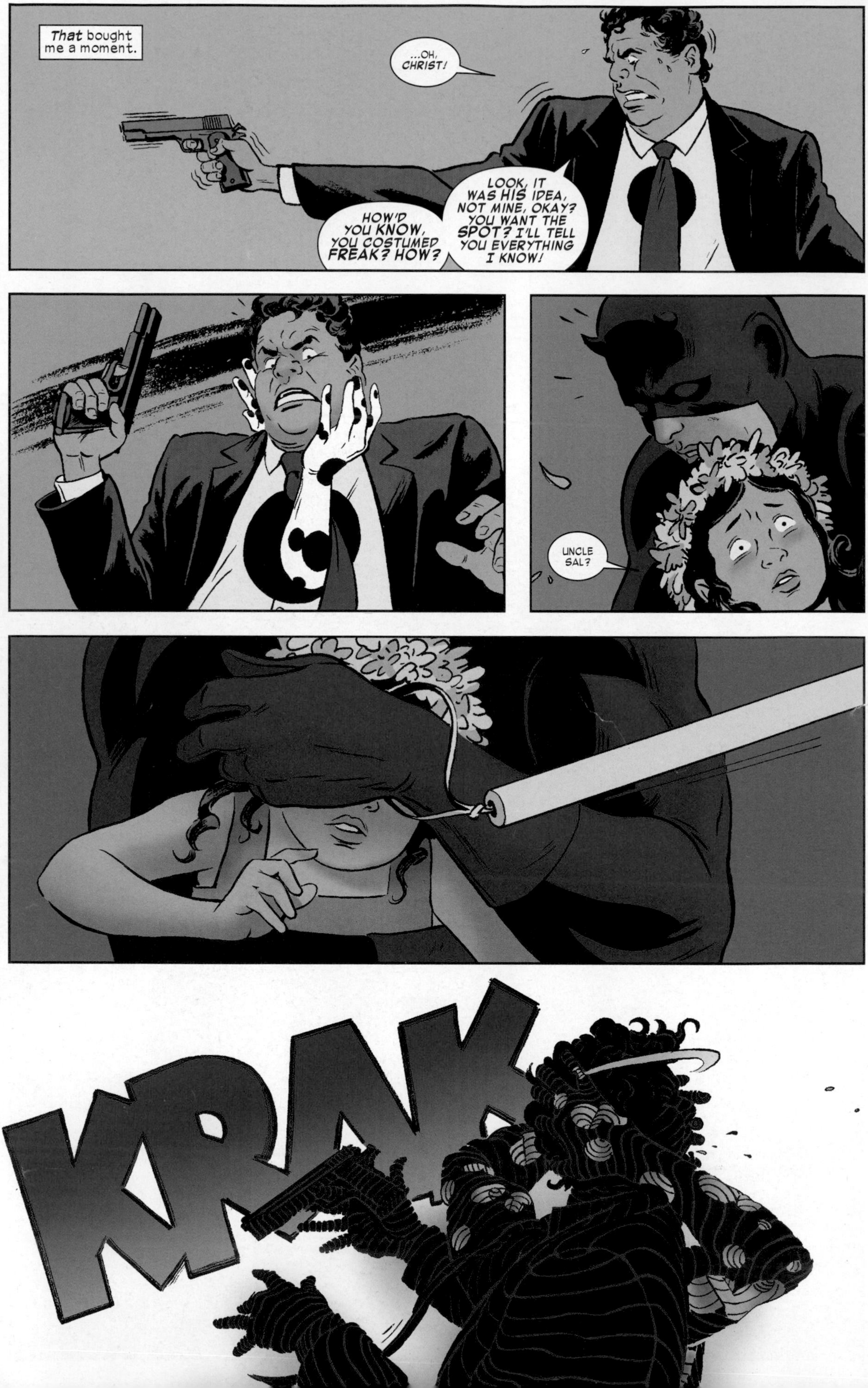
That bought me a moment.
...OH, CHRIST!
LOOK, IT WAS HIS IDEA, NOT MINE, OKAY? YOU WANT THE SPOT? I'LL TELL YOU EVERYTHING I KNOW!
HOW'D YOU KNOW, YOU COSTUMED FREAK? HOW?
UNCLE SAL?
KRAK

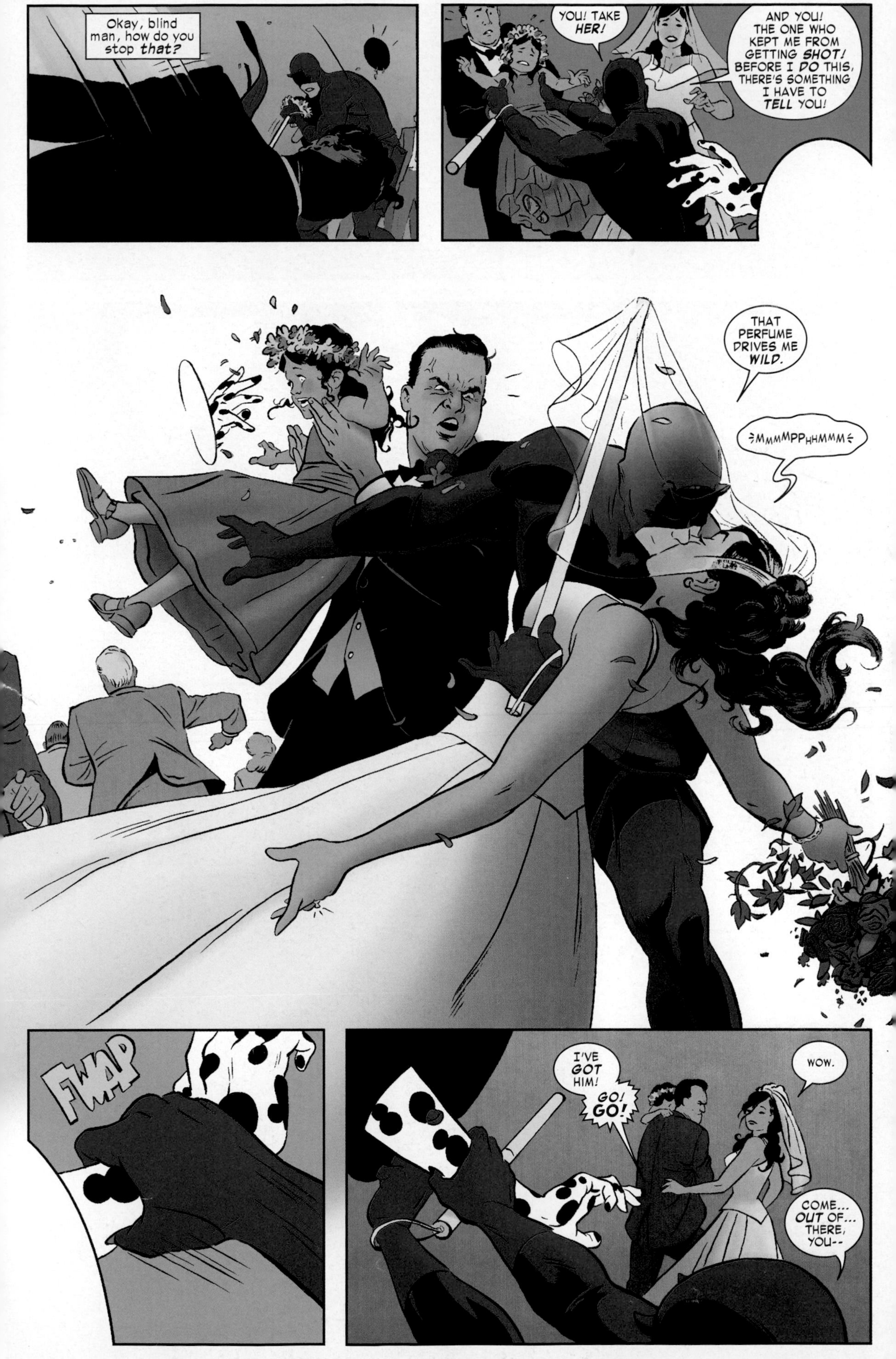
Okay, blind man, how do you stop that?
YOU! TAKE HER!
AND YOU! THE ONE WHO KEPT ME FROM GETTING SHOT! BEFORE I DO THIS, THERE'S SOMETHING I HAVE TO TELL YOU!
THAT PERFUME DRIVES ME WILD.
MMMMPPHHMMM
FWAP
I'VE GOT HIM! GO! GO!
WOW.
COME... OUT OF... THERE, YOU--

YAA AAAA

Didn't-- *expect* that--!

Whatever's-- on the other *side*--like jagged *ice*--!

What the holy hell am I *dealing* with--?

I could just let go and *run.*

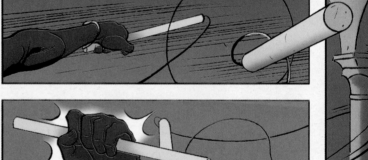

Yeah, right.

FINAL ☆☆☆☆

DAILY BUGLE

NEW YORK'S FINEST DAILY NEWSPAPER

SINCE 1897 ☆☆☆☆
$1.00 (in NYC)
$1.50 (outside city)

INSIDE: ROX STOX ON THE RISE; URICH ON JAMESON'S FALLING POLL NUMBERS; WINTERS ON PUNISHER COPYCAT; RUMOR: METS CONTACT GRIMM; MORE

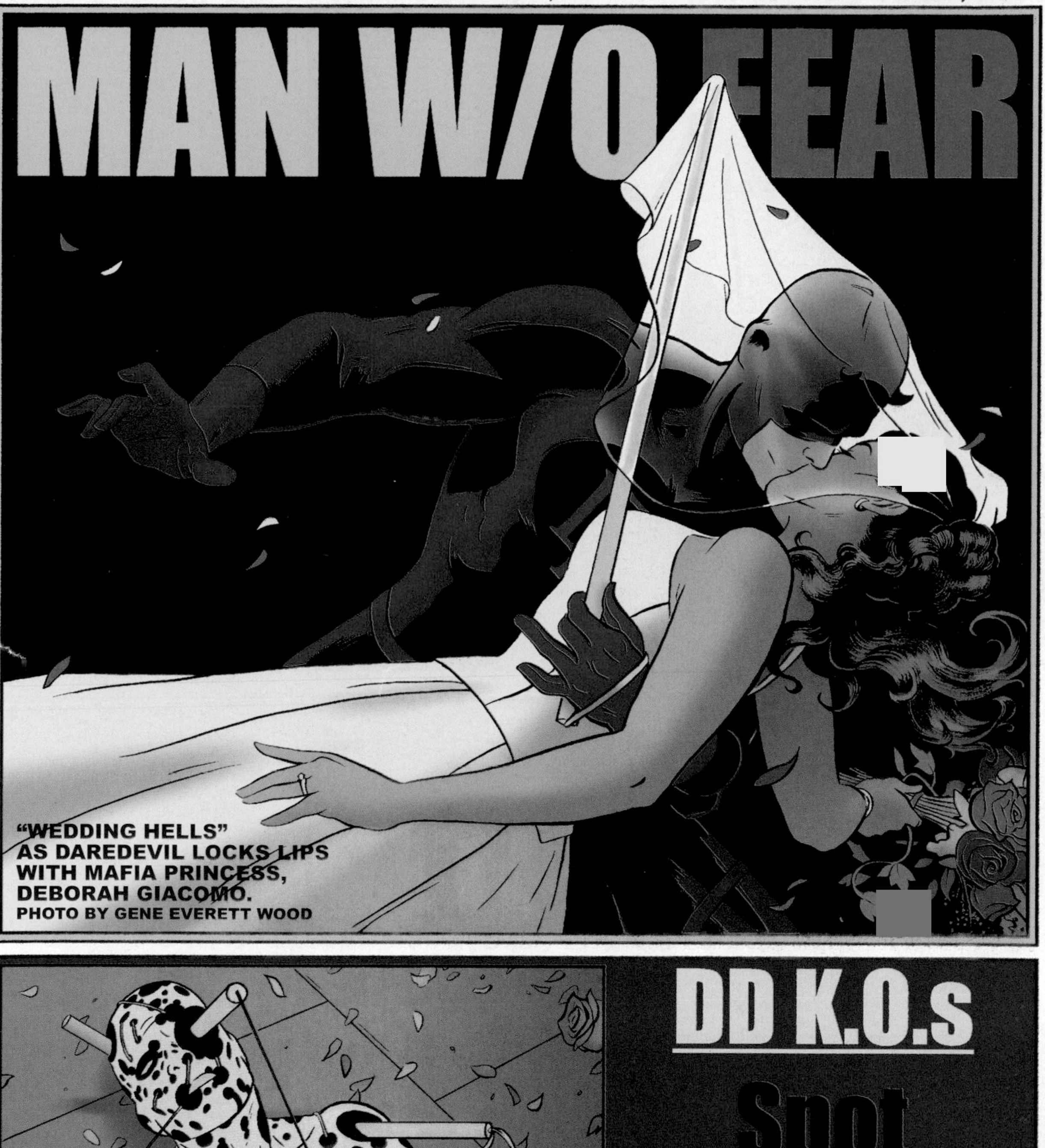
MAN W/O FEAR
"WEDDING HELLS" AS DAREDEVIL LOCKS LIPS WITH MAFIA PRINCESS, DEBORAH GIACOMO.
PHOTO BY GENE EVERETT WOOD

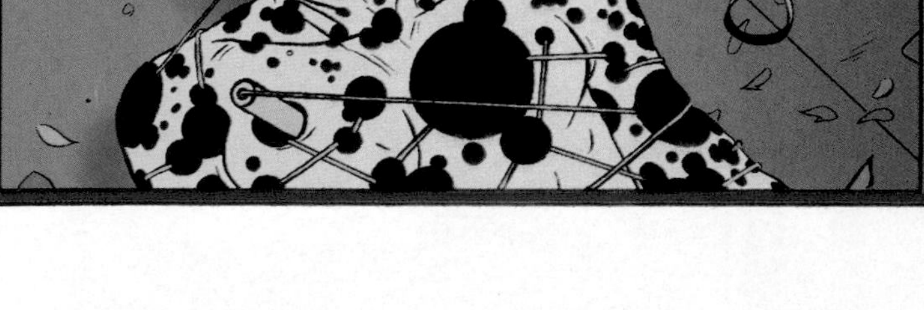

DD K.O.s Spot P.O.s Mob

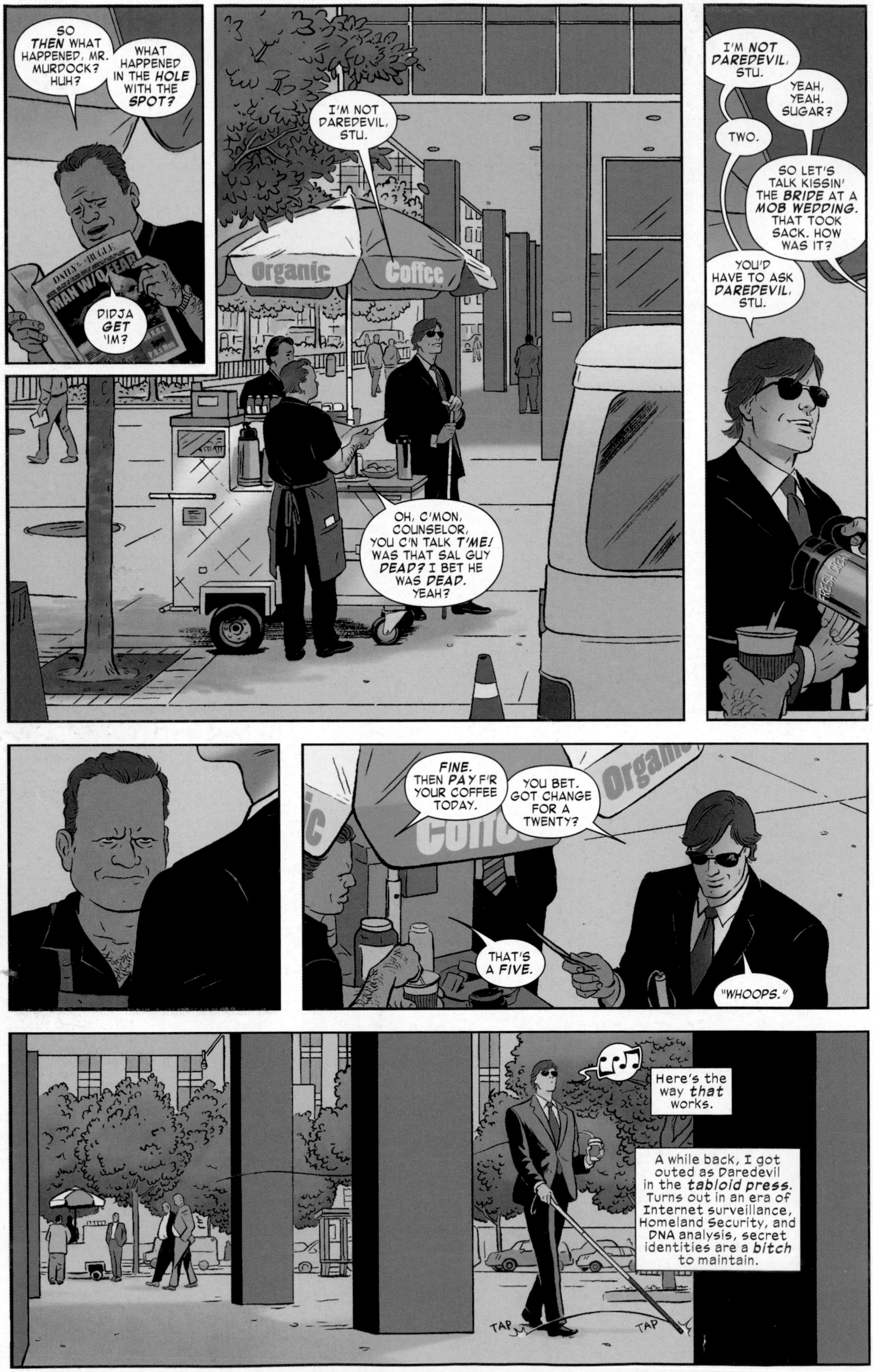
SO THEN WHAT HAPPENED, MR. MURDOCK? HUH?
WHAT HAPPENED IN THE HOLE WITH THE SPOT?
DAILY BUGLE
MAN W/O FEAR
DIDJA GET 'IM?
I'M NOT DAREDEVIL, STU.
Organic
Coffee
OH, C'MON, COUNSELOR, YOU C'N TALK T'ME! WAS THAT SAL GUY DEAD? I BET HE WAS DEAD. YEAH?
I'M NOT DAREDEVIL, STU.
YEAH, YEAH. SUGAR?
TWO.
SO LET'S TALK KISSIN' THE BRIDE AT A MOB WEDDING. THAT TOOK SACK. HOW WAS IT?
YOU'D HAVE TO ASK DAREDEVIL, STU.
FRESH CREAM
FINE. THEN PAY F'R YOUR COFFEE TODAY.
YOU BET. GOT CHANGE FOR A TWENTY?
Organic
Coffee
THAT'S A FIVE.
"WHOOPS."
Here's the way that works.
A while back, I got outed as Daredevil in the tabloid press. Turns out in an era of Internet surveillance, Homeland Security, and DNA analysis, secret identities are a bitch to maintain.
TAP
TAP

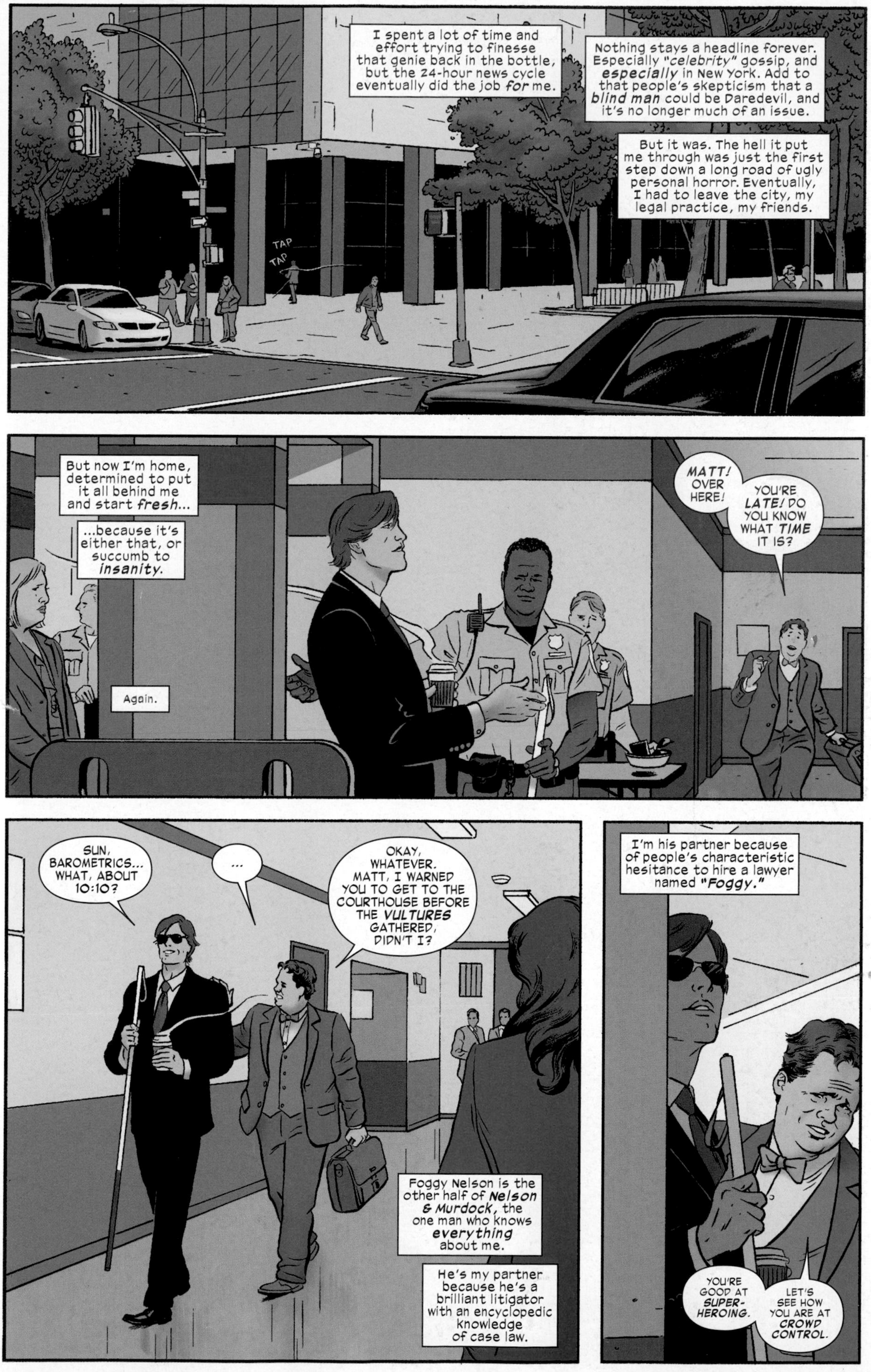

I spent a lot of time and effort trying to finesse that genie back in the bottle, but the 24-hour news cycle eventually did the job *for* me.
Nothing stays a headline forever. Especially *"celebrity"* gossip, and *especially* in New York. Add to that people's skepticism that a *blind man* could be Daredevil, and it's no longer much of an issue.
But it was. The hell it put me through was just the first step down a long road of ugly personal horror. Eventually, I had to leave the city, my legal practice, my friends.
TAP
TAP
But now I'm home, determined to put it all behind me and start *fresh*...
...because it's either that, or succumb to *insanity*.
Again.
MATT! OVER HERE!
YOU'RE *LATE!* DO YOU KNOW WHAT *TIME* IT IS?
SUN, BAROMETRICS... WHAT, ABOUT 10:10?
...
OKAY, WHATEVER. MATT, I WARNED YOU TO GET TO THE COURTHOUSE BEFORE THE *VULTURES* GATHERED, DIDN'T I?
Foggy Nelson is the other half of *Nelson & Murdock*, the one man who knows *everything* about me.
He's my partner because he's a brilliant litigator with an encyclopedic knowledge of case law.
I'm his partner because of people's characteristic hesitance to hire a lawyer named *"Foggy."*
YOU'RE GOOD AT *SUPER-HEROING.*
LET'S SEE HOW YOU ARE AT *CROWD CONTROL.*

BACK IN COURT, DAREDEVIL? HOW'S IT FEEL TO BE ANSWER A QUESTION FOR "LAW BLAWG"?

CREAK

PAF

"CA CLICK"

YO, DAREDEVIL, YOU HAVE A DAREDIVA IN YOUR LIFE?!

PAF

DO YOU EXPECT THE JURY TO ASK FOR AUTOGRAPHS?

IS IT *TRUE* JUSTICE *ISN'T* BLIND IN THIS CASE?

--TRUE YOU'RE GONNA BE ON "DANCING WITH THE STARS"?

BABABOOEY! BABABOOEY!!

ZZZT

I THOUGHT FOR *SURE* WE'D BE *PAST* THIS BY NOW.

AT LEAST IT'S NOT THE NETWORKS. MOSTLY PAPARAZZI AND BLOGGERS. IT COULD BE WORSE.

PAF   PAF

It gets worse.

...AND YOU CLAIM THE OFFICER IN QUESTION HURLED RACIAL EPITHETS AT YOU AS HE DRAGGED YOU FROM YOUR VEHICLE, MR. JOBRANI. COULD YOU *REPEAT*--

OBJECTION, YOUR HONOR!

THE DEFENSE QUESTIONS THE MOTIVATION OF COUNSEL IN BRINGING CHARGES OF "*POLICE BRUTALITY*."

AFTER ALL, AS THE VIGILANTE *DAREDEVIL*, MR. MURDOCK ALREADY MAINTAINS AN *ADVERSARIAL* RELATIONSHIP WITH PATROLMEN, DOES HE *NOT?*

SIGH.

And so it goes.

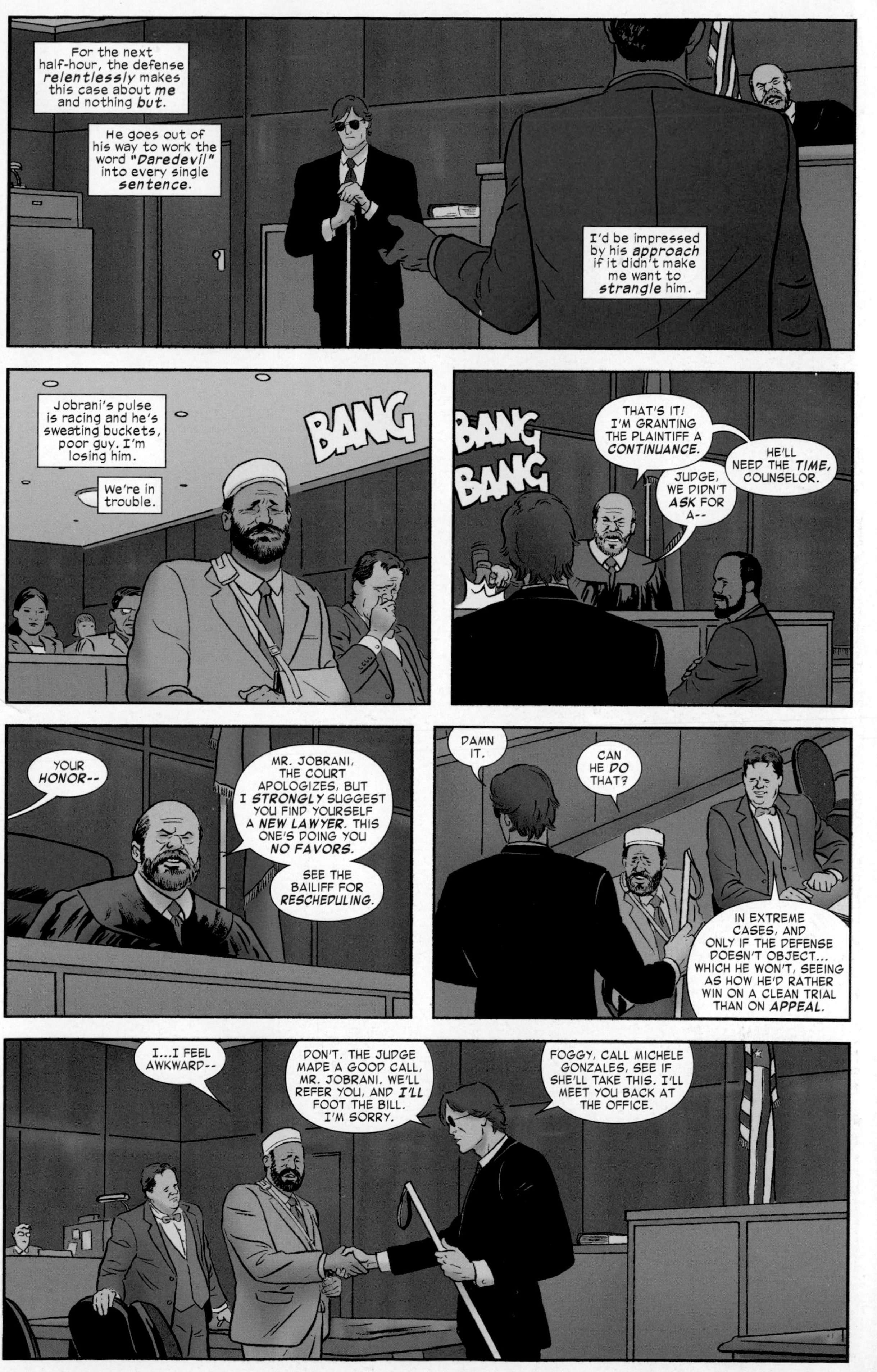
For the next half-hour, the defense relentlessly makes this case about me and nothing but.
He goes out of his way to work the word "Daredevil" into every single sentence.
I'd be impressed by his approach if it didn't make me want to strangle him.
Jobrani's pulse is racing and he's sweating buckets, poor guy. I'm losing him.
We're in trouble.
BANG
BANG
BANG
THAT'S IT! I'M GRANTING THE PLAINTIFF A CONTINUANCE.
JUDGE, WE DIDN'T ASK FOR A--
HE'LL NEED THE TIME, COUNSELOR.
YOUR HONOR--
MR. JOBRANI, THE COURT APOLOGIZES, BUT I STRONGLY SUGGEST YOU FIND YOURSELF A NEW LAWYER. THIS ONE'S DOING YOU NO FAVORS.
SEE THE BAILIFF FOR RESCHEDULING.
DAMN IT.
CAN HE DO THAT?
IN EXTREME CASES, AND ONLY IF THE DEFENSE DOESN'T OBJECT... WHICH HE WON'T, SEEING AS HOW HE'D RATHER WIN ON A CLEAN TRIAL THAN ON APPEAL.
I...I FEEL AWKWARD--
DON'T. THE JUDGE MADE A GOOD CALL, MR. JOBRANI. WE'LL REFER YOU, AND I'LL FOOT THE BILL. I'M SORRY.
FOGGY, CALL MICHELE GONZALES, SEE IF SHE'LL TAKE THIS. I'LL MEET YOU BACK AT THE OFFICE.

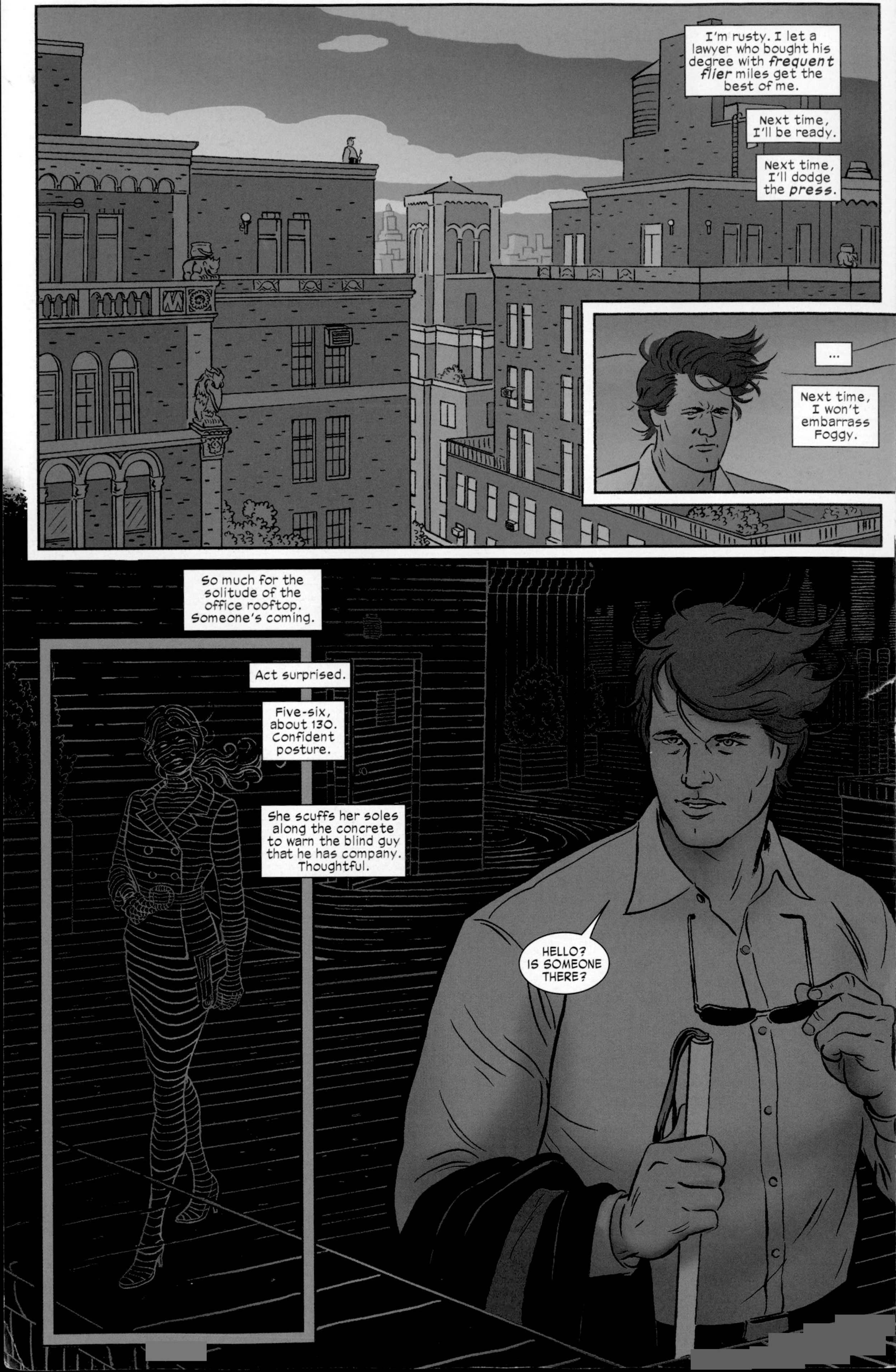
I'm rusty. I let a lawyer who bought his degree with *frequent flier* miles get the best of me.
Next time, I'll be ready.
Next time, I'll dodge the *press*.
...
Next time, I won't embarrass Foggy.
So much for the solitude of the office rooftop. Someone's coming.
Act surprised.
Five-six, about 130. Confident posture.
She scuffs her soles along the concrete to warn the blind guy that he has company. Thoughtful.
HELLO? IS SOMEONE THERE?

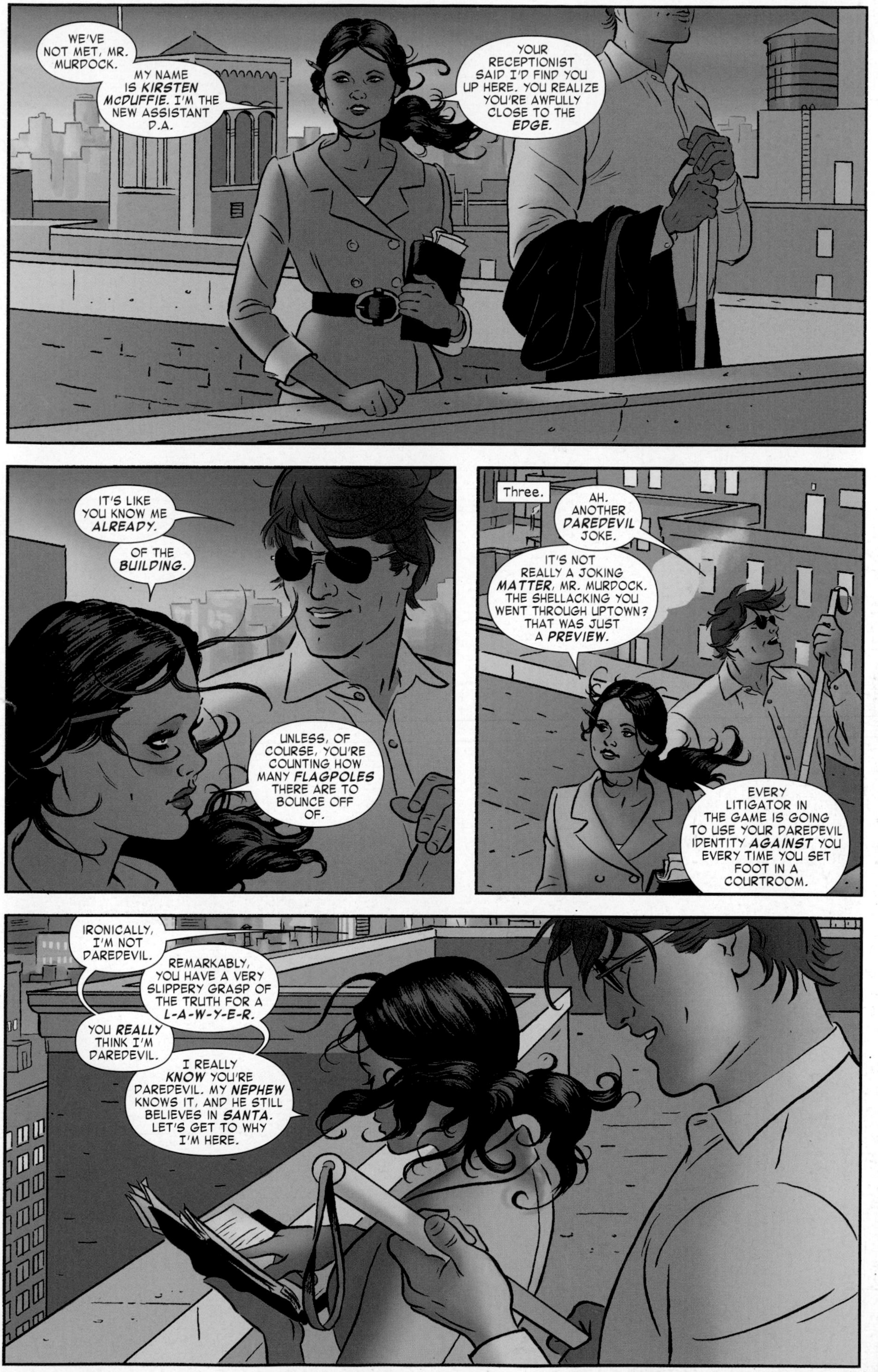
WE'VE NOT MET, MR. MURDOCK.
MY NAME IS KIRSTEN McDUFFIE. I'M THE NEW ASSISTANT D.A.
YOUR RECEPTIONIST SAID I'D FIND YOU UP HERE. YOU REALIZE YOU'RE AWFULLY CLOSE TO THE EDGE.
IT'S LIKE YOU KNOW ME ALREADY.
OF THE BUILDING.
UNLESS, OF COURSE, YOU'RE COUNTING HOW MANY FLAGPOLES THERE ARE TO BOUNCE OFF OF.
Three.
AH. ANOTHER DAREDEVIL JOKE.
IT'S NOT REALLY A JOKING MATTER, MR. MURDOCK. THE SHELLACKING YOU WENT THROUGH UPTOWN? THAT WAS JUST A PREVIEW.
EVERY LITIGATOR IN THE GAME IS GOING TO USE YOUR DAREDEVIL IDENTITY AGAINST YOU EVERY TIME YOU SET FOOT IN A COURTROOM.
IRONICALLY, I'M NOT DAREDEVIL.
REMARKABLY, YOU HAVE A VERY SLIPPERY GRASP OF THE TRUTH FOR A L-A-W-Y-E-R.
YOU REALLY THINK I'M DAREDEVIL.
I REALLY KNOW YOU'RE DAREDEVIL. MY NEPHEW KNOWS IT, AND HE STILL BELIEVES IN SANTA. LET'S GET TO WHY I'M HERE.

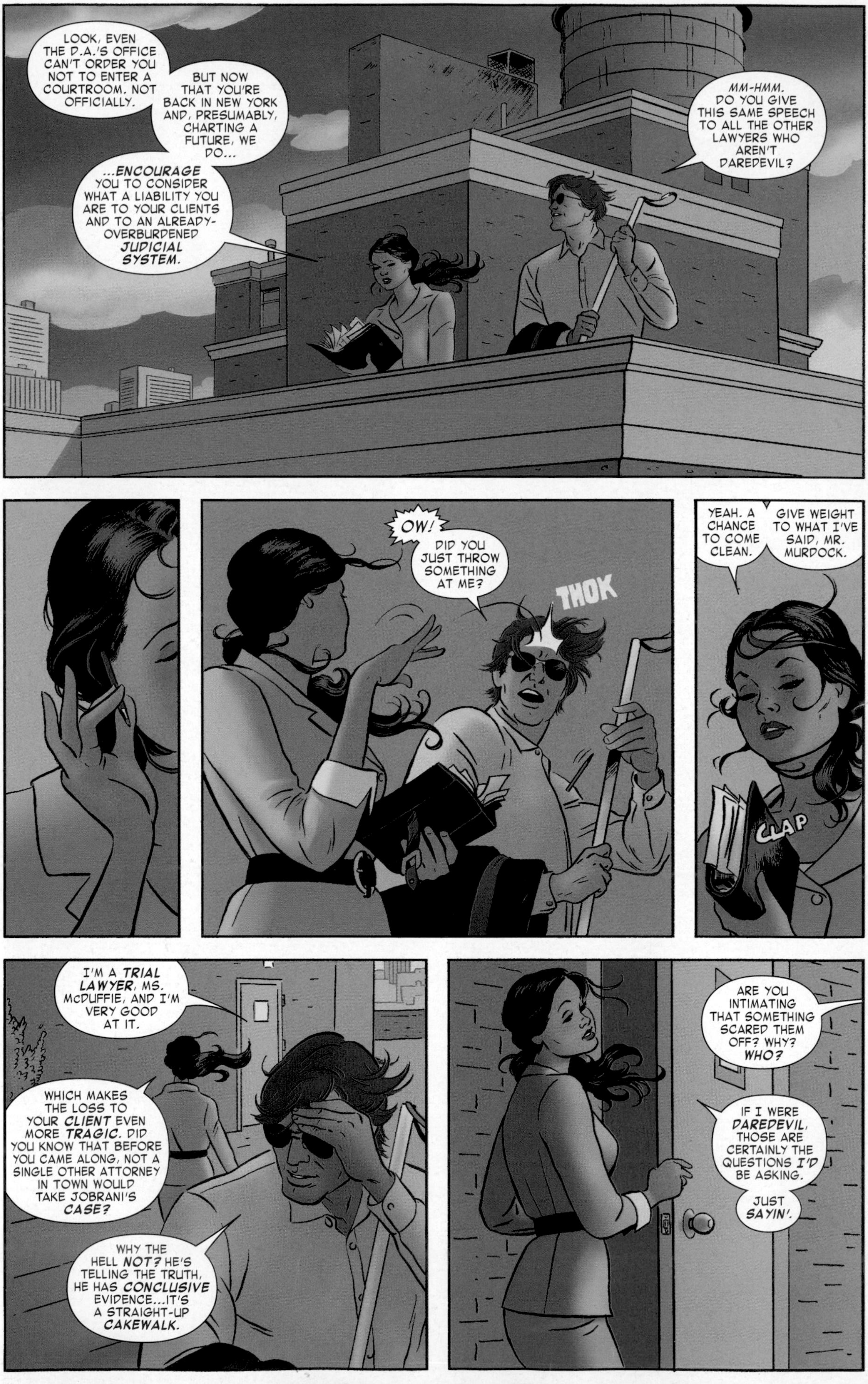
LOOK, EVEN THE D.A.'S OFFICE CAN'T ORDER YOU NOT TO ENTER A COURTROOM. NOT OFFICIALLY.
BUT NOW THAT YOU'RE BACK IN NEW YORK AND, PRESUMABLY, CHARTING A FUTURE, WE DO...
...ENCOURAGE YOU TO CONSIDER WHAT A LIABILITY YOU ARE TO YOUR CLIENTS AND TO AN ALREADY-OVERBURDENED JUDICIAL SYSTEM.
MM-HMM. DO YOU GIVE THIS SAME SPEECH TO ALL THE OTHER LAWYERS WHO AREN'T DAREDEVIL?
OW!
DID YOU JUST THROW SOMETHING AT ME?
THOK
YEAH. A CHANCE TO COME CLEAN.
GIVE WEIGHT TO WHAT I'VE SAID, MR. MURDOCK.
CLAP
I'M A TRIAL LAWYER, MS. McDUFFIE, AND I'M VERY GOOD AT IT.
WHICH MAKES THE LOSS TO YOUR CLIENT EVEN MORE TRAGIC. DID YOU KNOW THAT BEFORE YOU CAME ALONG, NOT A SINGLE OTHER ATTORNEY IN TOWN WOULD TAKE JOBRANI'S CASE?
WHY THE HELL NOT? HE'S TELLING THE TRUTH, HE HAS CONCLUSIVE EVIDENCE...IT'S A STRAIGHT-UP CAKEWALK.
ARE YOU INTIMATING THAT SOMETHING SCARED THEM OFF? WHY? WHO?
IF I WERE DAREDEVIL, THOSE ARE CERTAINLY THE QUESTIONS I'D BE ASKING.
JUST SAYIN'.

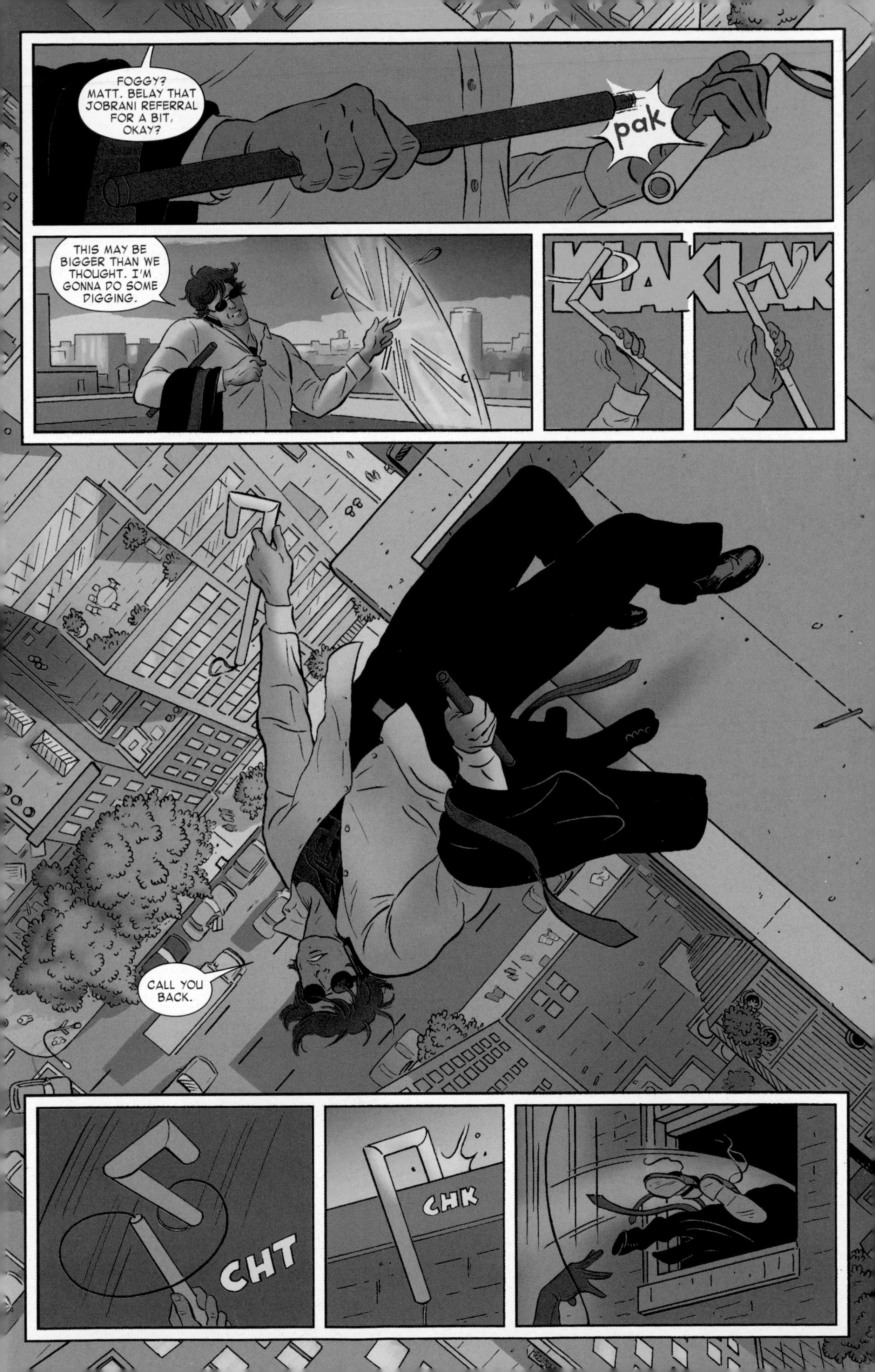
FOGGY? MATT. BELAY THAT JOBRANI REFERRAL FOR A BIT, OKAY?
pak
THIS MAY BE BIGGER THAN WE THOUGHT. I'M GONNA DO SOME DIGGING.
KLAKKLAK
CALL YOU BACK.
CHT
CHK

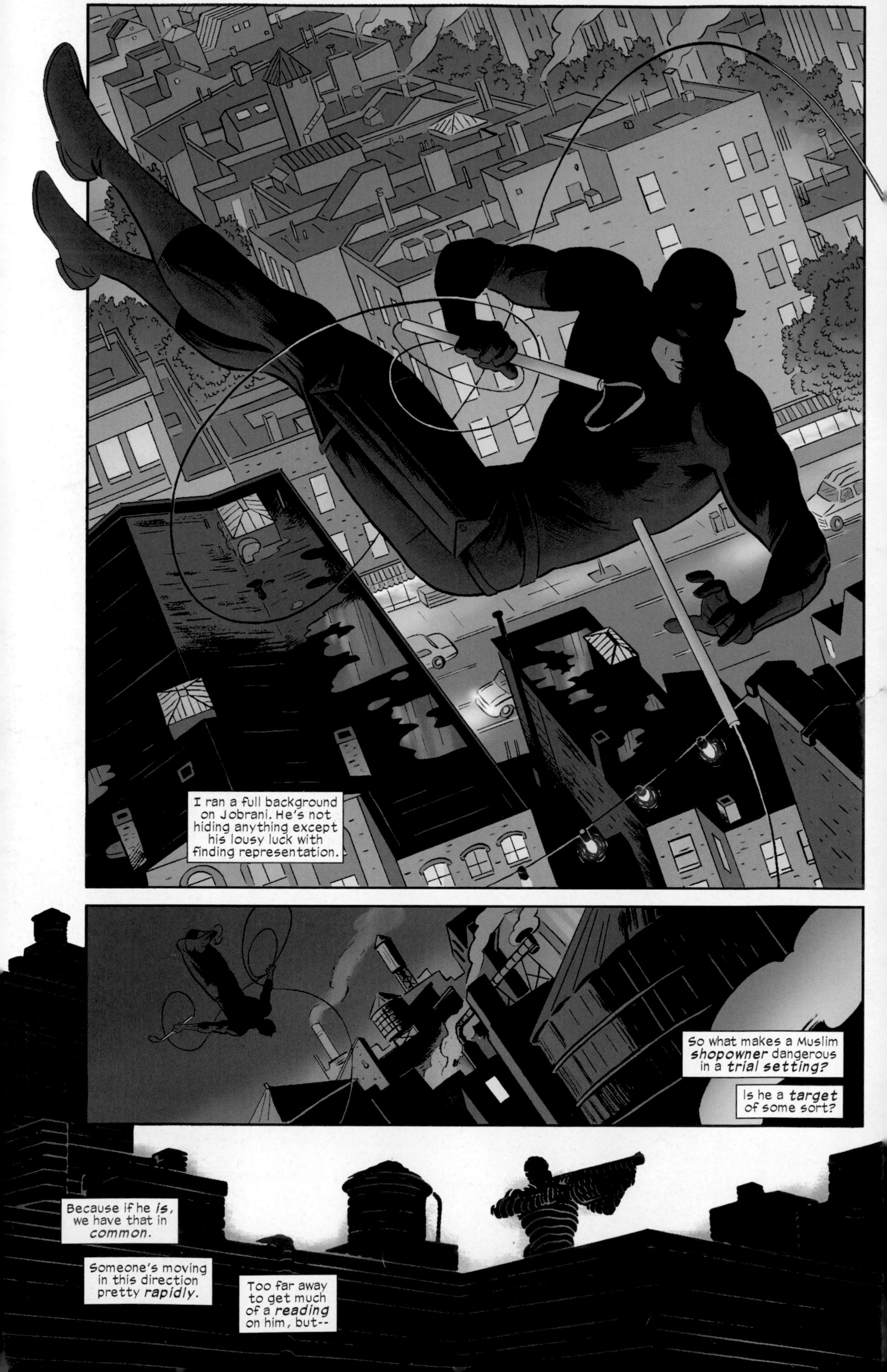

I ran a full background on Jobrani. He's not hiding anything except his lousy luck with finding representation.
So what makes a Muslim *shopowner* dangerous in a *trial setting?*
Is he a *target* of some sort?
Because if he *is*, we have that in *common*.
Someone's moving in this direction pretty *rapidly*.
Too far away to get much of a *reading* on him, but--

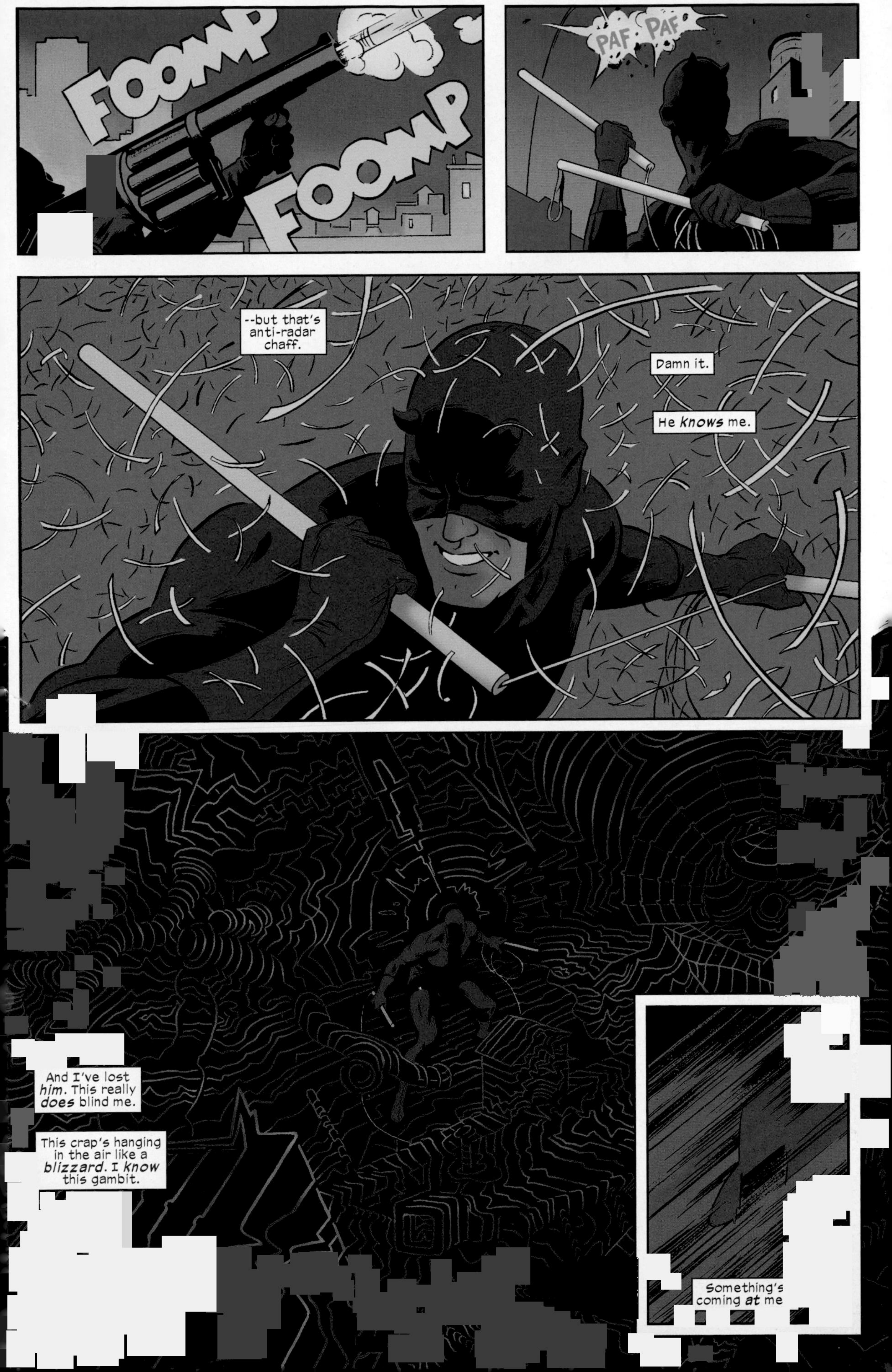
FOOMP
FOOMP
PAF PAF
--but that's anti-radar chaff.
Damn it.
He *knows* me.
And I've lost *him*. This really *does* blind me.
This crap's hanging in the air like a *blizzard*. I *know* this gambit.
Something's coming *at* me

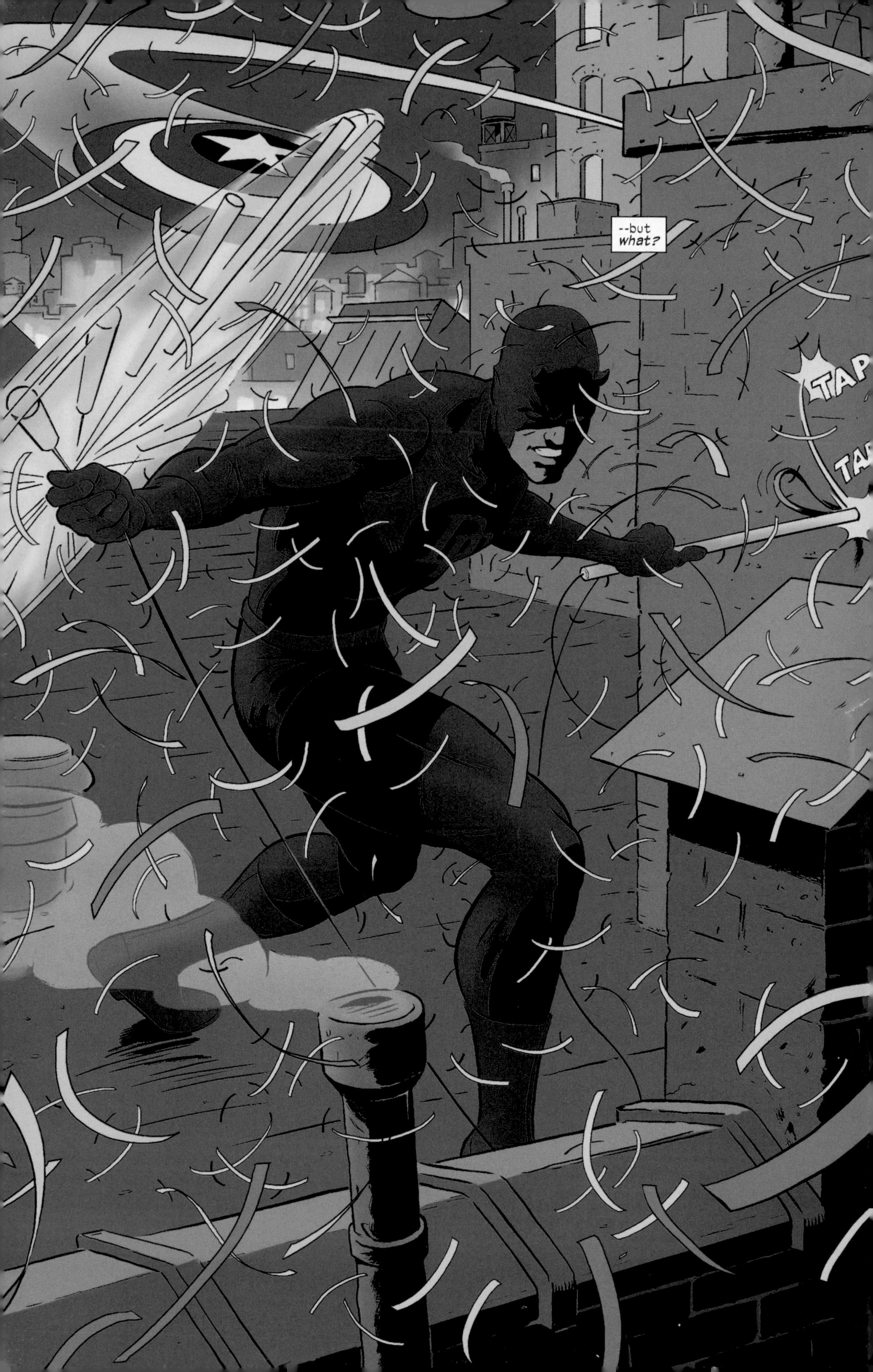
--but what?
TAP
TAP

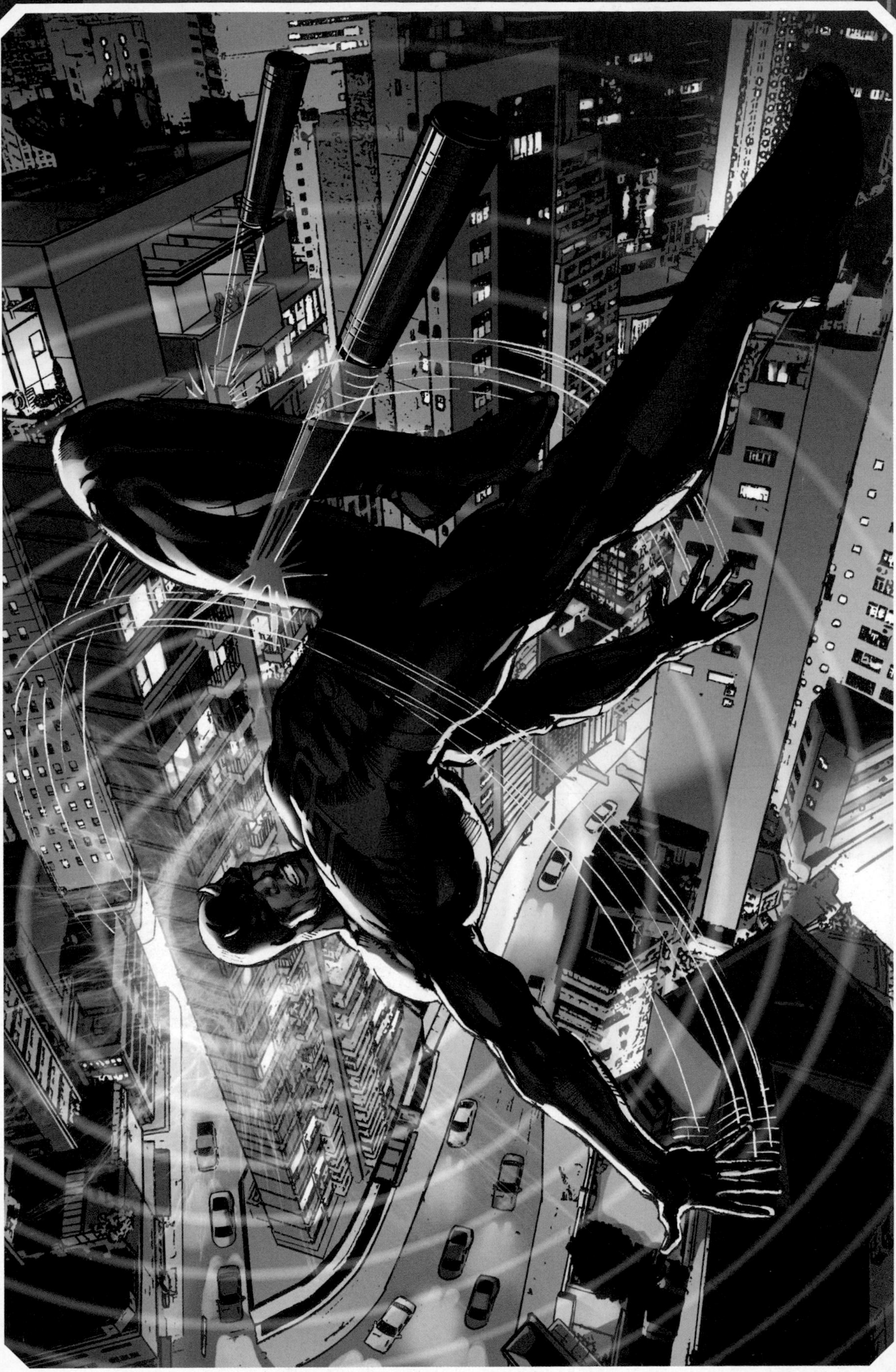

ISSUE #1 ***VARIANT BY NEAL ADAMS & JUSTIN PONSOR***

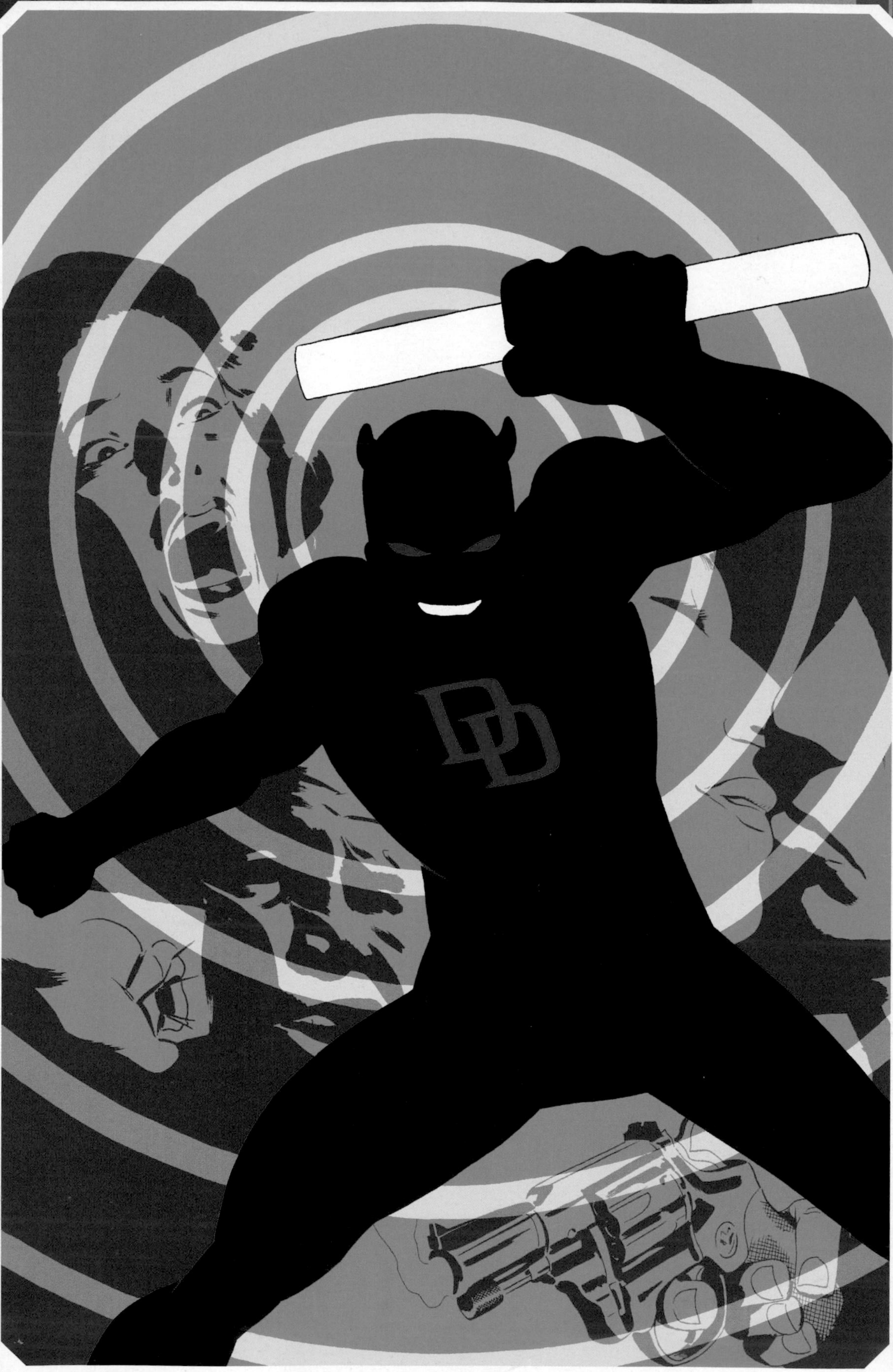
DD

ISSUE #1 ***VARIANT BY MARCOS MARTIN***

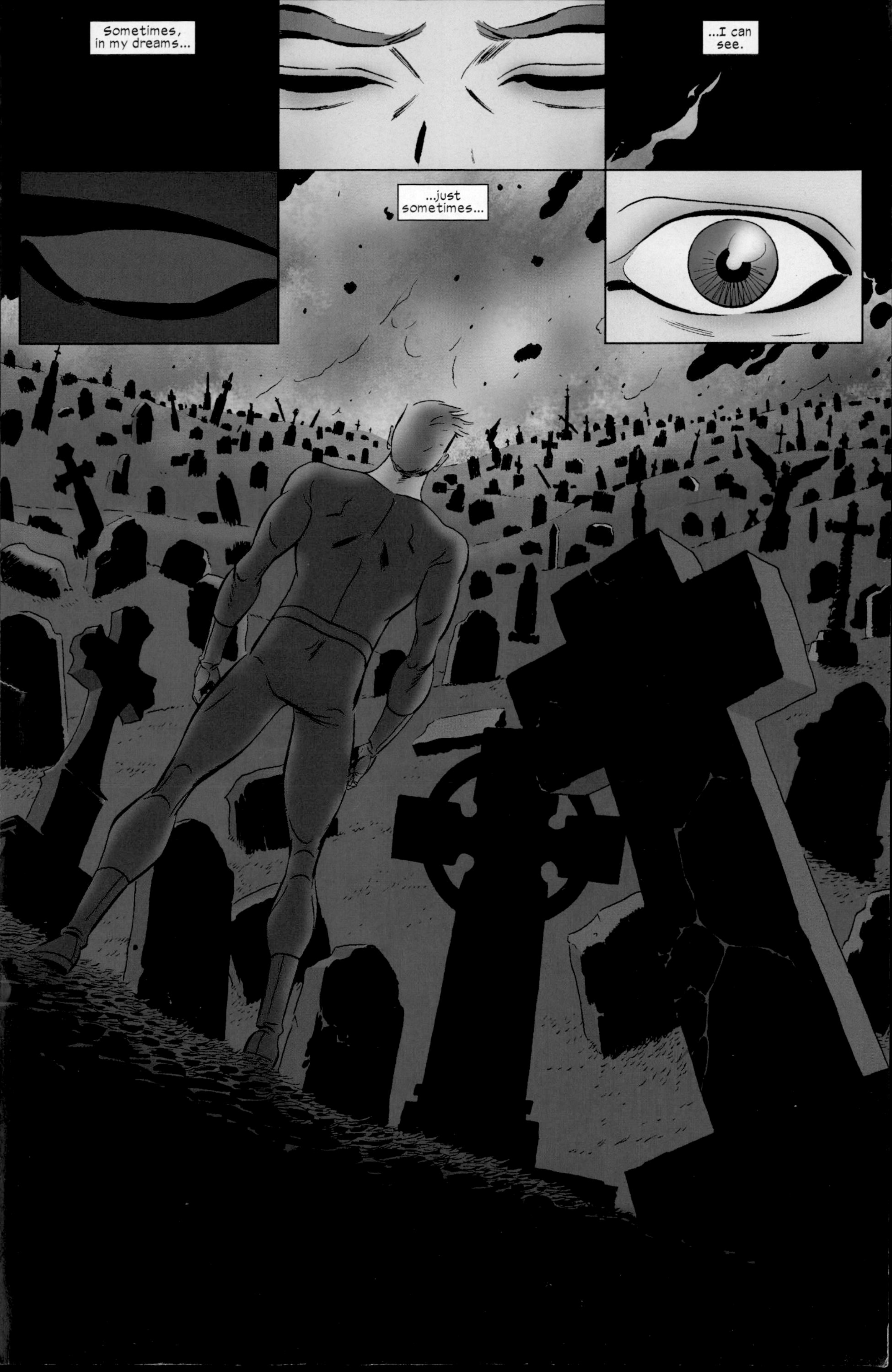
Sometimes, in my dreams...
...I can see.
...just sometimes...

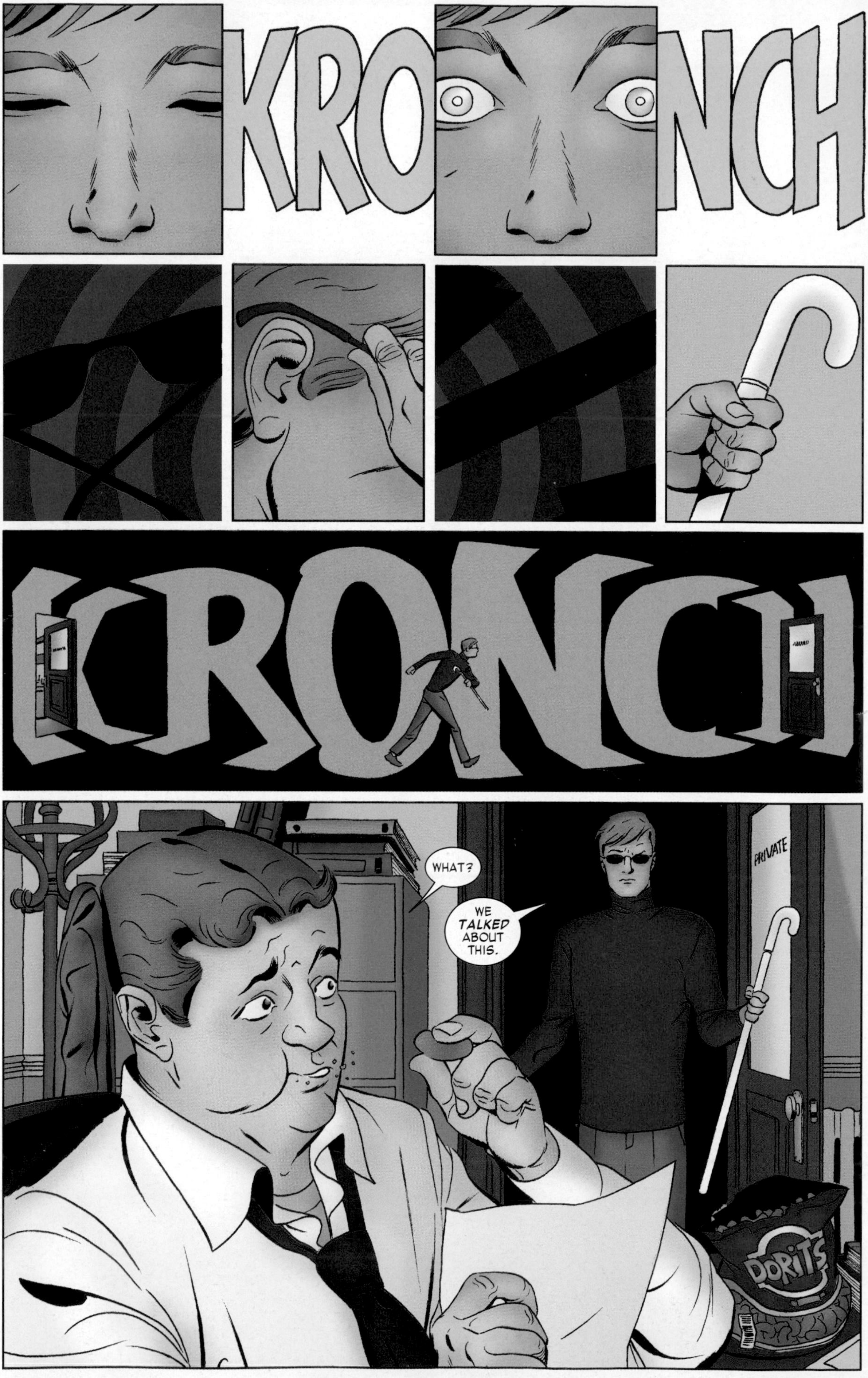
KRO
NCH
KRONCH
PRIVATE
WHAT?
WE TALKED ABOUT THIS.
DORITS

SORRY. SORRY. SORRY. TODAY'S THE DAY, RIGHT?

‡KAAF‡ YEP. AND YOU'RE COMING *WITH.*

PLOOF

ME? NO. CAN'T. NO TIME. TOO MUCH TO *DO.*

REBUILDING *NELSON & MURDOCK* IS AN *EXPENSIVE PROPOSITION,* MY FRIEND.

SO RIGHT NOW, WE ARE A *VOLUME BUSINESS.*

I'VE GOT BRIEFS TO FILE, CLERKS TO CALL, DEPOSITIONS TO CHECK, AFFIDA--

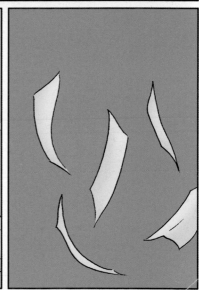

YOU ARE A *MYSTERY.*

I AM AN *OPEN BOOK.*

EVEN BOOKS *TRAVEL.* I DON'T UNDERSTAND HOW YOU CAN BE SO *SEDENTARY* AND SO *COOPED-UP* AND SO...SO...

RESPONSIBLE?

...NUMB. OH, MY *GOD,* FOGGY...WE LIVE IN *NEW YORK.*

THE GREATEST CITY ON *EARTH.*

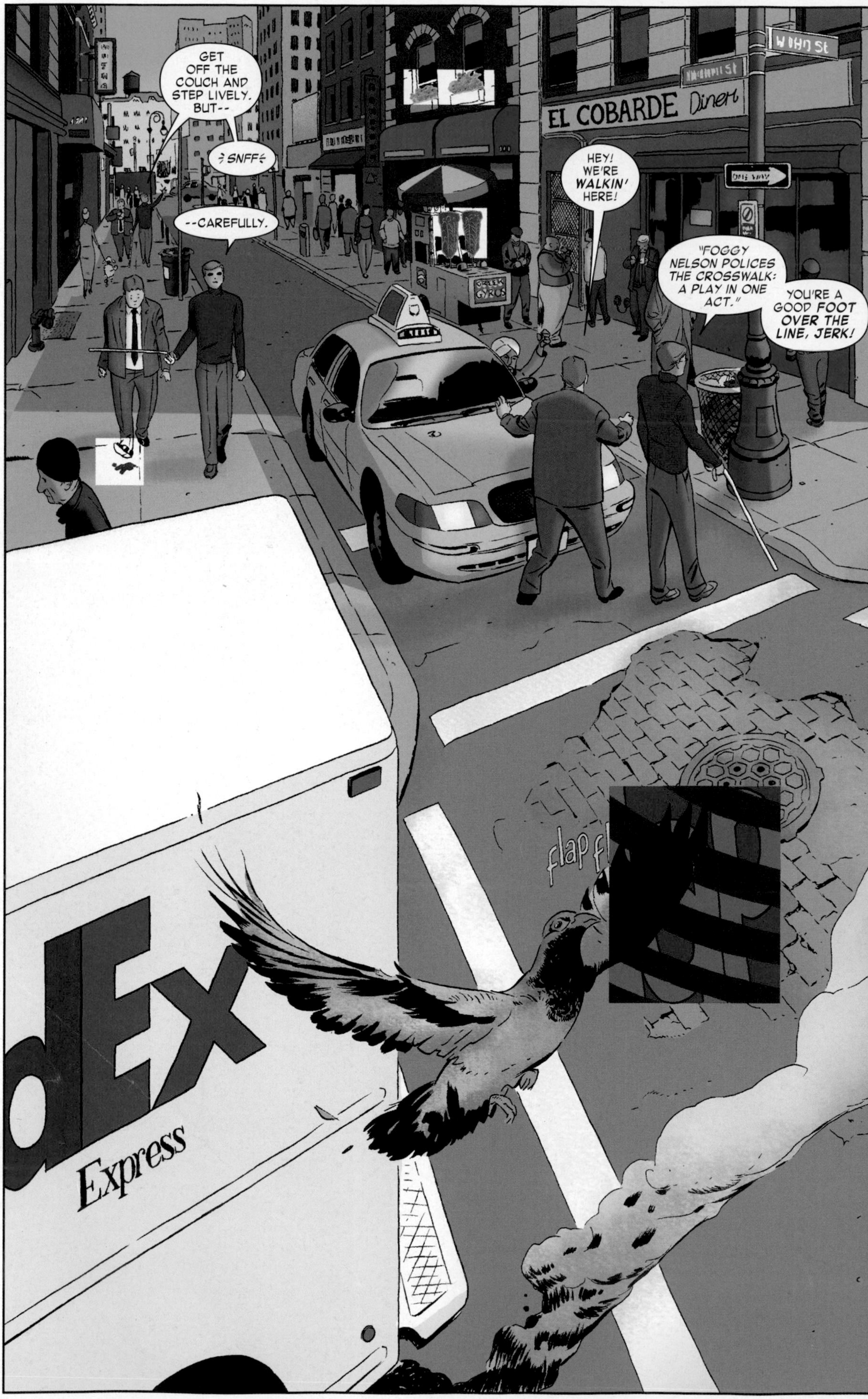
GET OFF THE COUCH AND STEP LIVELY. BUT--
SNFF
--CAREFULLY.
HEY! WE'RE WALKIN' HERE!
"FOGGY NELSON POLICES THE CROSSWALK: A PLAY IN ONE ACT."
YOU'RE A GOOD FOOT OVER THE LINE, JERK!
EL COBARDE Diner
GREEK GYROS
flap
Express

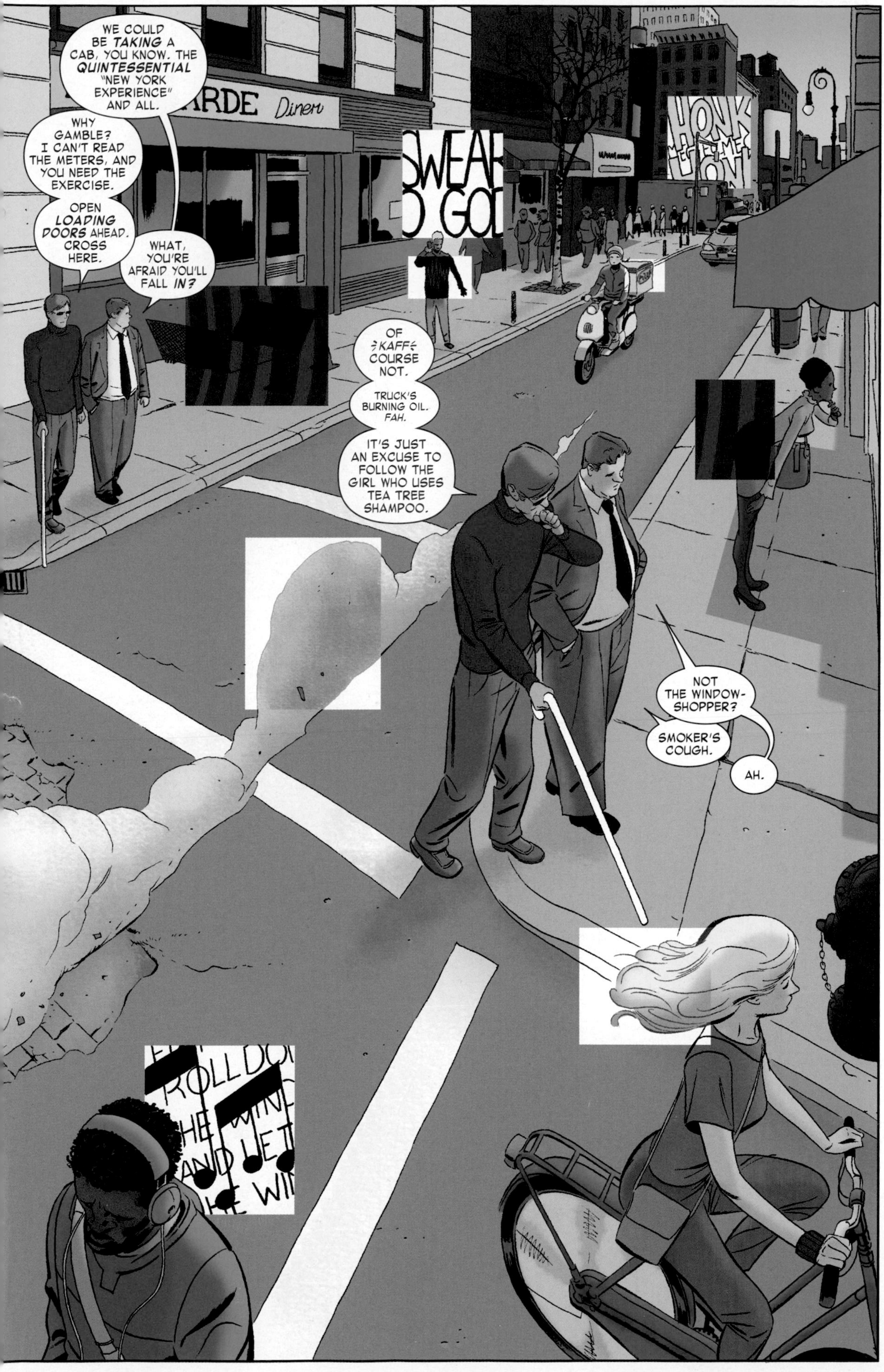
WE COULD BE *TAKING* A CAB, YOU KNOW. THE ***QUINTESSENTIAL*** "NEW YORK EXPERIENCE" AND ALL.
WHY GAMBLE? I CAN'T READ THE METERS, AND YOU NEED THE EXERCISE.
OPEN ***LOADING DOORS*** AHEAD. CROSS HERE.
WHAT, YOU'RE AFRAID YOU'LL FALL ***IN?***
OF *KAFF* COURSE NOT.
TRUCK'S BURNING OIL. *FAH.*
IT'S JUST AN EXCUSE TO FOLLOW THE GIRL WHO USES TEA TREE SHAMPOO.
NOT THE WINDOW-SHOPPER?
SMOKER'S COUGH.
AH.

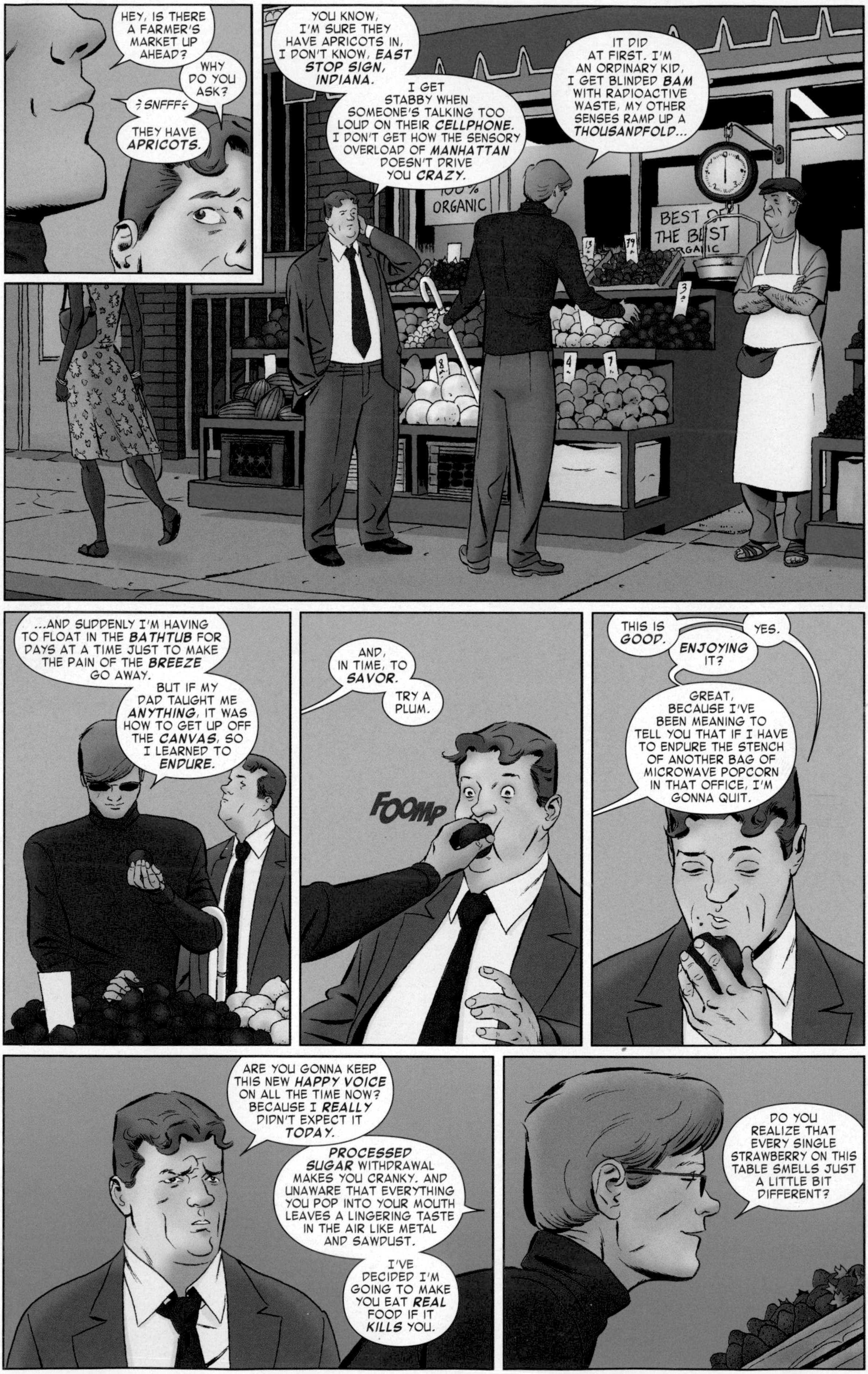

HEY, IS THERE A FARMER'S MARKET UP AHEAD?
WHY DO YOU ASK?
SNFFF
THEY HAVE APRICOTS.
YOU KNOW, I'M SURE THEY HAVE APRICOTS IN, I DON'T KNOW, EAST STOP SIGN, INDIANA.
I GET STABBY WHEN SOMEONE'S TALKING TOO LOUD ON THEIR CELLPHONE. I DON'T GET HOW THE SENSORY OVERLOAD OF MANHATTAN DOESN'T DRIVE YOU CRAZY.
IT DID AT FIRST. I'M AN ORDINARY KID, I GET BLINDED BAM WITH RADIOACTIVE WASTE, MY OTHER SENSES RAMP UP A THOUSANDFOLD...
ORGANIC
BEST OF THE BEST
...AND SUDDENLY I'M HAVING TO FLOAT IN THE BATHTUB FOR DAYS AT A TIME JUST TO MAKE THE PAIN OF THE BREEZE GO AWAY.
BUT IF MY DAD TAUGHT ME ANYTHING, IT WAS HOW TO GET UP OFF THE CANVAS, SO I LEARNED TO ENDURE.
AND, IN TIME, TO SAVOR.
TRY A PLUM.
FOOMP
THIS IS GOOD.
YES.
ENJOYING IT?
GREAT, BECAUSE I'VE BEEN MEANING TO TELL YOU THAT IF I HAVE TO ENDURE THE STENCH OF ANOTHER BAG OF MICROWAVE POPCORN IN THAT OFFICE, I'M GONNA QUIT.
ARE YOU GONNA KEEP THIS NEW HAPPY VOICE ON ALL THE TIME NOW? BECAUSE I REALLY DIDN'T EXPECT IT TODAY.
PROCESSED SUGAR WITHDRAWAL MAKES YOU CRANKY. AND UNAWARE THAT EVERYTHING YOU POP INTO YOUR MOUTH LEAVES A LINGERING TASTE IN THE AIR LIKE METAL AND SAWDUST.
I'VE DECIDED I'M GOING TO MAKE YOU EAT REAL FOOD IF IT KILLS YOU.
DO YOU REALIZE THAT EVERY SINGLE STRAWBERRY ON THIS TABLE SMELLS JUST A LITTLE BIT DIFFERENT?

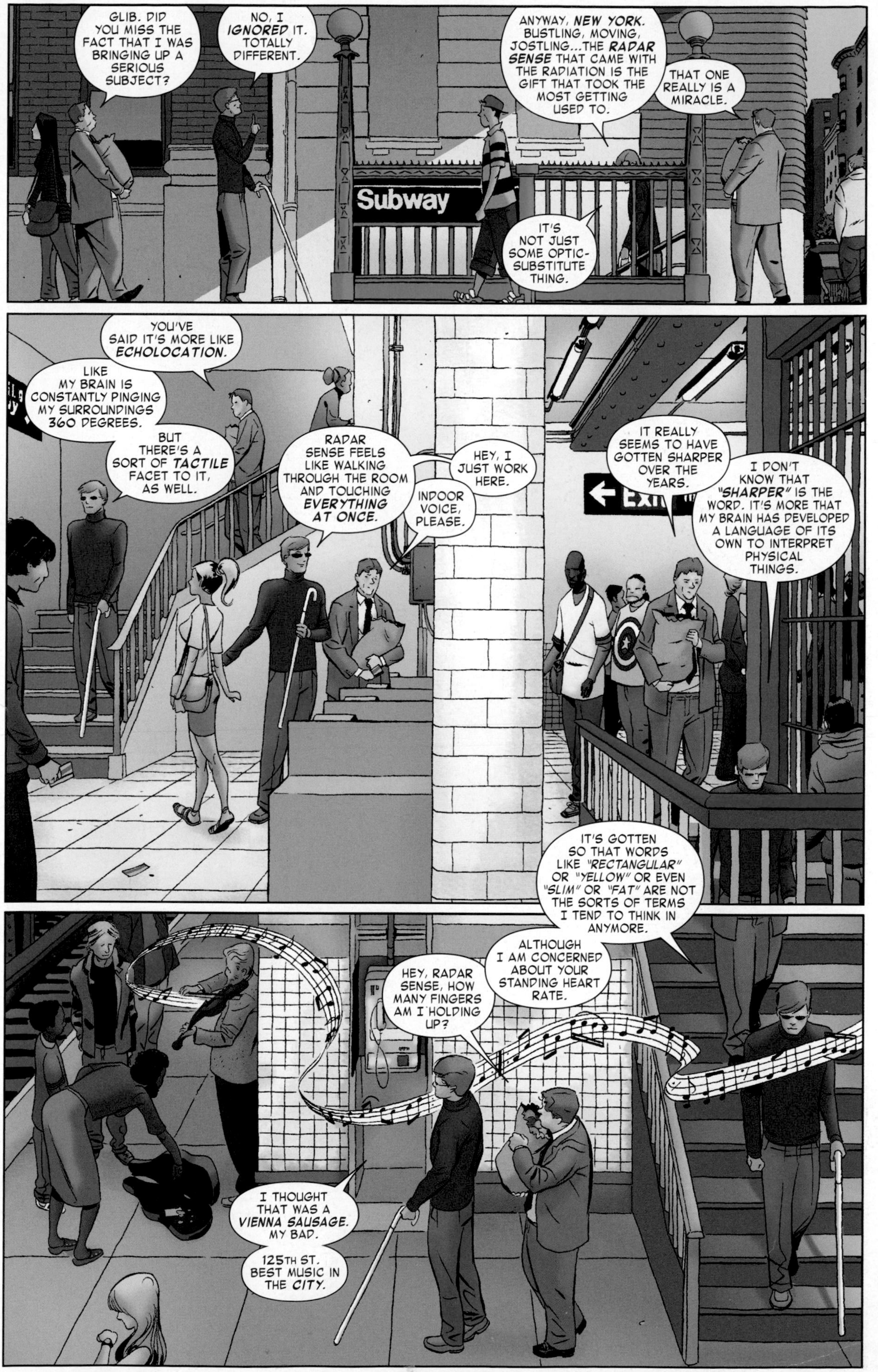
GLIB. DID YOU MISS THE FACT THAT I WAS BRINGING UP A SERIOUS SUBJECT?
NO, I IGNORED IT. TOTALLY DIFFERENT.
ANYWAY, NEW YORK. BUSTLING, MOVING, JOSTLING...THE RADAR SENSE THAT CAME WITH THE RADIATION IS THE GIFT THAT TOOK THE MOST GETTING USED TO.
THAT ONE REALLY IS A MIRACLE.
Subway
IT'S NOT JUST SOME OPTIC-SUBSTITUTE THING.
YOU'VE SAID IT'S MORE LIKE ECHOLOCATION.
LIKE MY BRAIN IS CONSTANTLY PINGING MY SURROUNDINGS 360 DEGREES.
BUT THERE'S A SORT OF TACTILE FACET TO IT, AS WELL.
RADAR SENSE FEELS LIKE WALKING THROUGH THE ROOM AND TOUCHING EVERYTHING AT ONCE.
HEY, I JUST WORK HERE.
INDOOR VOICE, PLEASE.
IT REALLY SEEMS TO HAVE GOTTEN SHARPER OVER THE YEARS.
I DON'T KNOW THAT "SHARPER" IS THE WORD. IT'S MORE THAT MY BRAIN HAS DEVELOPED A LANGUAGE OF ITS OWN TO INTERPRET PHYSICAL THINGS.
IT'S GOTTEN SO THAT WORDS LIKE "RECTANGULAR" OR "YELLOW" OR EVEN "SLIM" OR "FAT" ARE NOT THE SORTS OF TERMS I TEND TO THINK IN ANYMORE.
ALTHOUGH I AM CONCERNED ABOUT YOUR STANDING HEART RATE.
HEY, RADAR SENSE, HOW MANY FINGERS AM I HOLDING UP?
I THOUGHT THAT WAS A VIENNA SAUSAGE. MY BAD.
125TH ST. BEST MUSIC IN THE CITY.

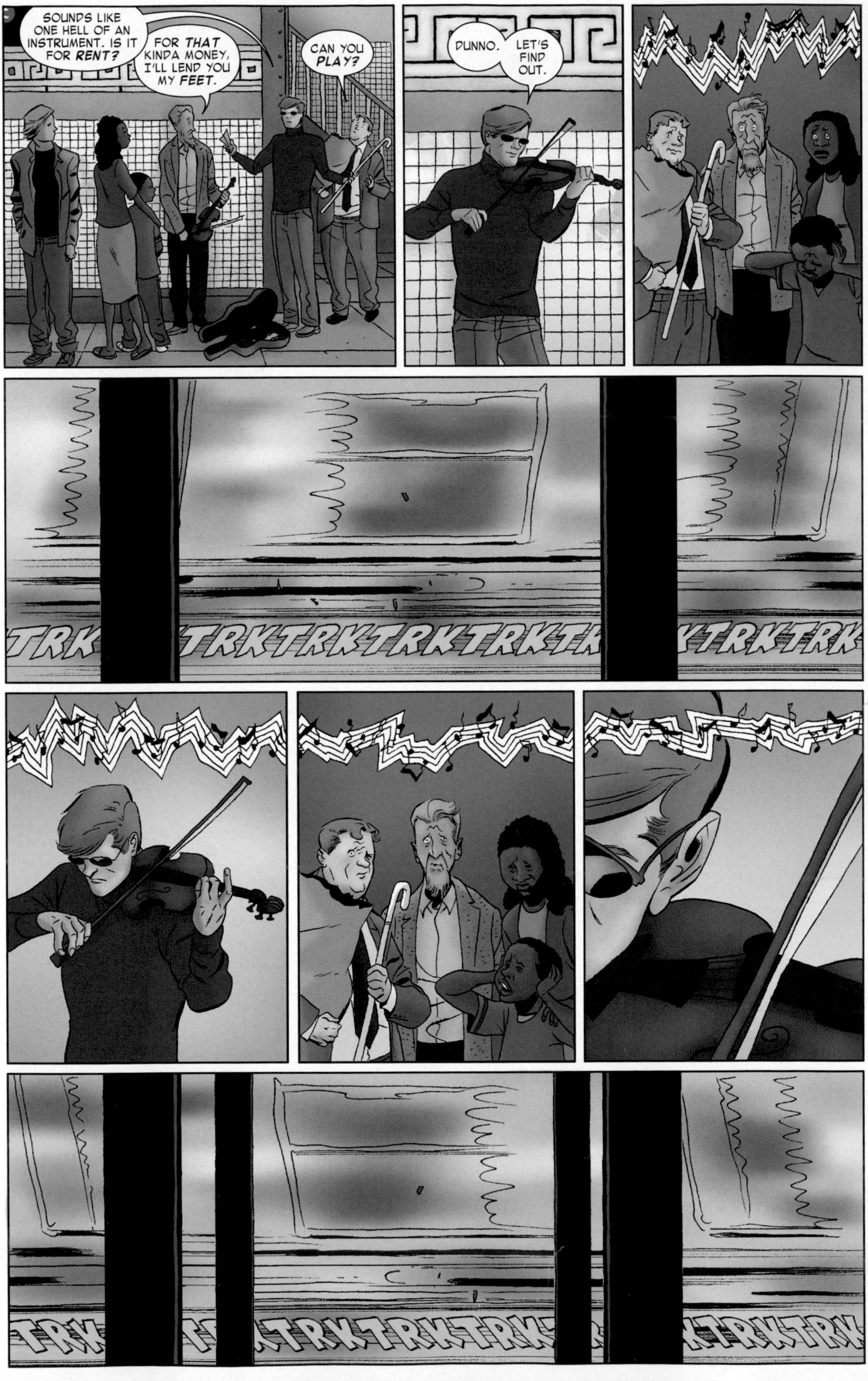
SOUNDS LIKE ONE HELL OF AN INSTRUMENT. IS IT FOR RENT?
FOR THAT KINDA MONEY, I'LL LEND YOU MY FEET.
CAN YOU PLAY?
DUNNO.
LET'S FIND OUT.
TRKTRKTRKTRKTRKTRKTRKTRKTRK
TRKTRKTRKTRKTRKTRKTRK

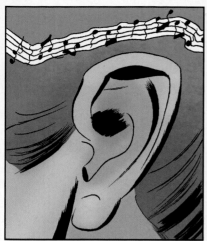

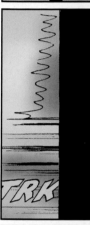
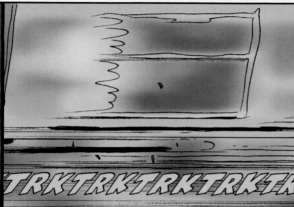

TRKTRKTRKTRKTRKTRKTRKTRKTRKTRK

CLAP CLAP CLAP CLAP

227

BRAVISSIMO. THERE'S A TRICK I'VE NEVER SEEN BEFORE.

NOW, CAN WE STOP PUTTING THIS OFF?

YES, DEAR.

LEAD THE WAY.

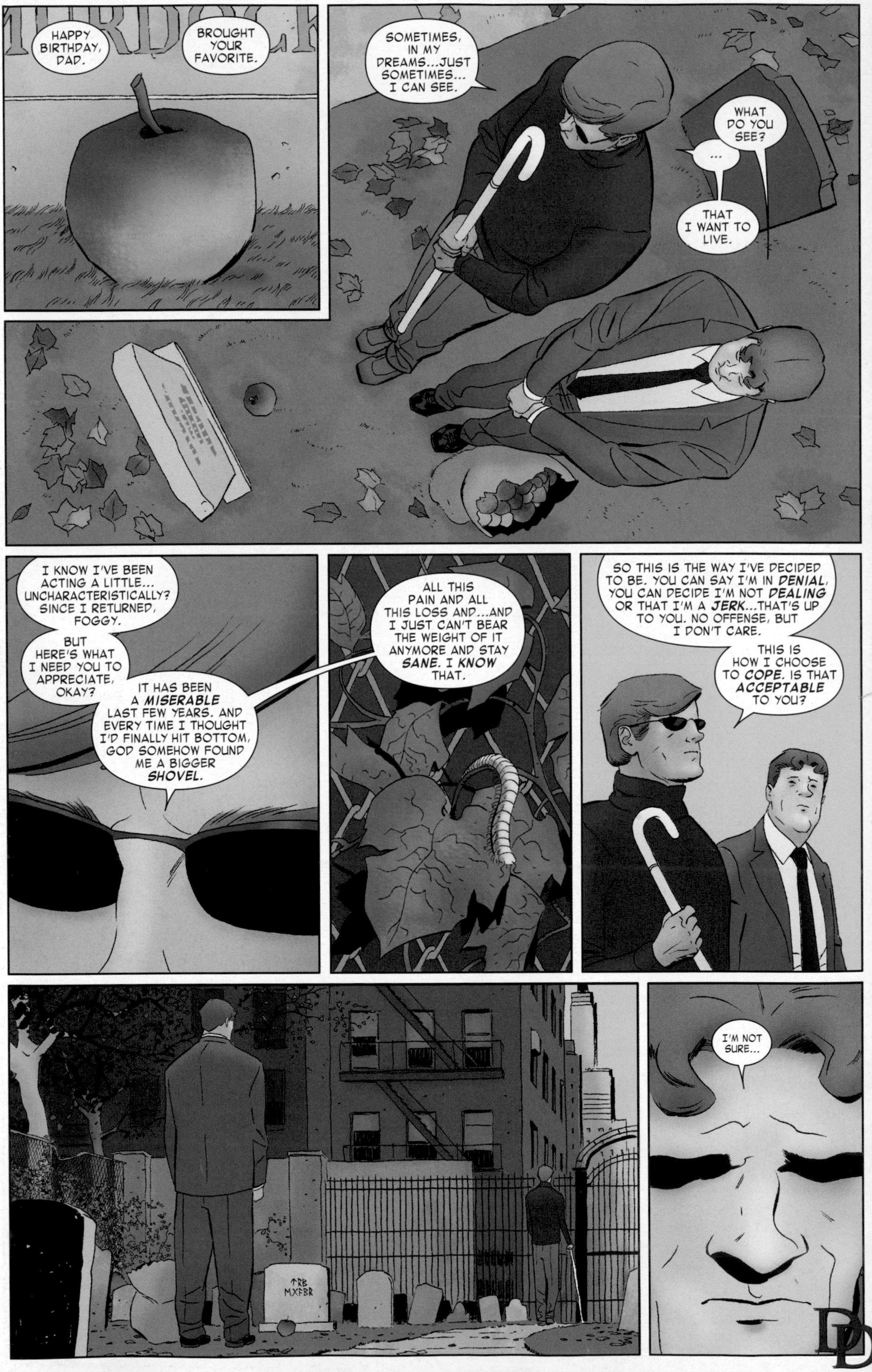
HAPPY BIRTHDAY, DAD.
BROUGHT YOUR FAVORITE.
SOMETIMES, IN MY DREAMS...JUST SOMETIMES... I CAN SEE.
WHAT DO YOU SEE?
...
THAT I WANT TO LIVE.
I KNOW I'VE BEEN ACTING A LITTLE... UNCHARACTERISTICALLY? SINCE I RETURNED, FOGGY.
BUT HERE'S WHAT I NEED YOU TO APPRECIATE, OKAY?
IT HAS BEEN A MISERABLE LAST FEW YEARS. AND EVERY TIME I THOUGHT I'D FINALLY HIT BOTTOM, GOD SOMEHOW FOUND ME A BIGGER SHOVEL.
ALL THIS PAIN AND ALL THIS LOSS AND...AND I JUST CAN'T BEAR THE WEIGHT OF IT ANYMORE AND STAY SANE. I KNOW THAT.
SO THIS IS THE WAY I'VE DECIDED TO BE. YOU CAN SAY I'M IN DENIAL, YOU CAN DECIDE I'M NOT DEALING OR THAT I'M A JERK...THAT'S UP TO YOU. NO OFFENSE, BUT I DON'T CARE.
THIS IS HOW I CHOOSE TO COPE. IS THAT ACCEPTABLE TO YOU?
I'M NOT SURE...

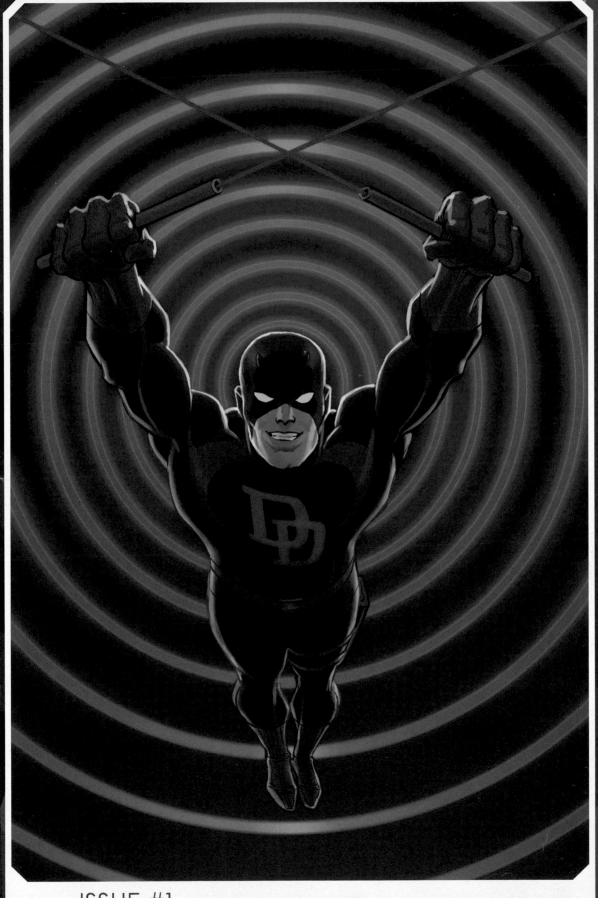

ISSUE #1 VARIANT BY JOHN ROMITA, TOM PALMER & DEAN WHITE

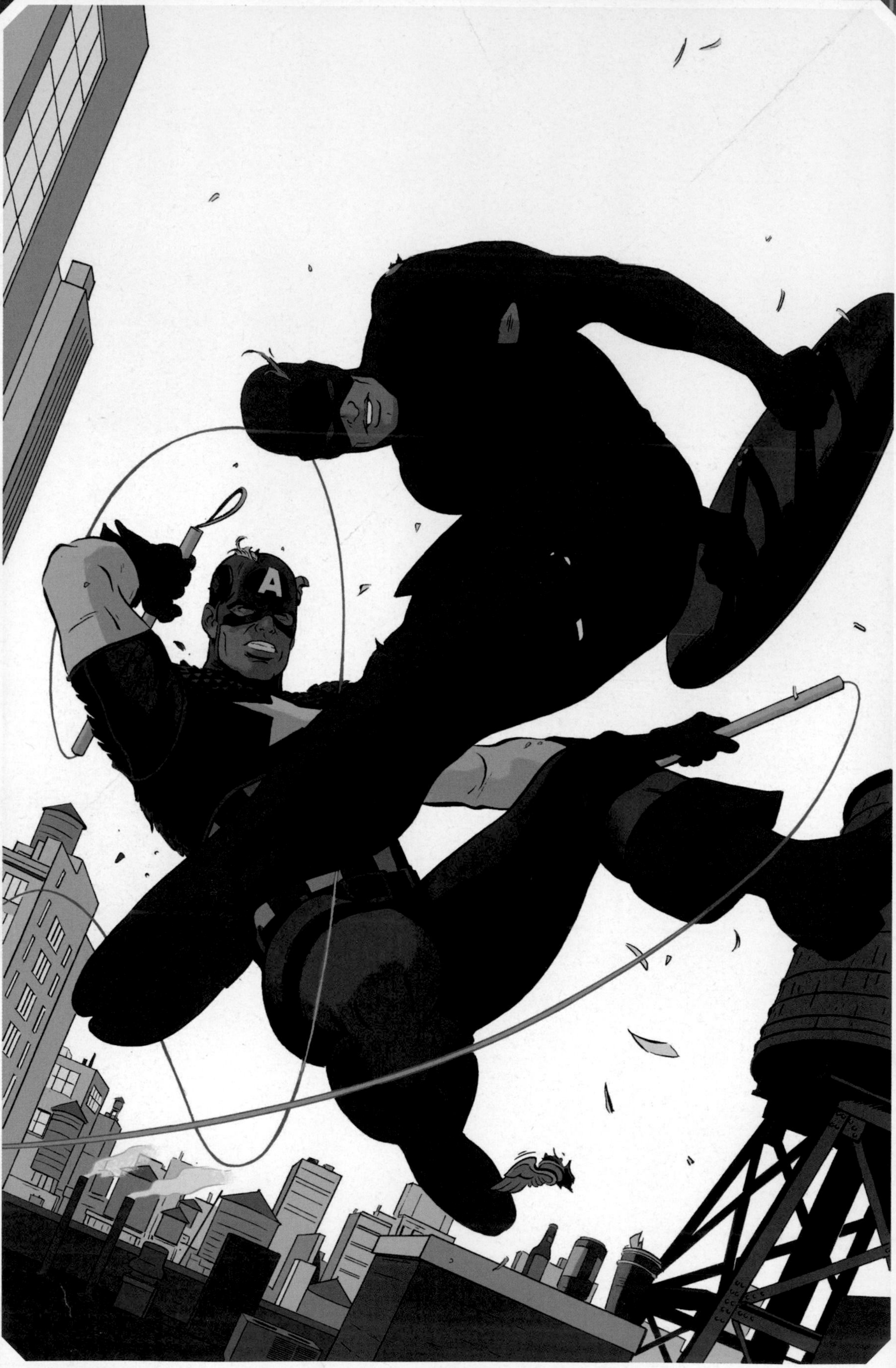

TWO

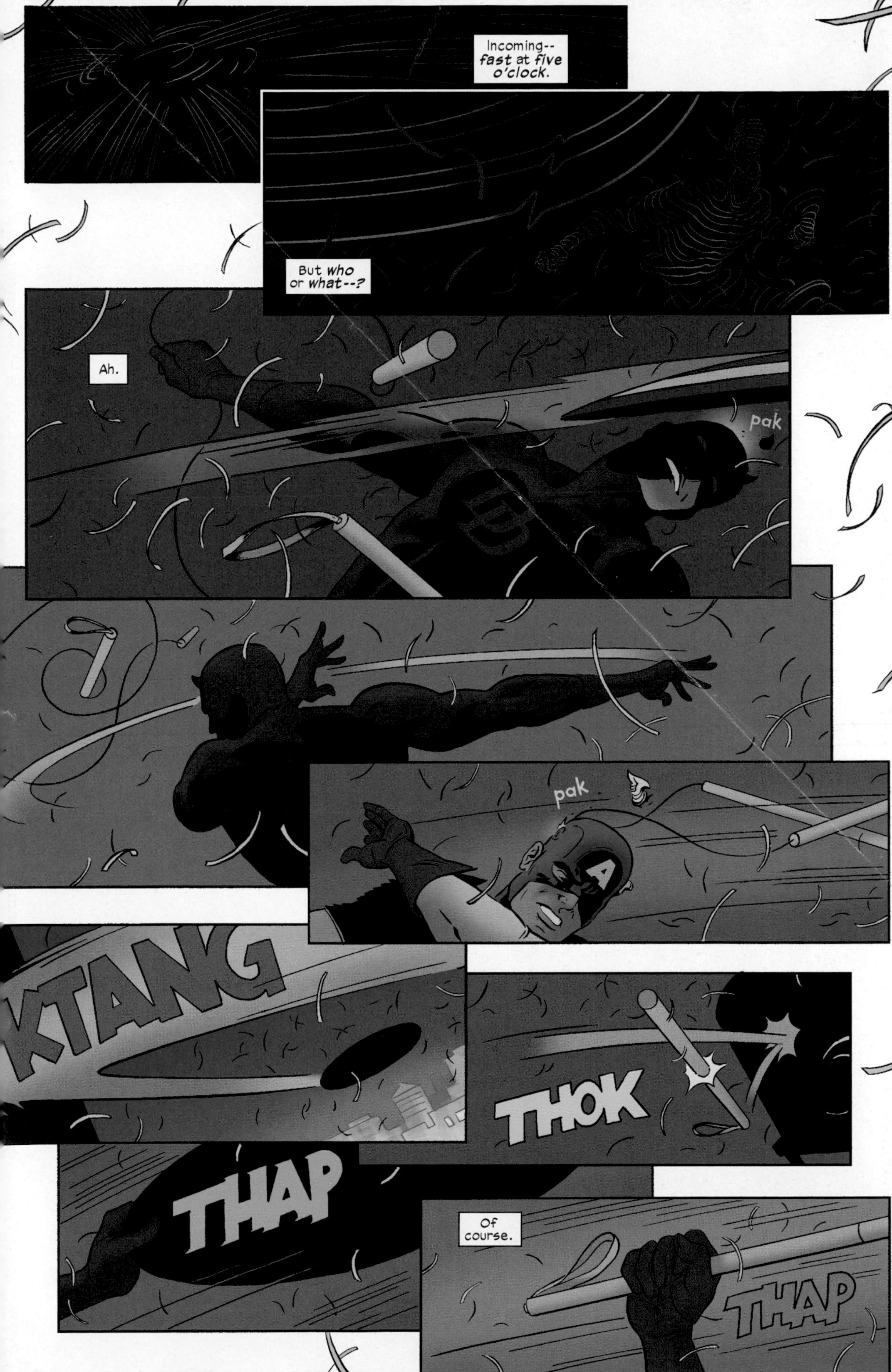
Incoming-- fast at five o'clock.
But who or what--?
Ah.
pak
pak
KTANG
THOK
THAP
Of course.
THAP

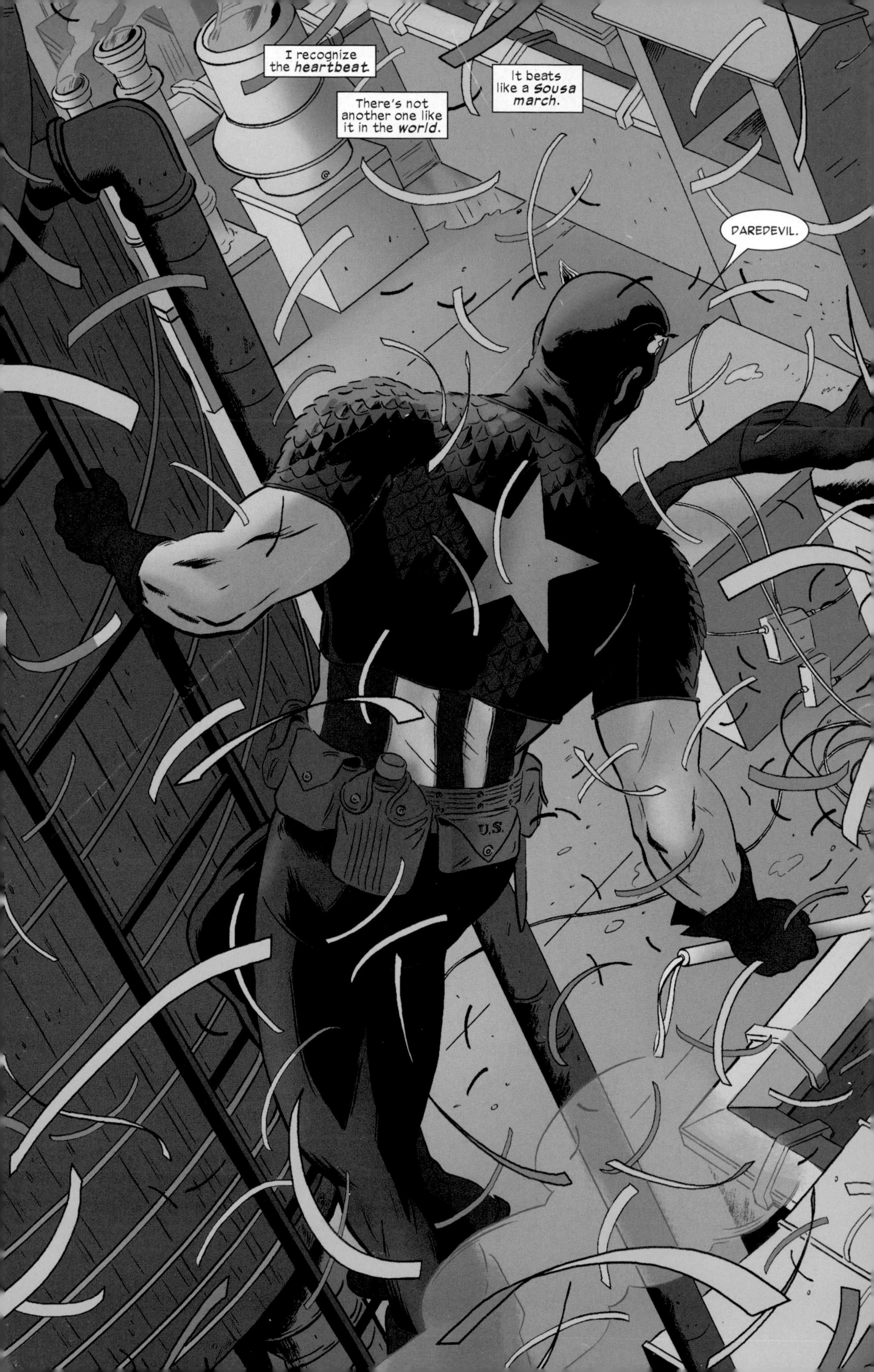
I recognize the *heartbeat*.
There's not another one like it in the *world*.
It beats like a *Sousa march*.
DAREDEVIL.

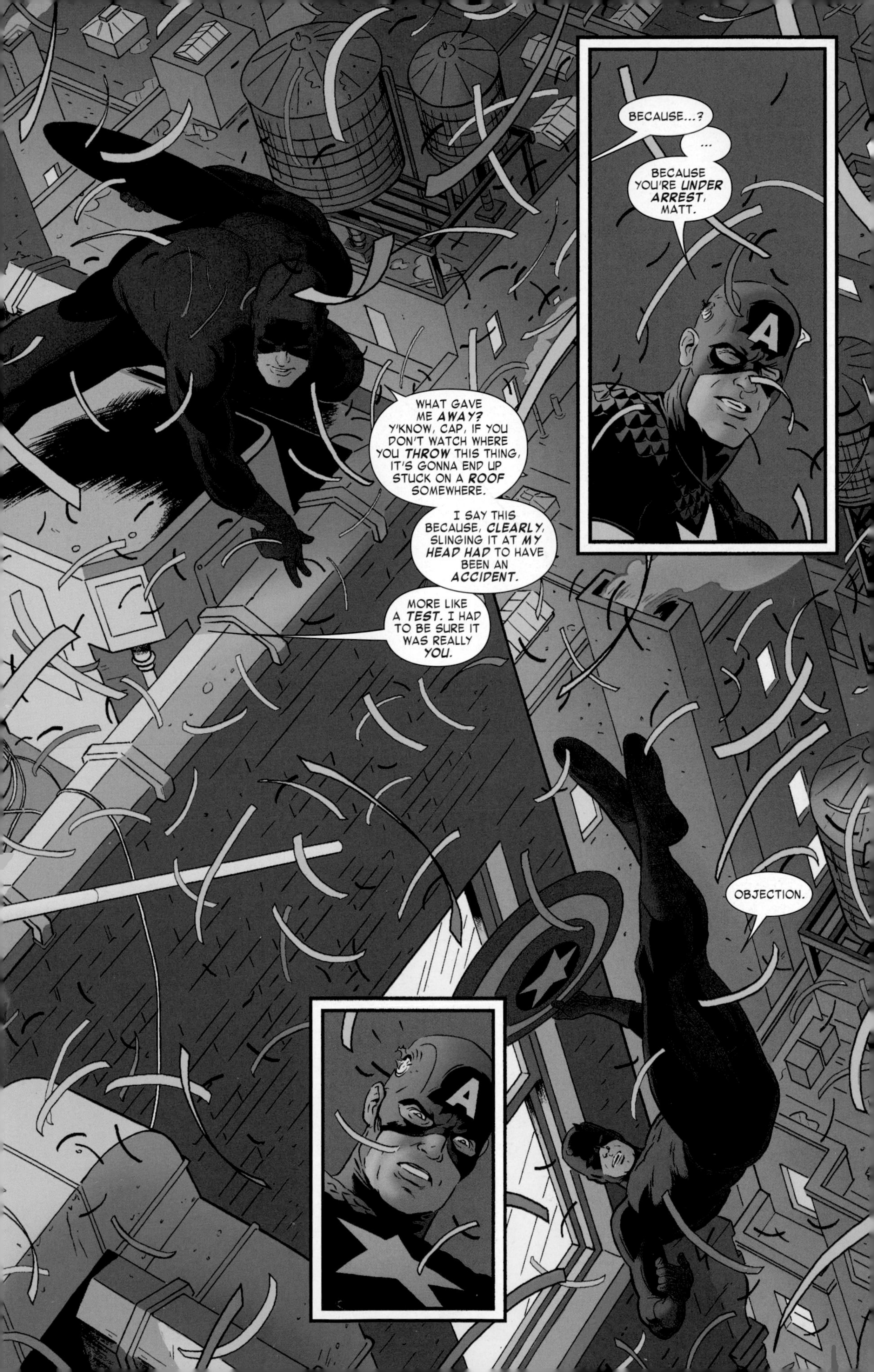
WHAT GAVE ME AWAY? Y'KNOW, CAP, IF YOU DON'T WATCH WHERE YOU THROW THIS THING, IT'S GONNA END UP STUCK ON A ROOF SOMEWHERE.
I SAY THIS BECAUSE, CLEARLY, SLINGING IT AT MY HEAD HAD TO HAVE BEEN AN ACCIDENT.
MORE LIKE A TEST. I HAD TO BE SURE IT WAS REALLY YOU.
BECAUSE...?
...
BECAUSE YOU'RE UNDER ARREST, MATT.
OBJECTION.

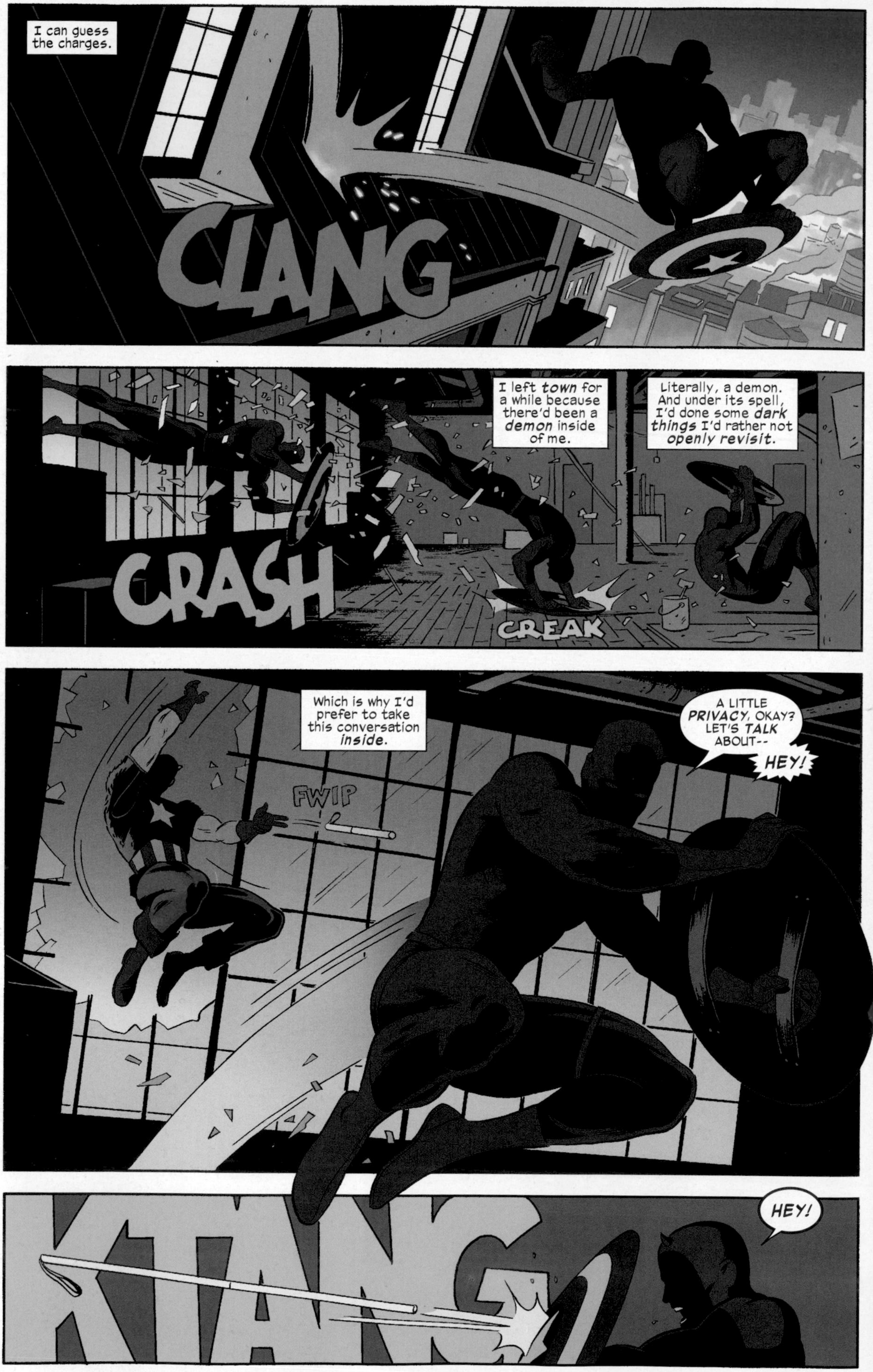

I can guess the charges.
CLANG
CRASH
I left *town* for a while because there'd been a *demon* inside of me.
Literally, a demon. And under its spell, I'd done some *dark things* I'd rather not *openly revisit*.
CREAK
Which is why I'd prefer to take this conversation *inside*.
A LITTLE *PRIVACY*, OKAY? LET'S *TALK* ABOUT--
HEY!
FWIP
KTANG
HEY!

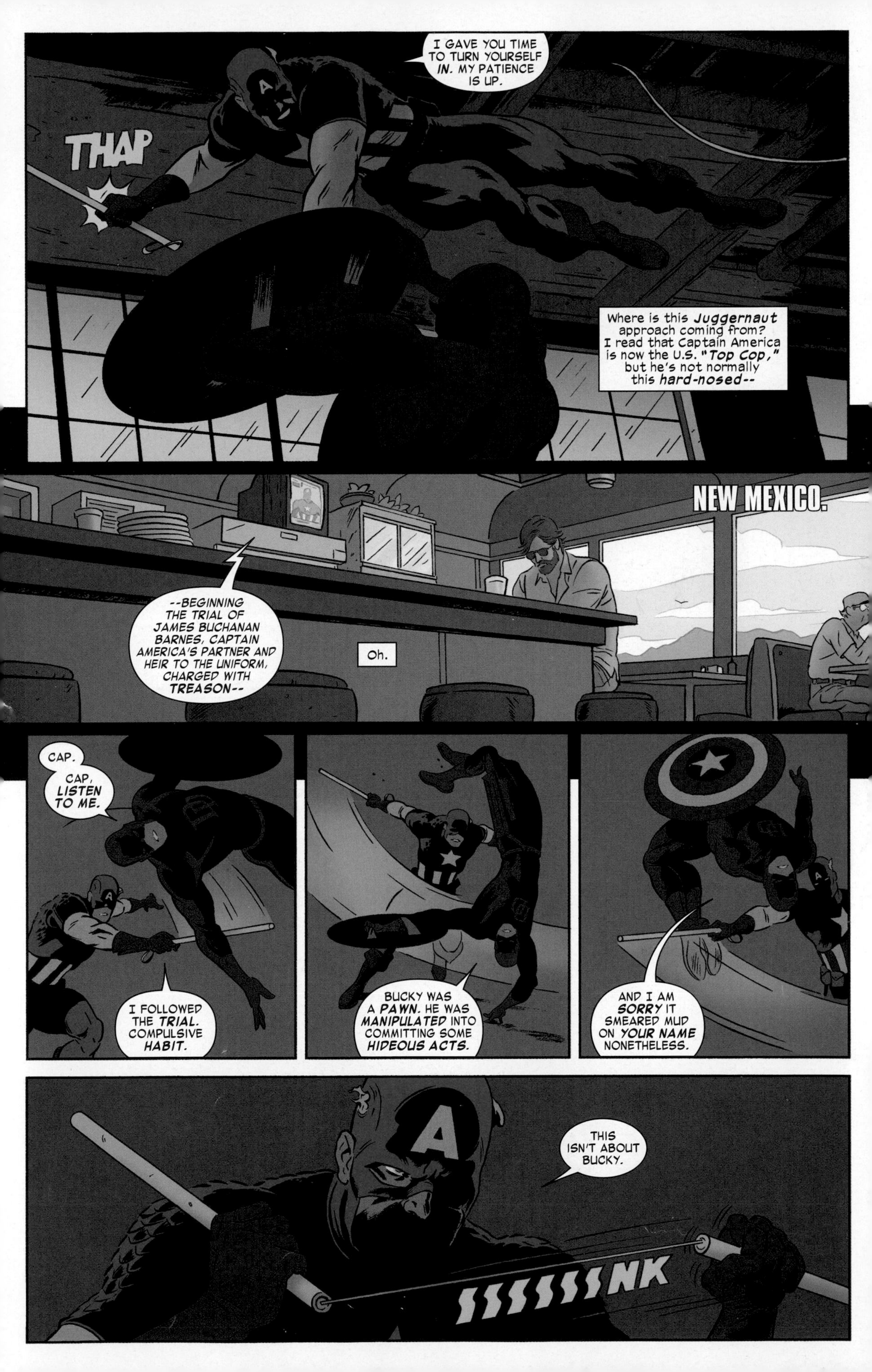
I GAVE YOU TIME TO TURN YOURSELF IN. MY PATIENCE IS UP.
THAP
Where is this Juggernaut approach coming from? I read that Captain America is now the U.S. "Top Cop," but he's not normally this hard-nosed--
NEW MEXICO.
--BEGINNING THE TRIAL OF JAMES BUCHANAN BARNES, CAPTAIN AMERICA'S PARTNER AND HEIR TO THE UNIFORM, CHARGED WITH TREASON--
Oh.
CAP.
CAP, LISTEN TO ME.
I FOLLOWED THE TRIAL. COMPULSIVE HABIT.
BUCKY WAS A PAWN. HE WAS MANIPULATED INTO COMMITTING SOME HIDEOUS ACTS.
AND I AM SORRY IT SMEARED MUD ON YOUR NAME NONETHELESS.
THIS ISN'T ABOUT BUCKY.
SSSSSSSNK

IT *TOTALLY* IS. BECAUSE NOW THAT YOU'VE BEEN PUT IN CHARGE OF HOLDING *EVERYONE* ACCOUNTABLE, YOU THINK *EVERYONE'S* MISSTEPS REFLECT ON YOU.

FWIP

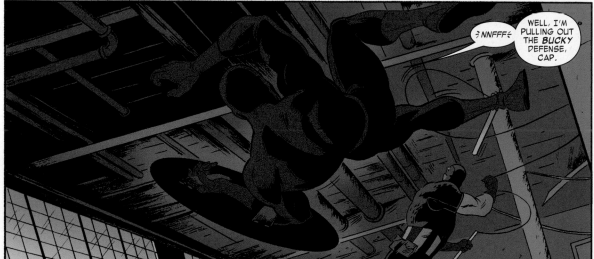

≥NNFFF≤

WELL, I'M PULLING OUT THE *BUCKY* DEFENSE, CAP.

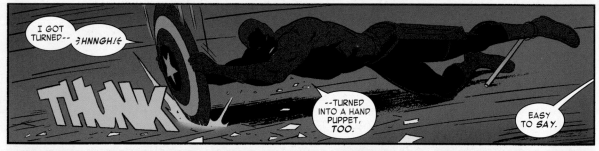

I GOT TURNED-- ≥HNNGH!≤

THNNK

--TURNED INTO A HAND PUPPET, *TOO.*

EASY TO *SAY.*

FPPPP

HARD TO *ADMIT.*

THINK. WHEN THE AVENGERS SPLASHED YOU INTO THE MODERN WORLD, DO YOU REMEMBER WHAT THE *PAGE TWO* HEADLINE WAS THAT *SAME* DAY?

"MASKED *'DAREDEVIL'* TOPPLES FIXER'S SYNDICATE."

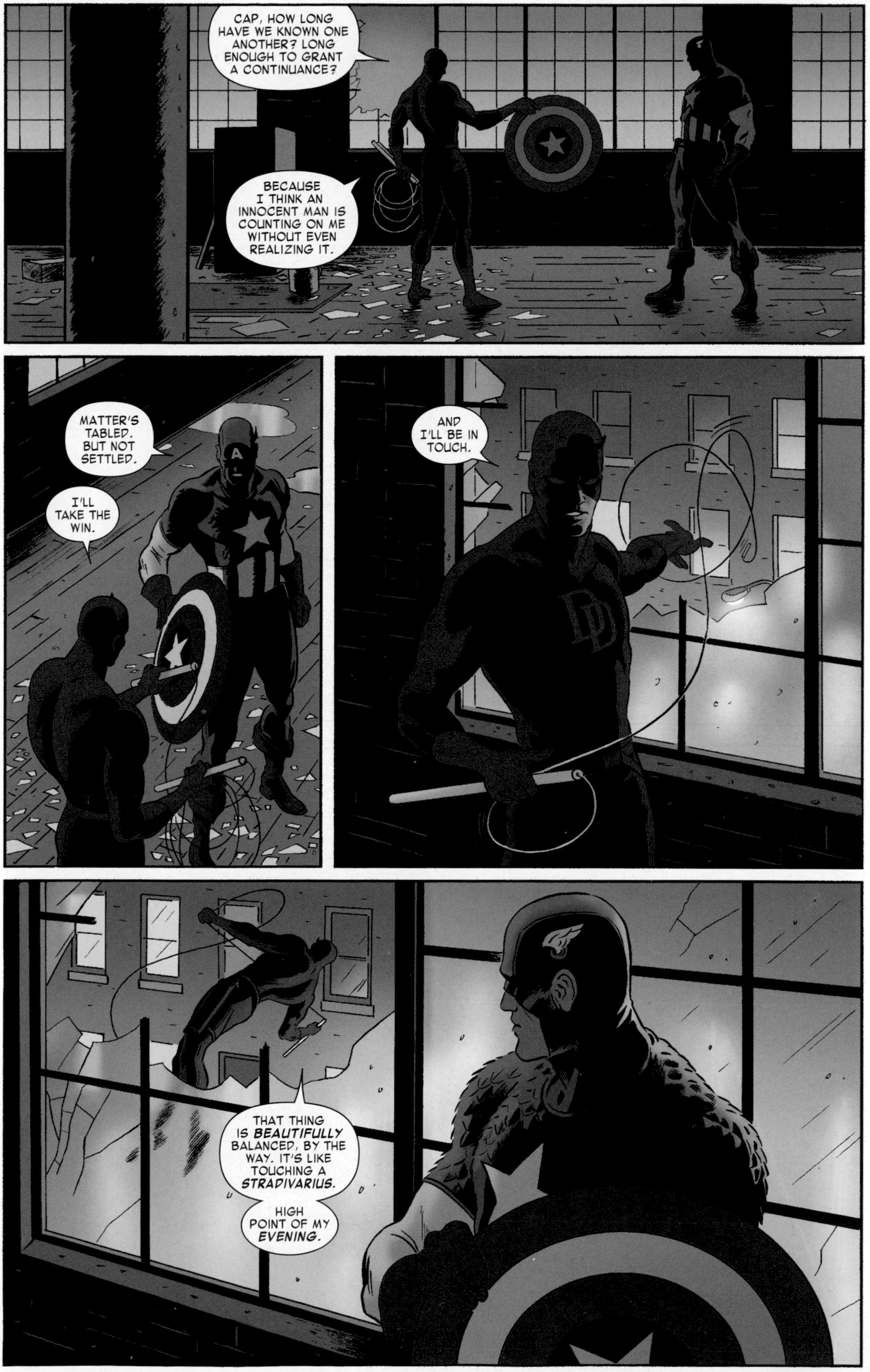
CAP, HOW LONG HAVE WE KNOWN ONE ANOTHER? LONG ENOUGH TO GRANT A CONTINUANCE?
BECAUSE I THINK AN INNOCENT MAN IS COUNTING ON ME WITHOUT EVEN REALIZING IT.
MATTER'S TABLED. BUT NOT SETTLED.
I'LL TAKE THE WIN.
AND I'LL BE IN TOUCH.
THAT THING IS *BEAUTIFULLY* BALANCED, BY THE WAY. IT'S LIKE TOUCHING A *STRADIVARIUS*.
HIGH POINT OF MY *EVENING*.

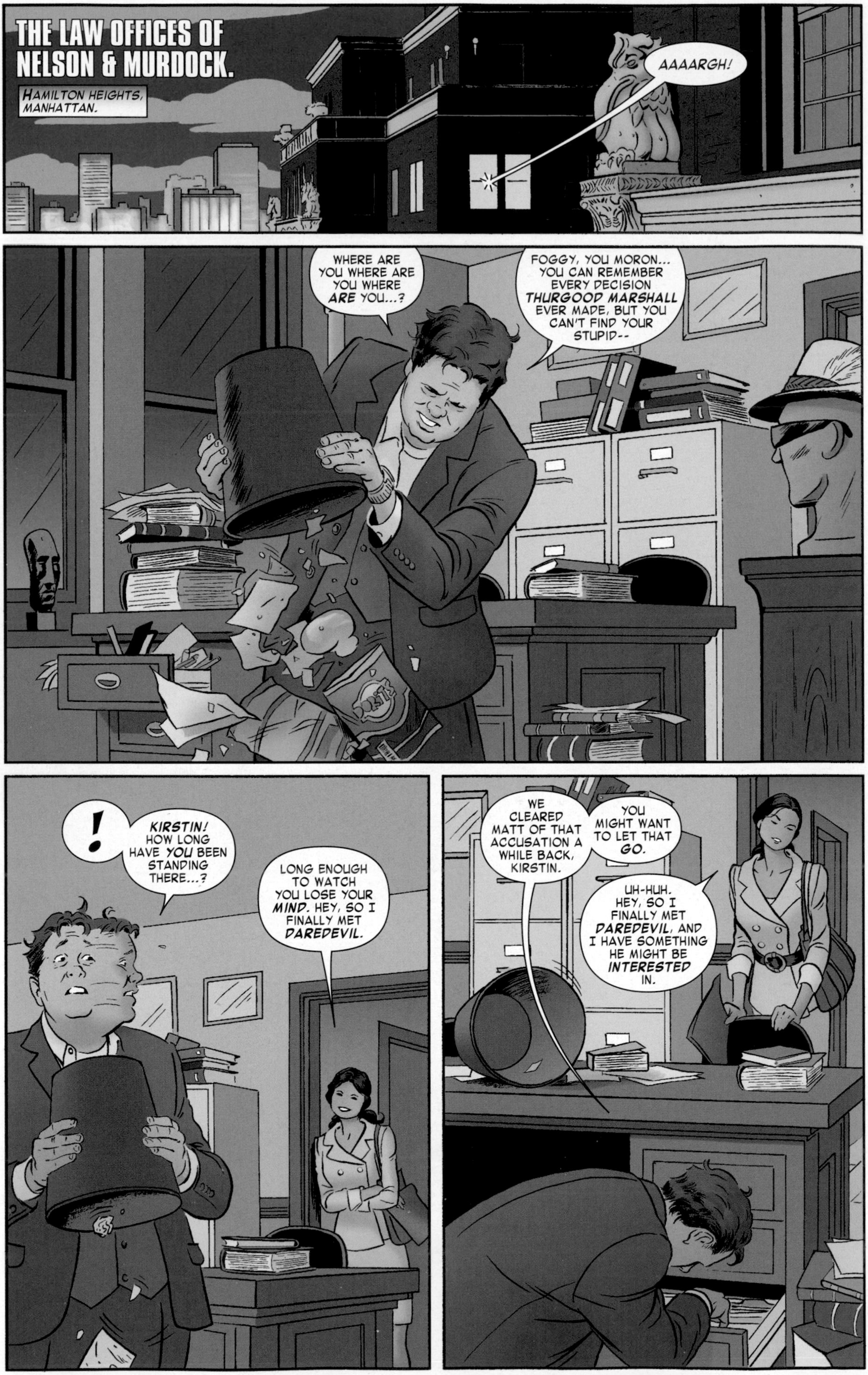
THE LAW OFFICES OF NELSON & MURDOCK.
HAMILTON HEIGHTS, MANHATTAN.
AAAARGH!
WHERE ARE YOU WHERE ARE YOU WHERE ARE YOU...?
FOGGY, YOU MORON... YOU CAN REMEMBER EVERY DECISION THURGOOD MARSHALL EVER MADE, BUT YOU CAN'T FIND YOUR STUPID--
!
KIRSTIN! HOW LONG HAVE YOU BEEN STANDING THERE...?
LONG ENOUGH TO WATCH YOU LOSE YOUR MIND. HEY, SO I FINALLY MET DAREDEVIL.
WE CLEARED MATT OF THAT ACCUSATION A WHILE BACK, KIRSTIN.
YOU MIGHT WANT TO LET THAT GO.
UH-HUH. HEY, SO I FINALLY MET DAREDEVIL, AND I HAVE SOMETHING HE MIGHT BE INTERESTED IN.

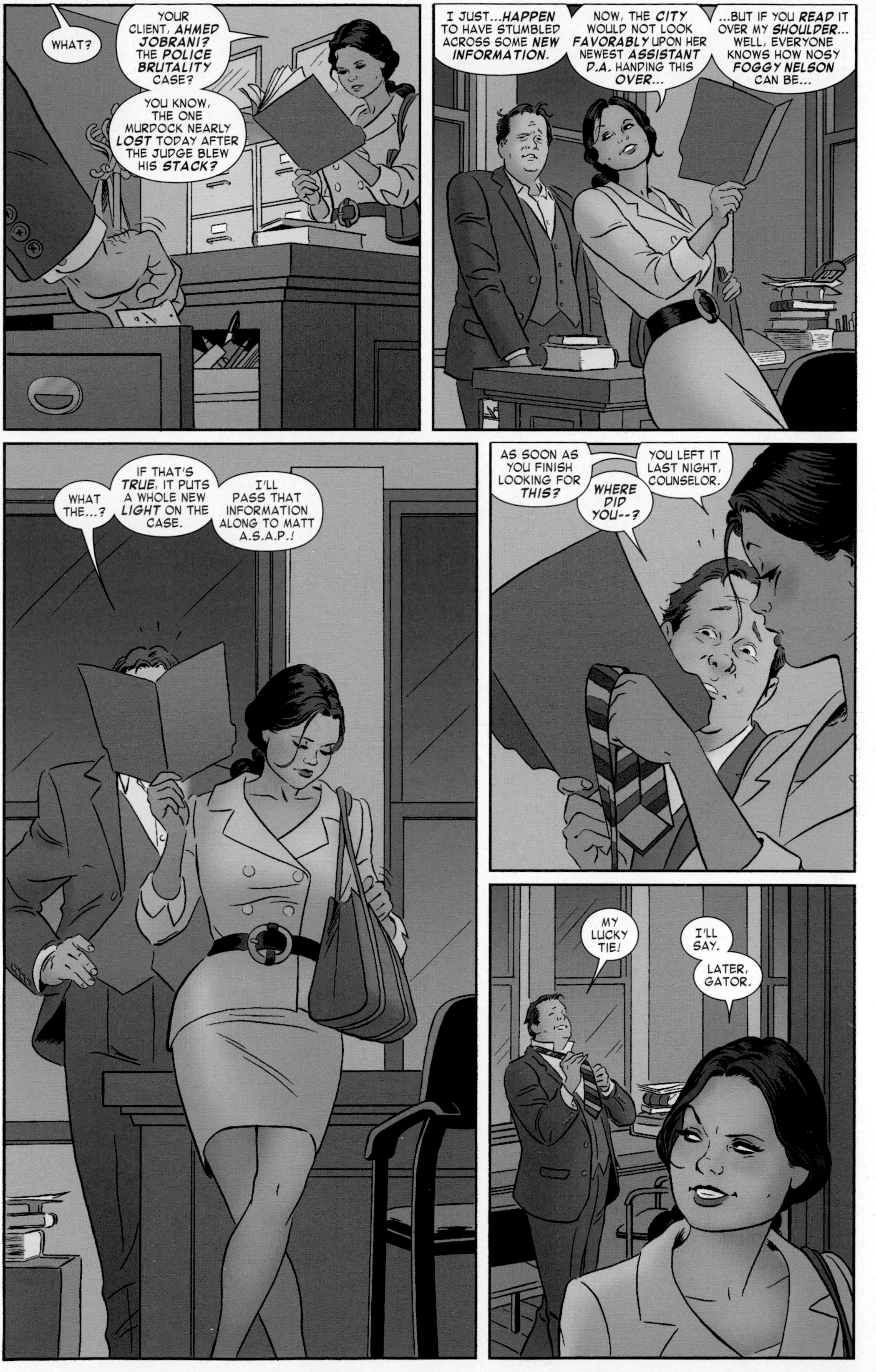
WHAT?
YOUR CLIENT, AHMED JOBRANI? THE POLICE BRUTALITY CASE?
YOU KNOW, THE ONE MURDOCK NEARLY LOST TODAY AFTER THE JUDGE BLEW HIS STACK?
I JUST...HAPPEN TO HAVE STUMBLED ACROSS SOME NEW INFORMATION.
NOW, THE CITY WOULD NOT LOOK FAVORABLY UPON HER NEWEST ASSISTANT D.A. HANDING THIS OVER...
...BUT IF YOU READ IT OVER MY SHOULDER... WELL, EVERYONE KNOWS HOW NOSY FOGGY NELSON CAN BE...
WHAT THE...?
IF THAT'S TRUE, IT PUTS A WHOLE NEW LIGHT ON THE CASE.
I'LL PASS THAT INFORMATION ALONG TO MATT A.S.A.P.!
AS SOON AS YOU FINISH LOOKING FOR THIS?
WHERE DID YOU--?
YOU LEFT IT LAST NIGHT, COUNSELOR.
MY LUCKY TIE!
I'LL SAY.
LATER, GATOR.

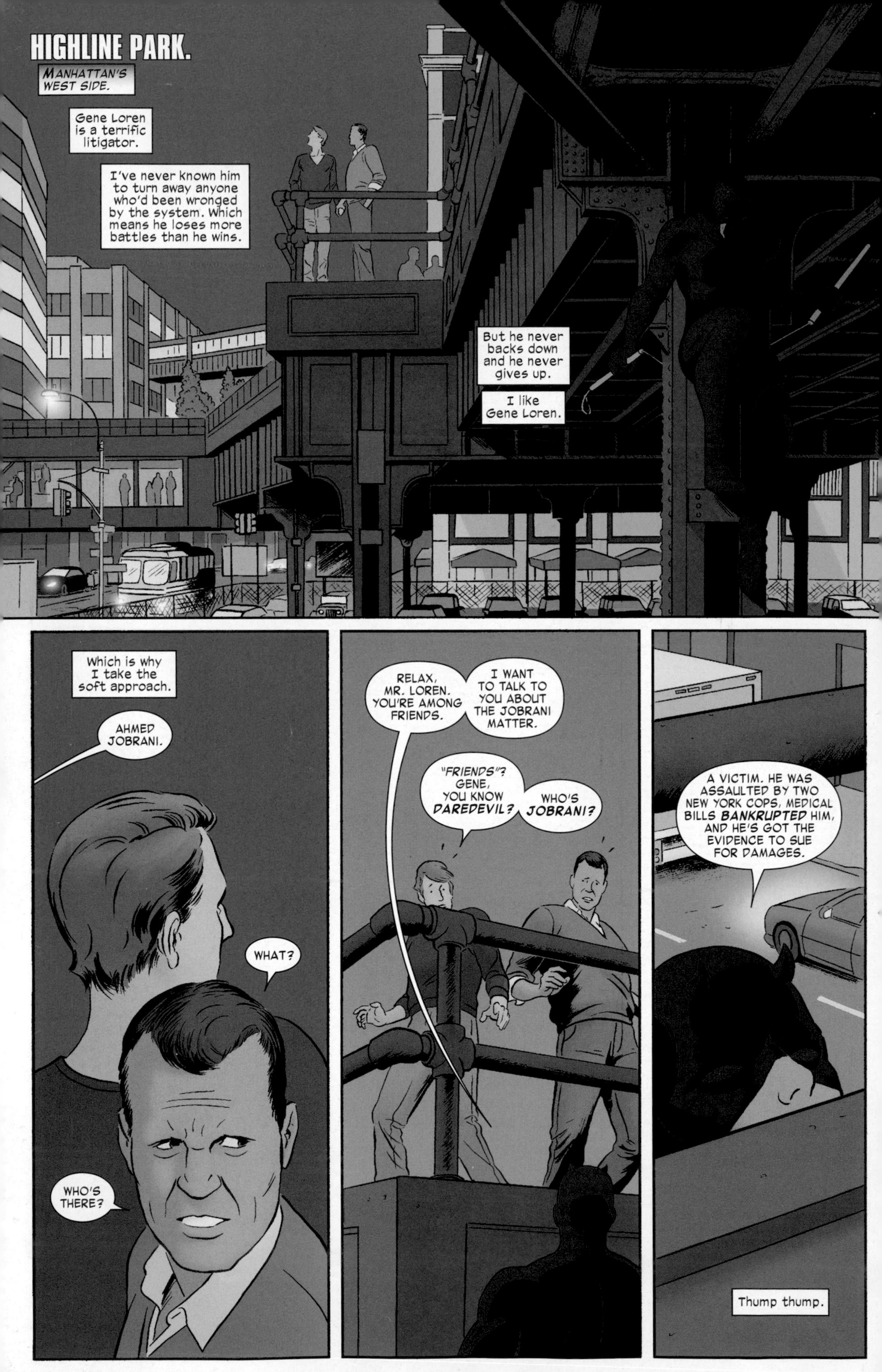
HIGHLINE PARK.
MANHATTAN'S WEST SIDE.
Gene Loren is a terrific litigator.
I've never known him to turn away anyone who'd been wronged by the system. Which means he loses more battles than he wins.
But he never backs down and he never gives up.
I like Gene Loren.
Which is why I take the soft approach.
AHMED JOBRANI.
WHAT?
WHO'S THERE?
RELAX, MR. LOREN. YOU'RE AMONG FRIENDS.
I WANT TO TALK TO YOU ABOUT THE JOBRANI MATTER.
"FRIENDS"? GENE, YOU KNOW DAREDEVIL?
WHO'S JOBRANI?
A VICTIM. HE WAS ASSAULTED BY TWO NEW YORK COPS, MEDICAL BILLS BANKRUPTED HIM, AND HE'S GOT THE EVIDENCE TO SUE FOR DAMAGES.
Thump thump.

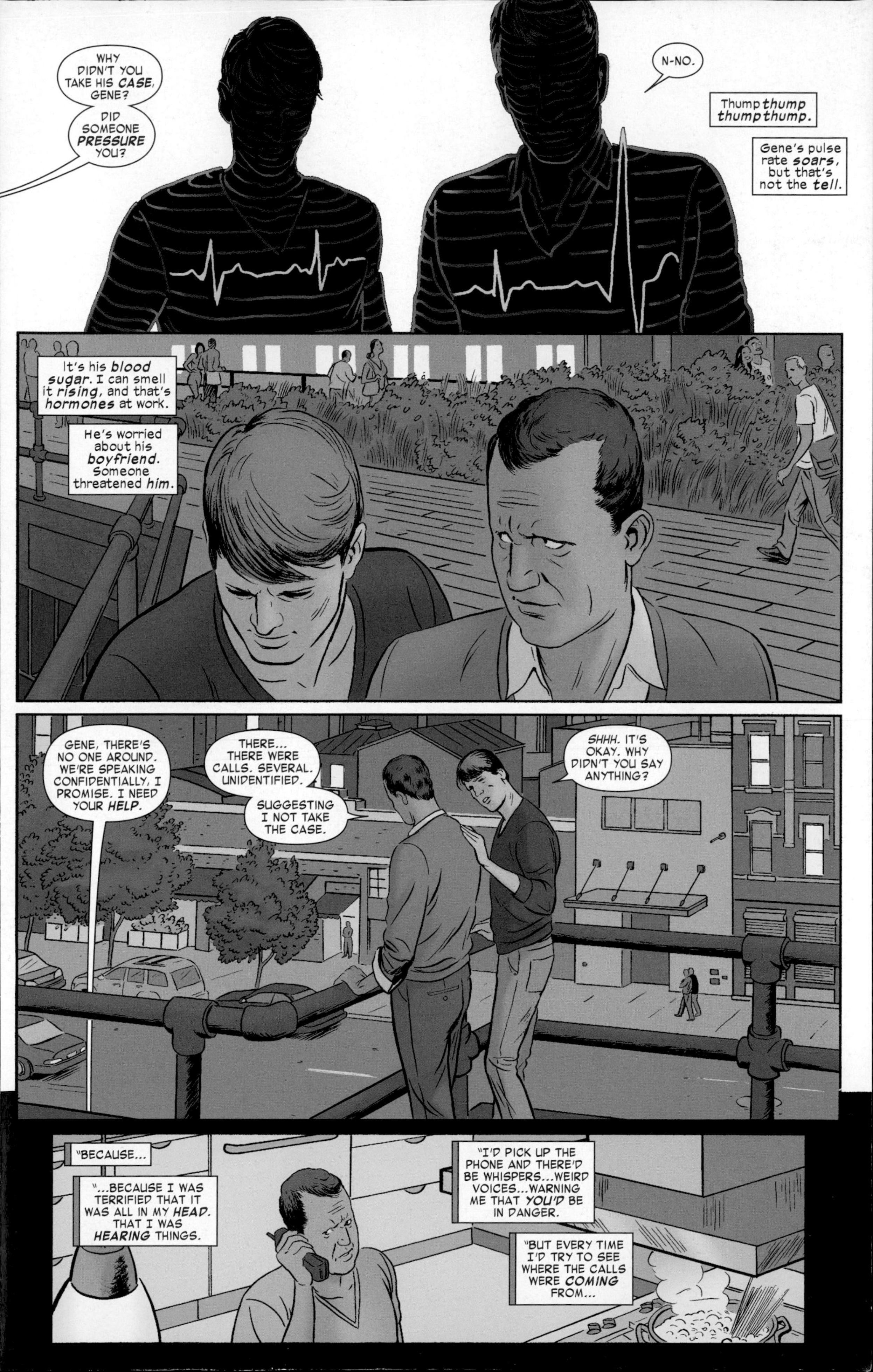

WHY DIDN'T YOU TAKE HIS CASE, GENE?
DID SOMEONE PRESSURE YOU?
N-NO.
Thump thump thump thump.
Gene's pulse rate soars, but that's not the tell.
It's his blood sugar. I can smell it rising, and that's hormones at work.
He's worried about his boyfriend. Someone threatened him.
GENE, THERE'S NO ONE AROUND. WE'RE SPEAKING CONFIDENTIALLY, I PROMISE. I NEED YOUR HELP.
THERE... THERE WERE CALLS. SEVERAL. UNIDENTIFIED.
SUGGESTING I NOT TAKE THE CASE.
SHHH. IT'S OKAY. WHY DIDN'T YOU SAY ANYTHING?
"BECAUSE...
"...BECAUSE I WAS TERRIFIED THAT IT WAS ALL IN MY HEAD. THAT I WAS HEARING THINGS.
"I'D PICK UP THE PHONE AND THERE'D BE WHISPERS...WEIRD VOICES...WARNING ME THAT YOU'D BE IN DANGER.
"BUT EVERY TIME I'D TRY TO SEE WHERE THE CALLS WERE COMING FROM...

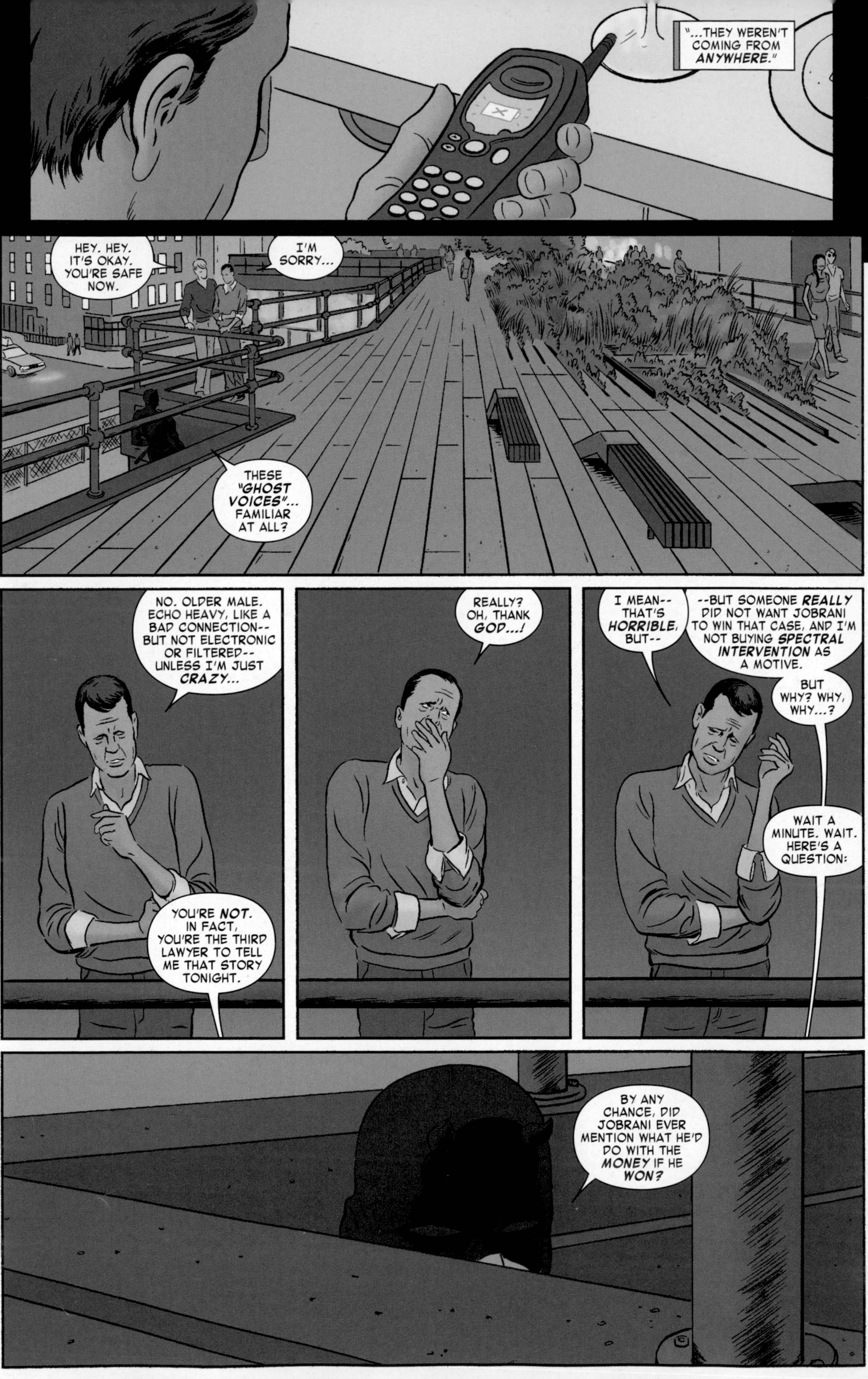
"...THEY WEREN'T COMING FROM ANYWHERE."
HEY. HEY. IT'S OKAY. YOU'RE SAFE NOW.
I'M SORRY...
THESE "GHOST VOICES"... FAMILIAR AT ALL?
NO. OLDER MALE. ECHO HEAVY, LIKE A BAD CONNECTION--BUT NOT ELECTRONIC OR FILTERED--UNLESS I'M JUST CRAZY...
YOU'RE NOT. IN FACT, YOU'RE THE THIRD LAWYER TO TELL ME THAT STORY TONIGHT.
REALLY? OH, THANK GOD...!
I MEAN--THAT'S HORRIBLE, BUT--
--BUT SOMEONE REALLY DID NOT WANT JOBRANI TO WIN THAT CASE, AND I'M NOT BUYING SPECTRAL INTERVENTION AS A MOTIVE.
BUT WHY? WHY, WHY...?
WAIT A MINUTE. WAIT. HERE'S A QUESTION:
BY ANY CHANCE, DID JOBRANI EVER MENTION WHAT HE'D DO WITH THE MONEY IF HE WON?

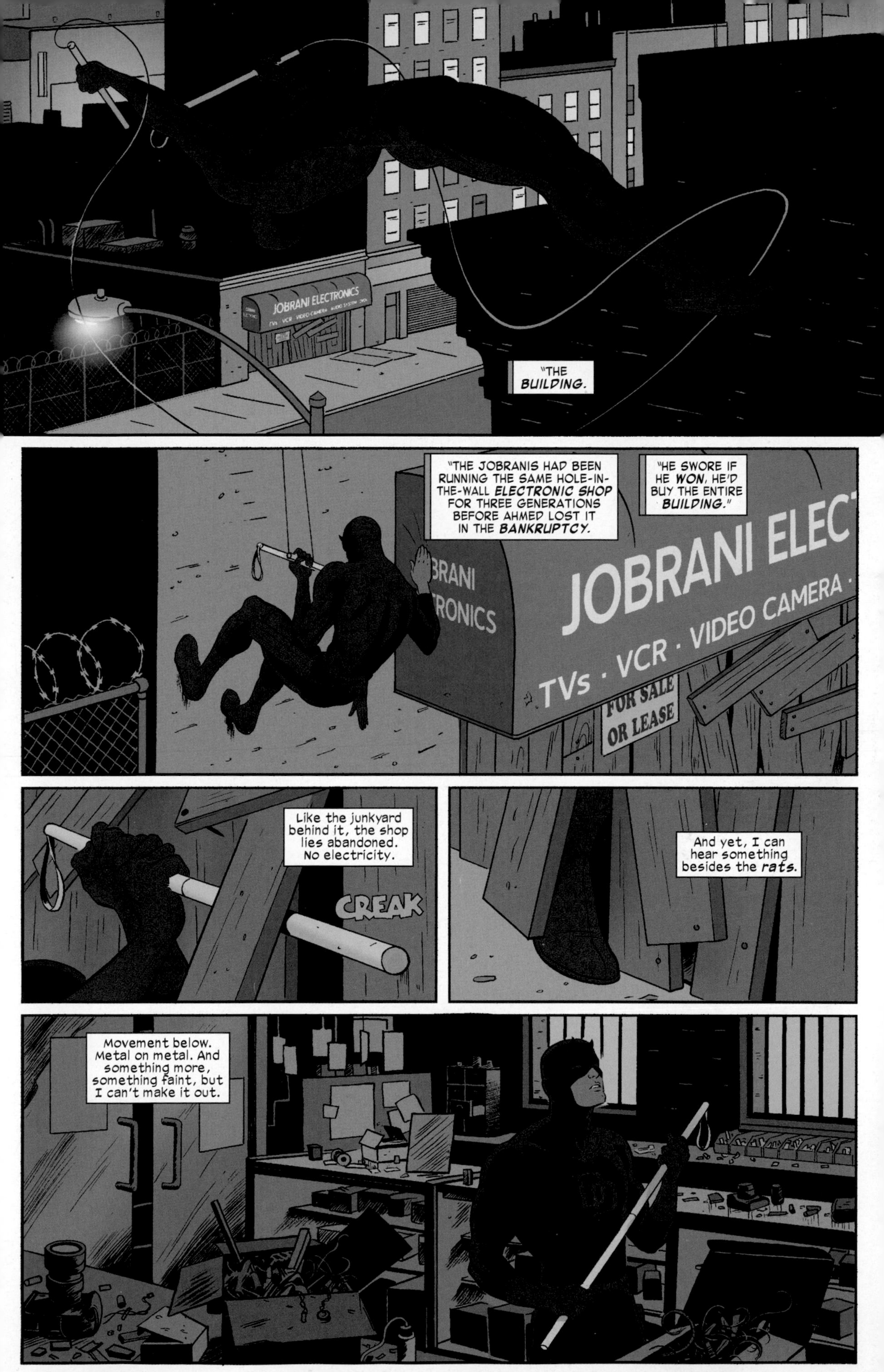
JOBRANI ELECTRONICS
TVs · VCR · VIDEO CAMERA
"THE BUILDING.
"THE JOBRANIS HAD BEEN RUNNING THE SAME HOLE-IN-THE-WALL ELECTRONIC SHOP FOR THREE GENERATIONS BEFORE AHMED LOST IT IN THE BANKRUPTCY.
"HE SWORE IF HE WON, HE'D BUY THE ENTIRE BUILDING."
JOBRANI ELECT
TVs · VCR · VIDEO CAMERA ·
FOR SALE OR LEASE
Like the junkyard behind it, the shop lies abandoned. No electricity.
CREAK
And yet, I can hear something besides the rats.
Movement below. Metal on metal. And something more, something faint, but I can't make it out.

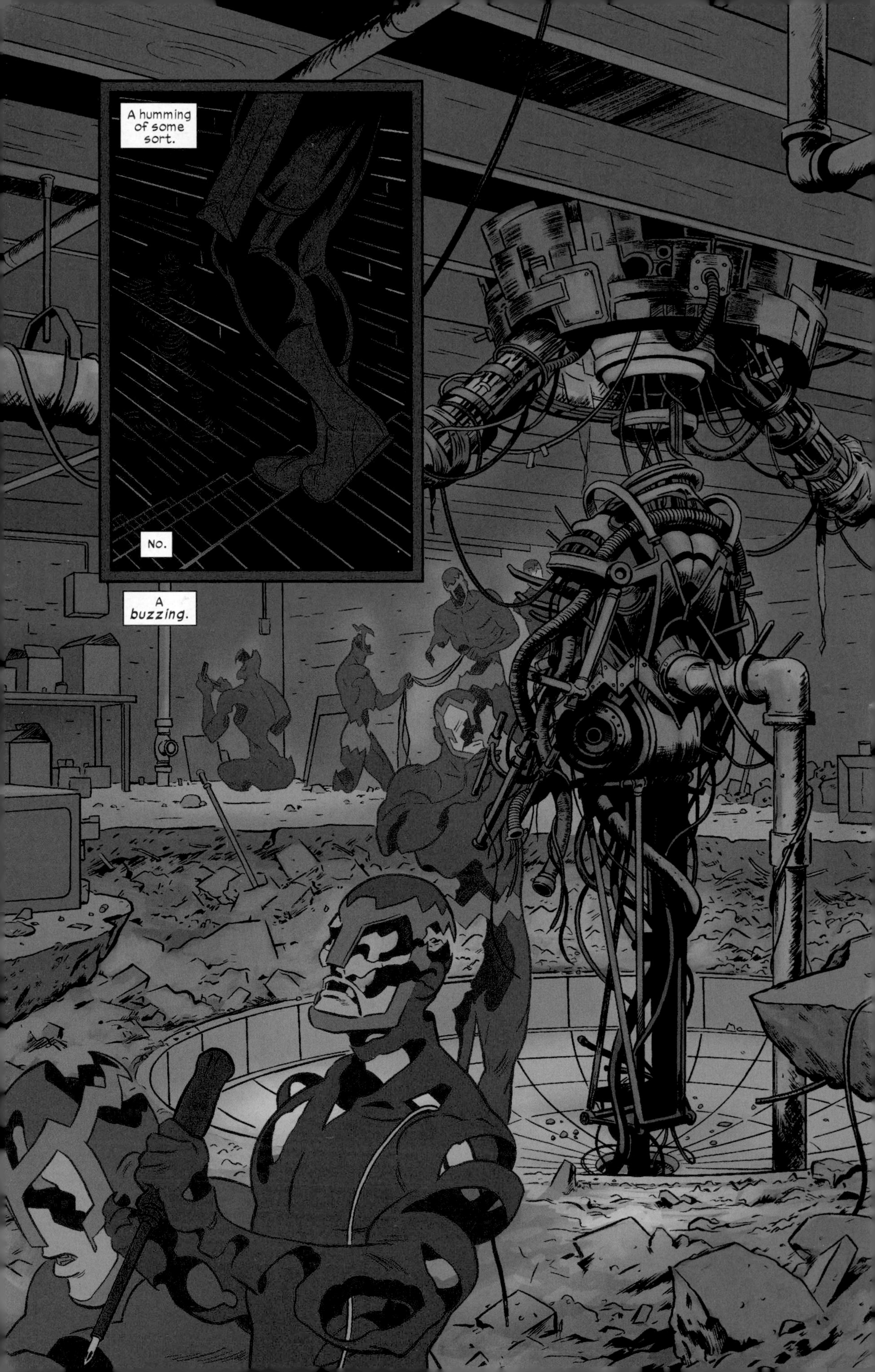

A humming of some sort.
No.
A *buzzing*.

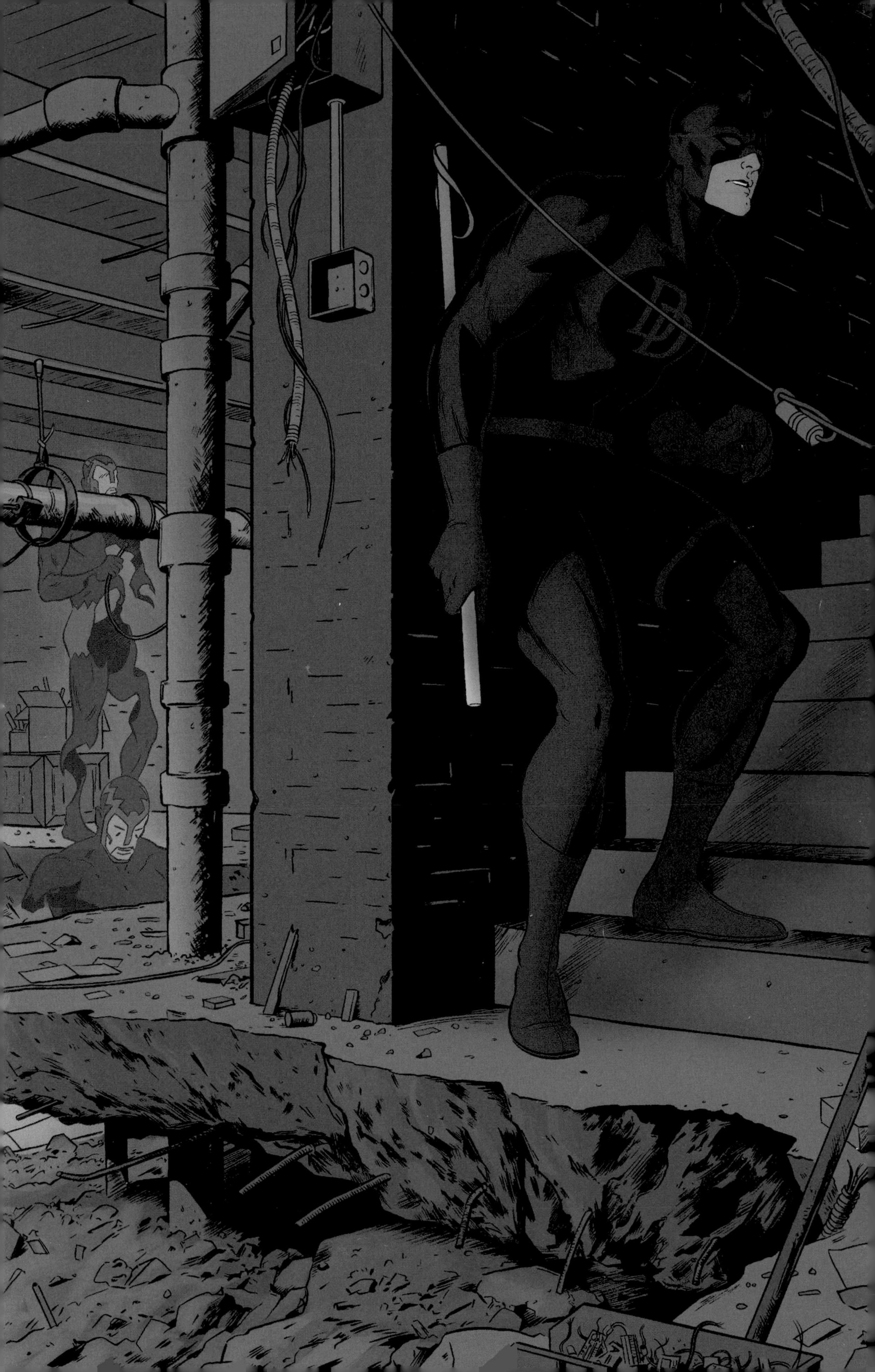

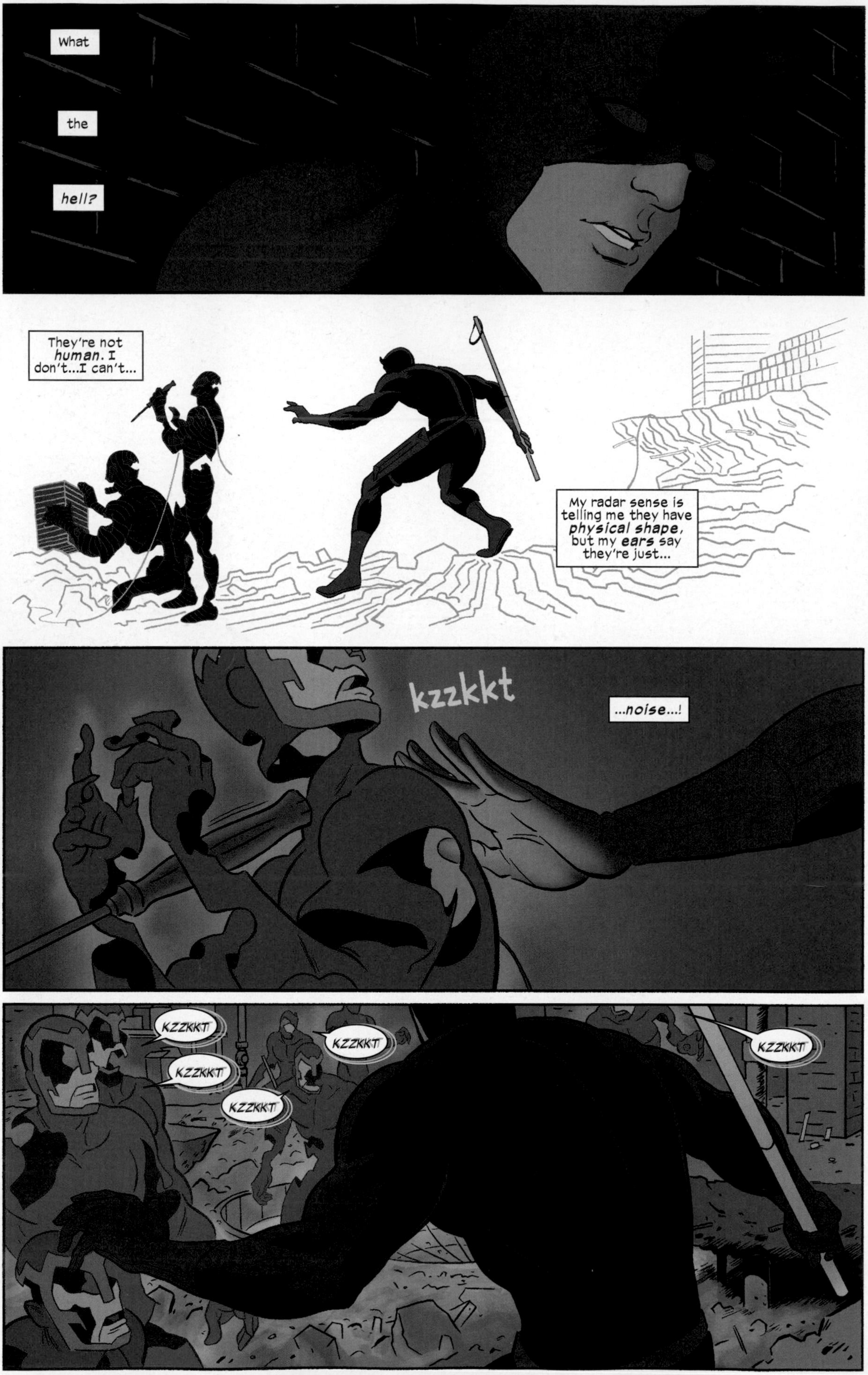
What
the
hell?
They're not *human*. I don't...I can't...
My radar sense is telling me they have *physical shape*, but my *ears* say they're just...
kzzkkt
...*noise*...!
KZZKKT
KZZKKT
KZZKKT
KZZKKT
KZZKKT

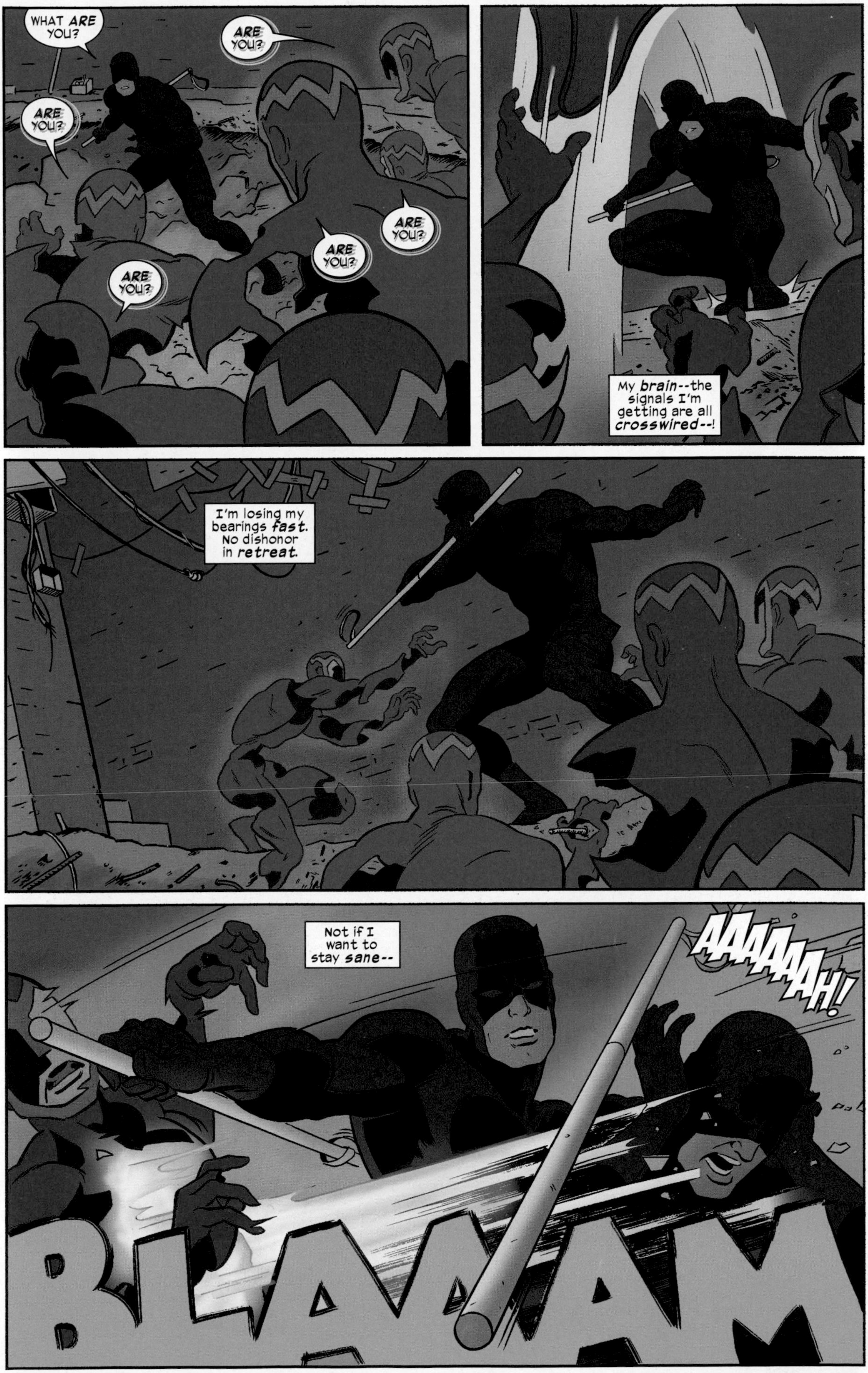
WHAT ARE YOU?
ARE YOU?
ARE YOU?
ARE YOU?
ARE YOU?
ARE YOU?
My brain--the signals I'm getting are all crosswired--!
I'm losing my bearings fast. No dishonor in retreat.
Not if I want to stay sane--
AAAAAAH!
BLAAM

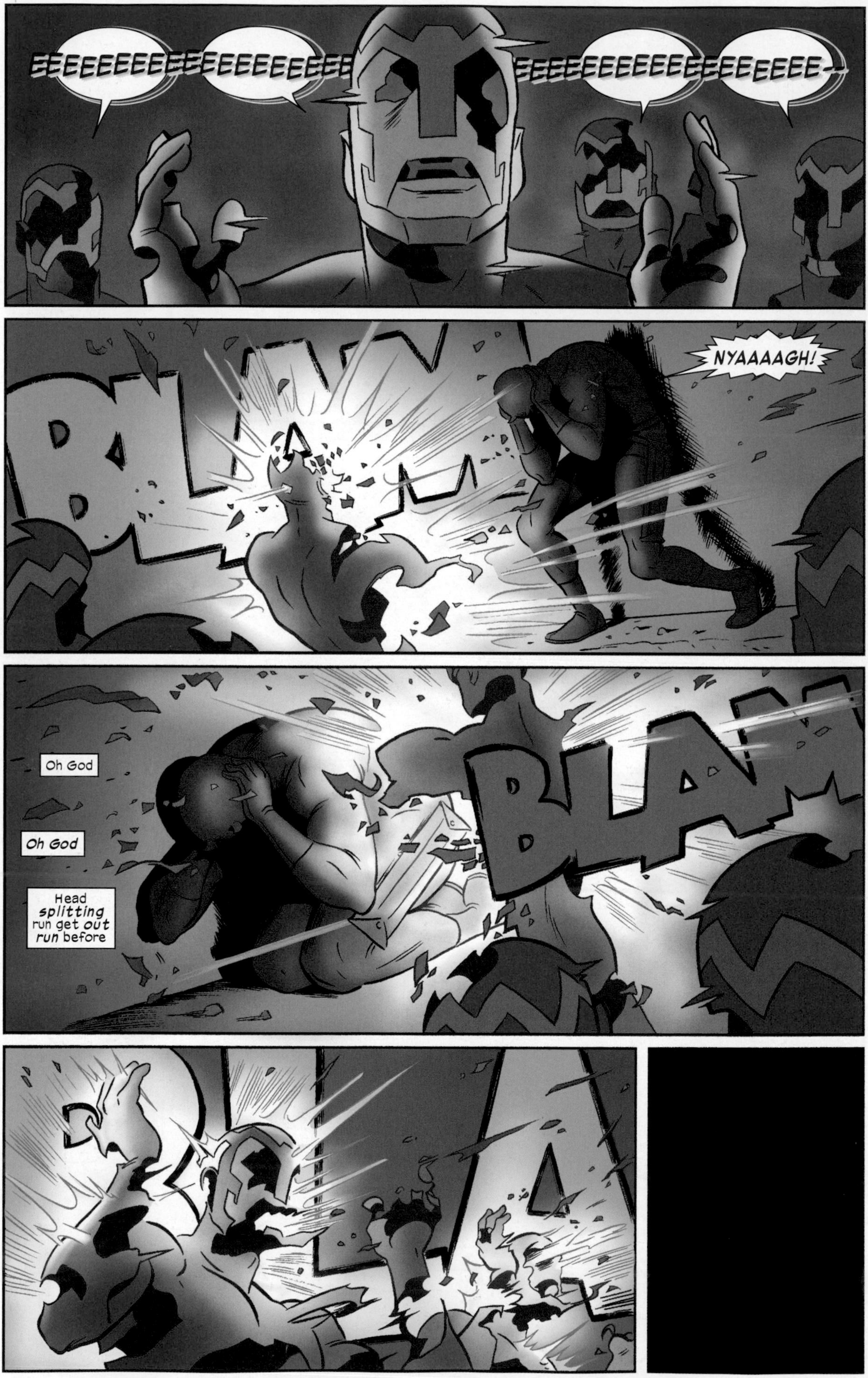
EEEEEEEEEEEEEEEEEEEEE
EEEEEEEEEEEEEEEEEEEEEE–
BLAM
NYAAAAGH!
Oh God
Oh God
Head splitting run get out run before
BLAM
BLAM

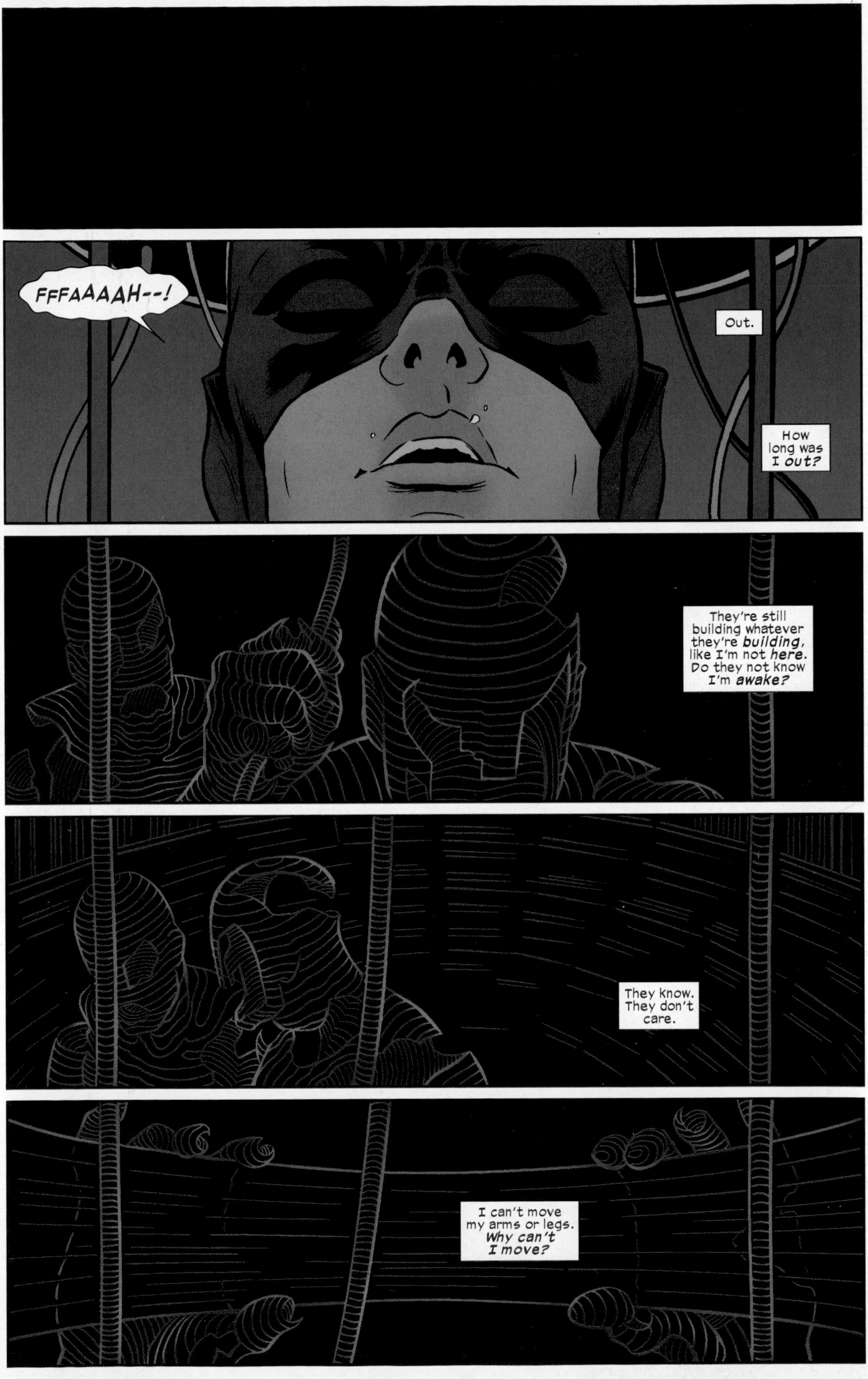
FFFAAAAH--!
Out.
How long was I *out?*
They're still building whatever they're *building,* like I'm not *here.* Do they not know I'm *awake?*
They know. They don't care.
I can't move my arms or legs. *Why can't I move?*

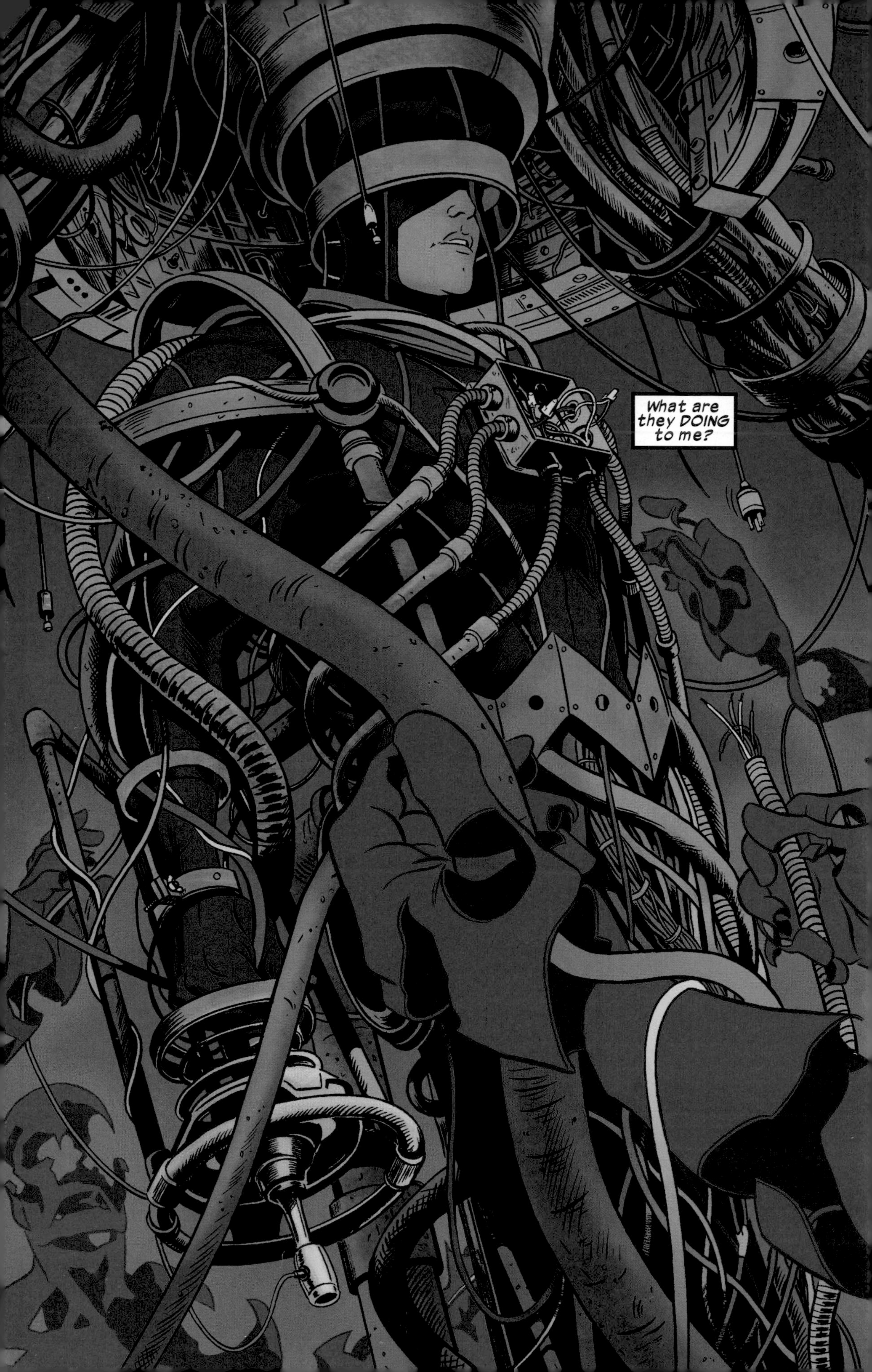
What are they DOING to me?

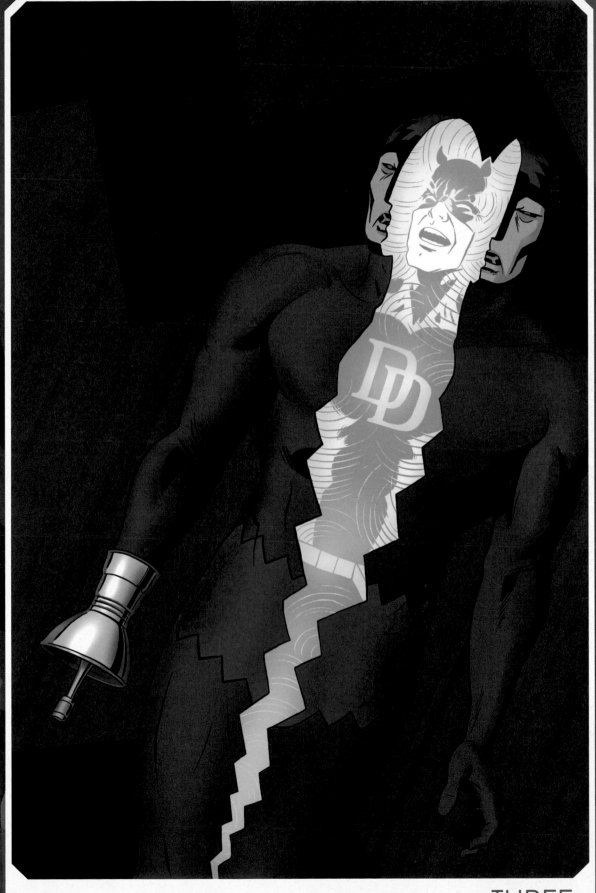

THREE

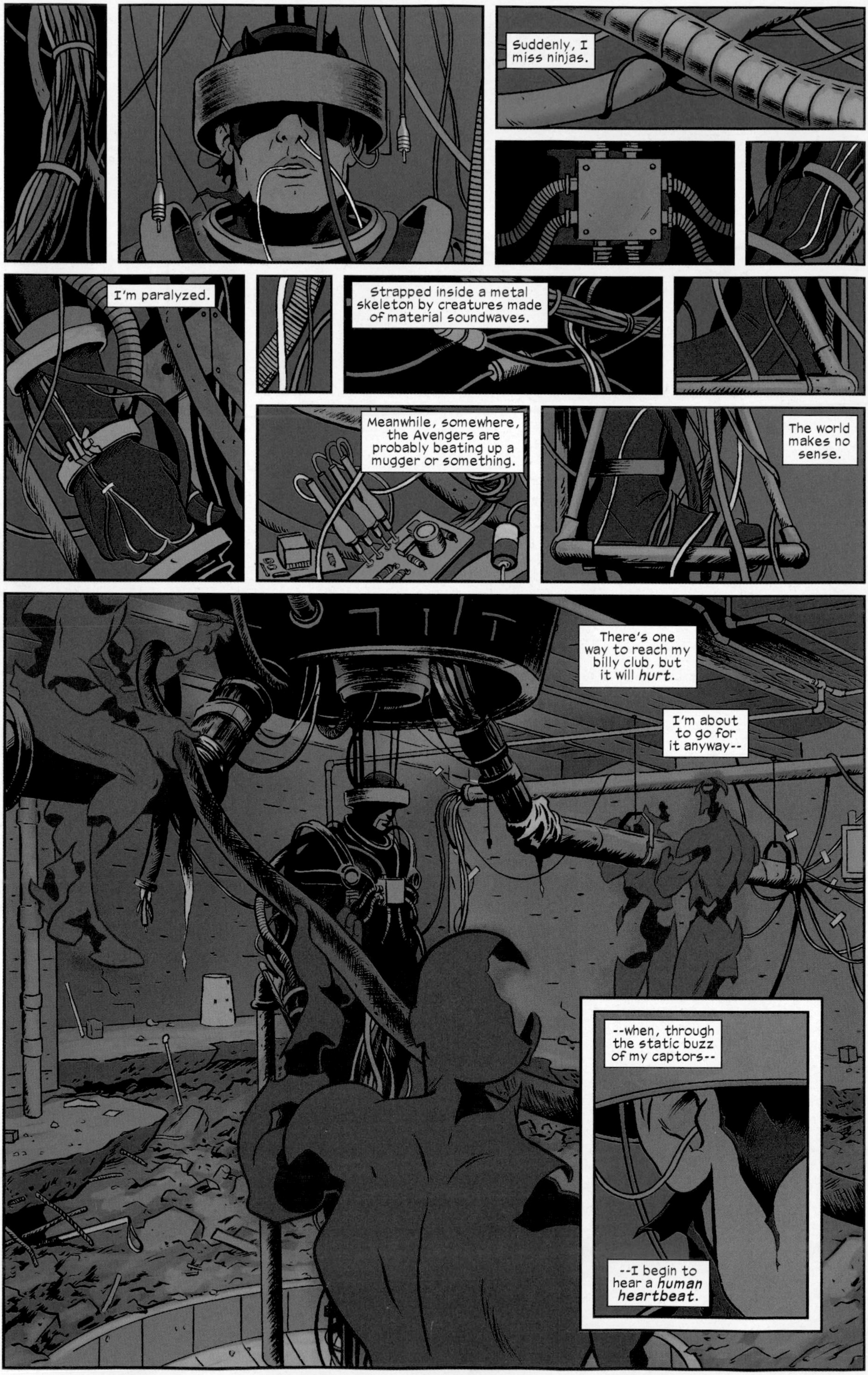
Suddenly, I miss ninjas.
I'm paralyzed.
Strapped inside a metal skeleton by creatures made of material soundwaves.
Meanwhile, somewhere, the Avengers are probably beating up a mugger or something.
The world makes no sense.
There's one way to reach my billy club, but it will *hurt*.
I'm about to go for it anyway--
--when, through the static buzz of my captors--
--I begin to hear a *human heartbeat*.

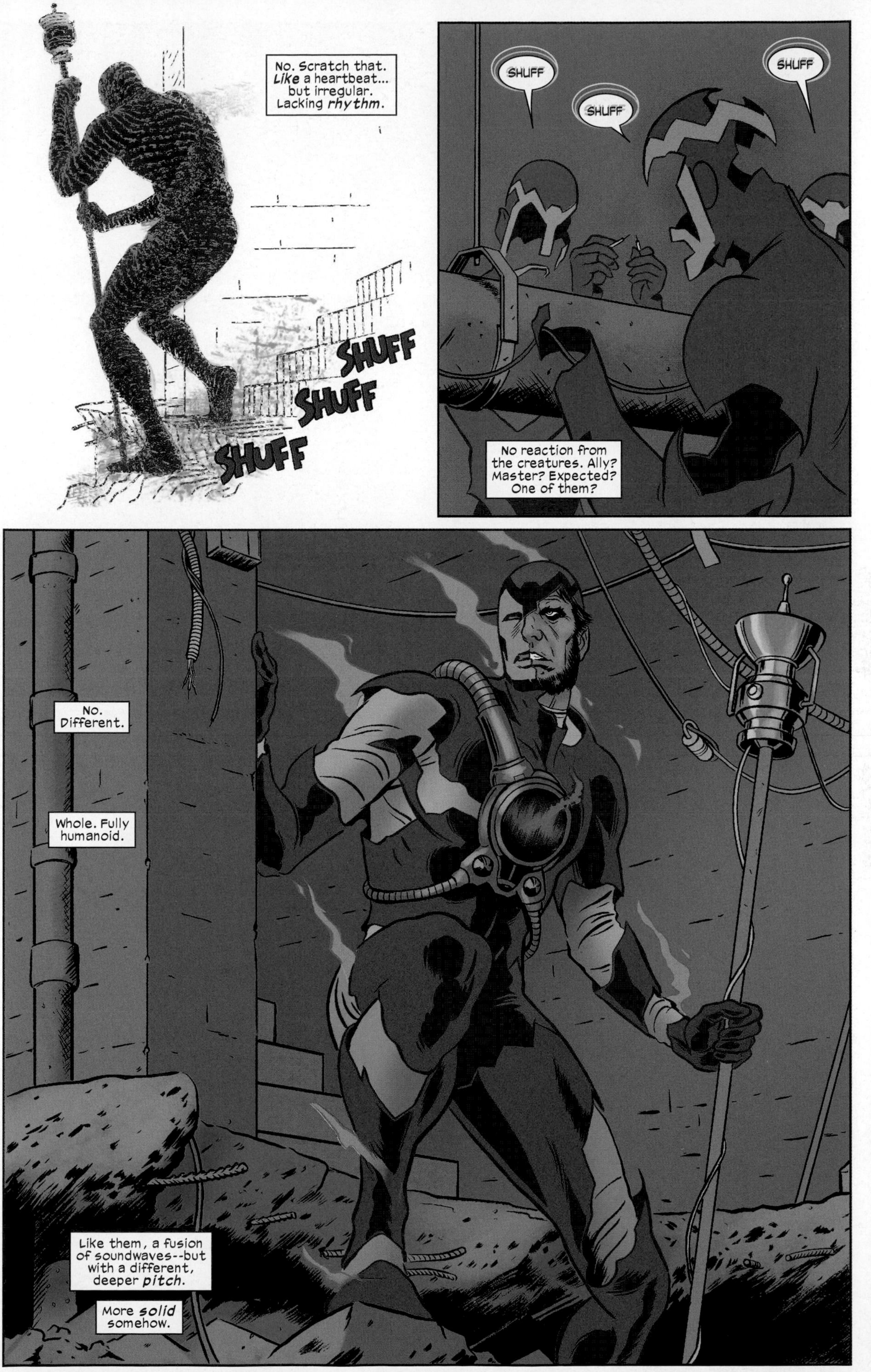
No. Scratch that. Like a heartbeat... but irregular. Lacking rhythm.
SHUFF
SHUFF
SHUFF
SHUFF
SHUFF
SHUFF
No reaction from the creatures. Ally? Master? Expected? One of them?
No. Different.
Whole. Fully humanoid.
Like them, a fusion of soundwaves--but with a different, deeper pitch.
More solid somehow.

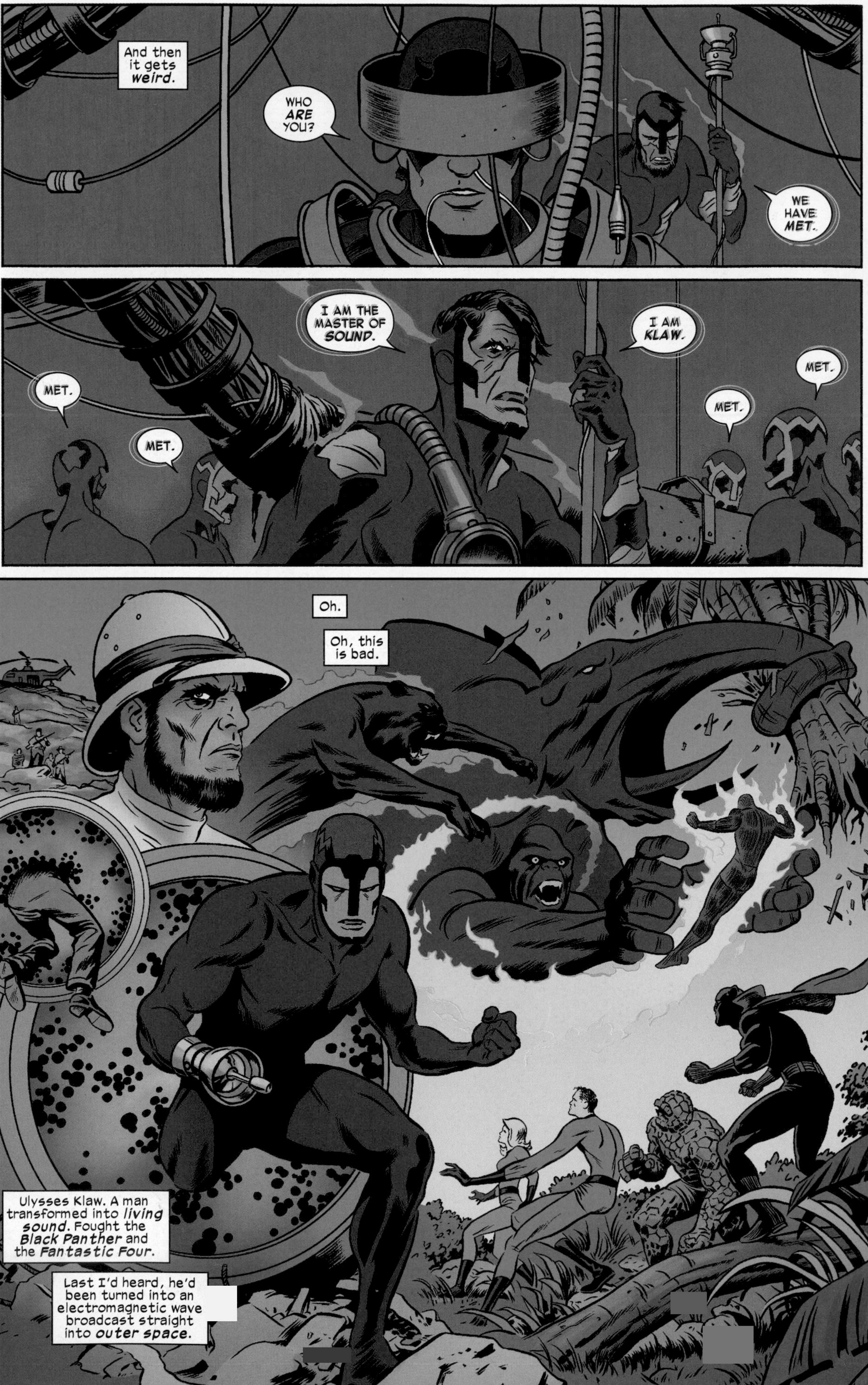
And then it gets *weird*.
WHO *ARE* YOU?
WE HAVE *MET*.
I AM THE MASTER OF *SOUND*.
I AM *KLAW*.
MET.
MET.
MET.
MET.
Oh.
Oh, this is bad.
Ulysses Klaw. A man transformed into *living sound*. Fought the *Black Panther* and the *Fantastic Four*.
Last I'd heard, he'd been turned into an electromagnetic wave broadcast straight into *outer space*.

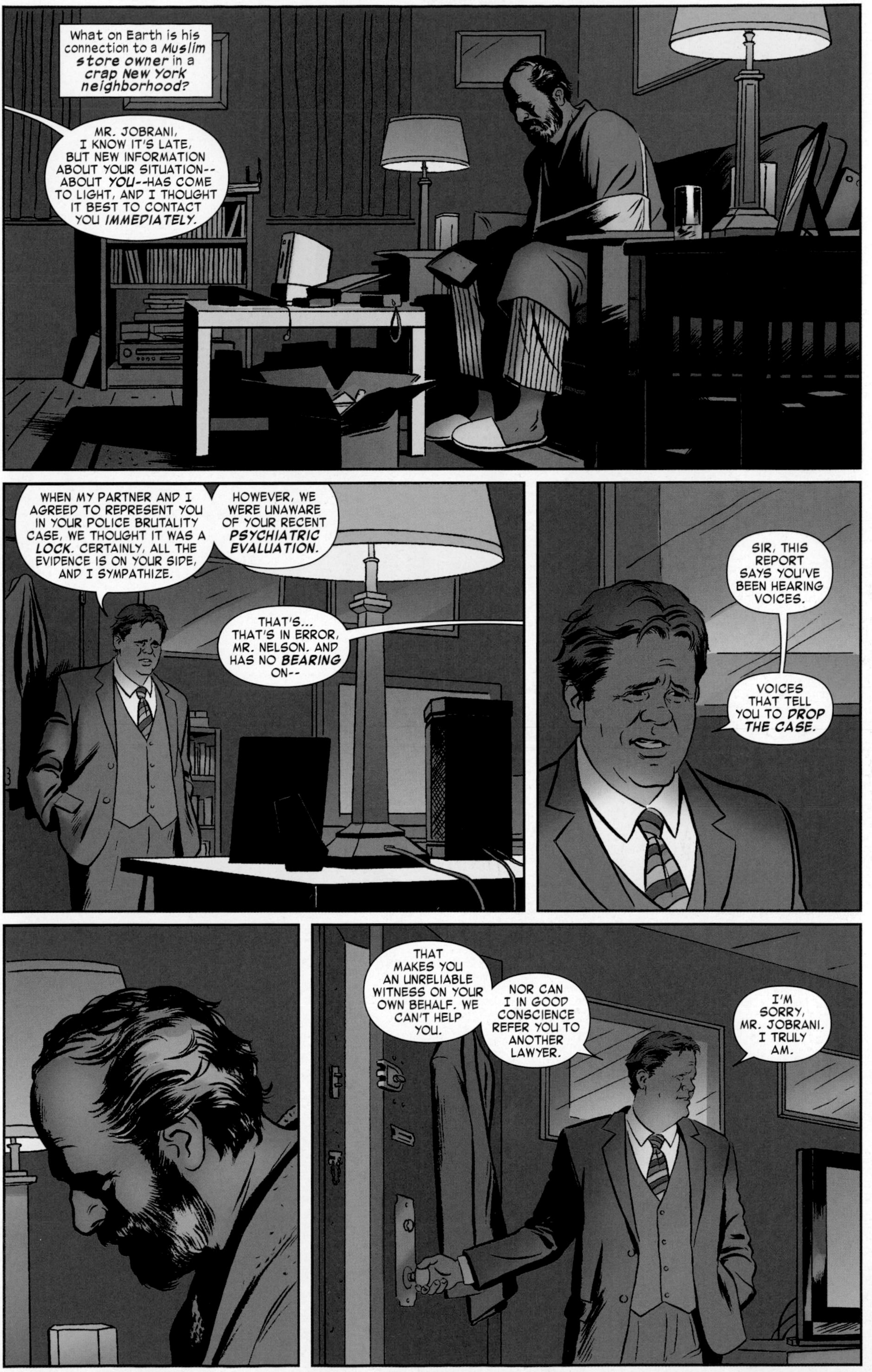
What on Earth is his connection to a *Muslim store owner* in a *crap New York neighborhood?*
MR. JOBRANI, I KNOW IT'S LATE, BUT NEW INFORMATION ABOUT YOUR SITUATION-- ABOUT *YOU*--HAS COME TO LIGHT, AND I THOUGHT IT BEST TO CONTACT YOU *IMMEDIATELY.*
WHEN MY PARTNER AND I AGREED TO REPRESENT YOU IN YOUR POLICE BRUTALITY CASE, WE THOUGHT IT WAS A *LOCK.* CERTAINLY, ALL THE EVIDENCE IS ON YOUR SIDE, AND I SYMPATHIZE.
HOWEVER, WE WERE UNAWARE OF YOUR RECENT *PSYCHIATRIC EVALUATION.*
THAT'S... THAT'S IN ERROR, MR. NELSON. AND HAS NO *BEARING* ON--
SIR, THIS REPORT SAYS YOU'VE BEEN HEARING VOICES.
VOICES THAT TELL YOU TO *DROP THE CASE.*
THAT MAKES YOU AN UNRELIABLE WITNESS ON YOUR OWN BEHALF. WE CAN'T HELP YOU.
NOR CAN I IN GOOD CONSCIENCE REFER YOU TO ANOTHER LAWYER.
I'M SORRY, MR. JOBRANI. I TRULY AM.

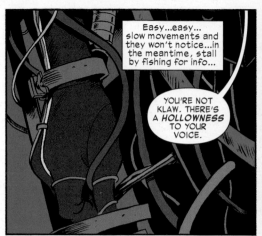

Easy...easy... slow movements and they won't notice...in the meantime, stall by fishing for info...

YOU'RE NOT KLAW. THERE'S A *HOLLOWNESS* TO YOUR VOICE.

I AM HIM. WE ARE *ALL* HIM. PIECES.

ECHOES OF A *GRAND HARMONY.*

PIECES.

PIECES.

PIECES.

"I WAS ONE OF HIS *SOUNDSHADOWS* ONCE...AN ABERRATION, A FORGOTTEN *FREAKCHANCE* MELODY OF ENERGIES THAT LIVED ON PAST MY PURPOSE OF *CREATION*...

"...UNNOTICED... APART...AND *ABANDONED.*"

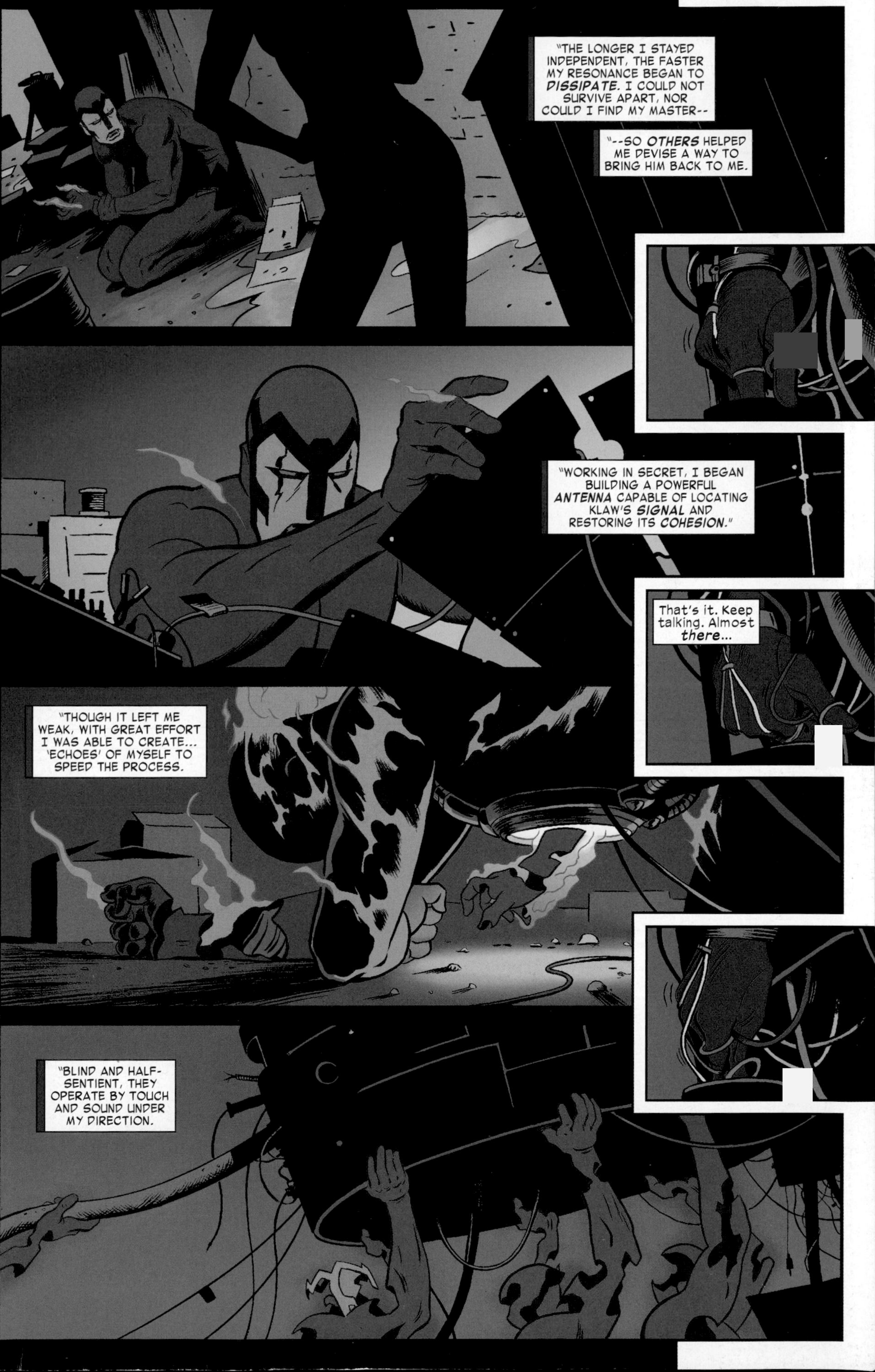
"THE LONGER I STAYED INDEPENDENT, THE FASTER MY RESONANCE BEGAN TO DISSIPATE. I COULD NOT SURVIVE APART, NOR COULD I FIND MY MASTER--
"--SO OTHERS HELPED ME DEVISE A WAY TO BRING HIM BACK TO ME.
"WORKING IN SECRET, I BEGAN BUILDING A POWERFUL ANTENNA CAPABLE OF LOCATING KLAW'S SIGNAL AND RESTORING ITS COHESION."
That's it. Keep talking. Almost there...
"THOUGH IT LEFT ME WEAK, WITH GREAT EFFORT I WAS ABLE TO CREATE... 'ECHOES' OF MYSELF TO SPEED THE PROCESS.
"BLIND AND HALF-SENTIENT, THEY OPERATE BY TOUCH AND SOUND UNDER MY DIRECTION.

"HIDDEN HERE, OUR ONLY THREAT OF EXPOSURE WAS THE MAN WHO ONCE *OWNED* THIS BUILDING."

"HE SWORE TO RECLAIM IT WITH MONEY FROM A *LAWSUIT*.

"I COULD DO NOTHING *PHYSICALLY* TO STOP HIM...NOT WITHOUT LEAVING THE PREMISES UNGUARDED..."

...BUT VOICES *CARRY.*

CHKK

CHKK

CHKK

CHKK

CHKK

CHKK

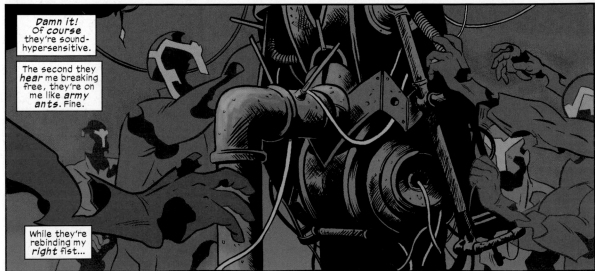

Damn it! Of *course* they're sound-hypersensitive.

The second they *hear* me breaking free, they're on me like *army ants.* Fine.

While they're rebinding my *right* fist...

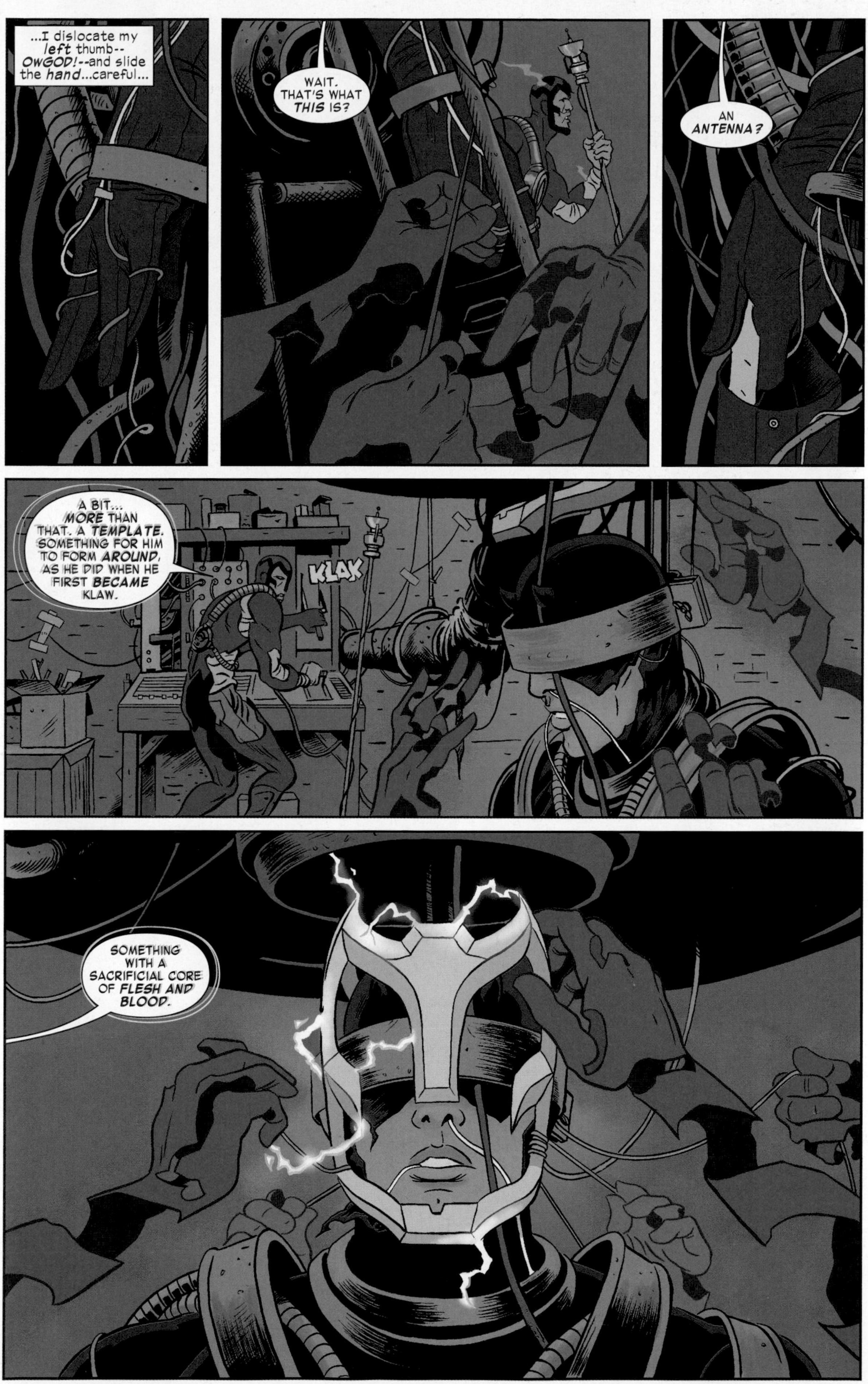
...I dislocate my left thumb-- OWGOD!--and slide the hand...careful...
WAIT. THAT'S WHAT THIS IS?
AN ANTENNA?
A BIT... MORE THAN THAT. A TEMPLATE. SOMETHING FOR HIM TO FORM AROUND, AS HE DID WHEN HE FIRST BECAME KLAW.
KLAK
SOMETHING WITH A SACRIFICIAL CORE OF FLESH AND BLOOD.

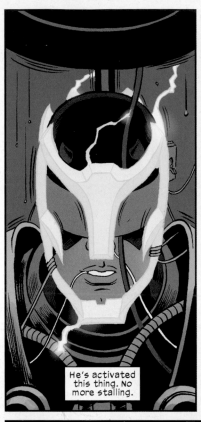

He's activated this thing. No more stalling.

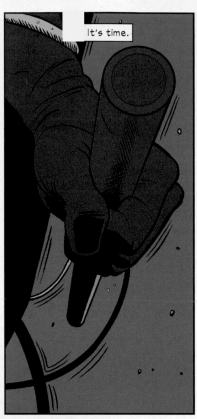

It's time.

I may not survive this. I certainly may not come out of it with all my senses intact.

But it's all I know to do.

If I need them not to hear me *escaping*--

--then I need a *big noise*.

AAAAAAAAAA

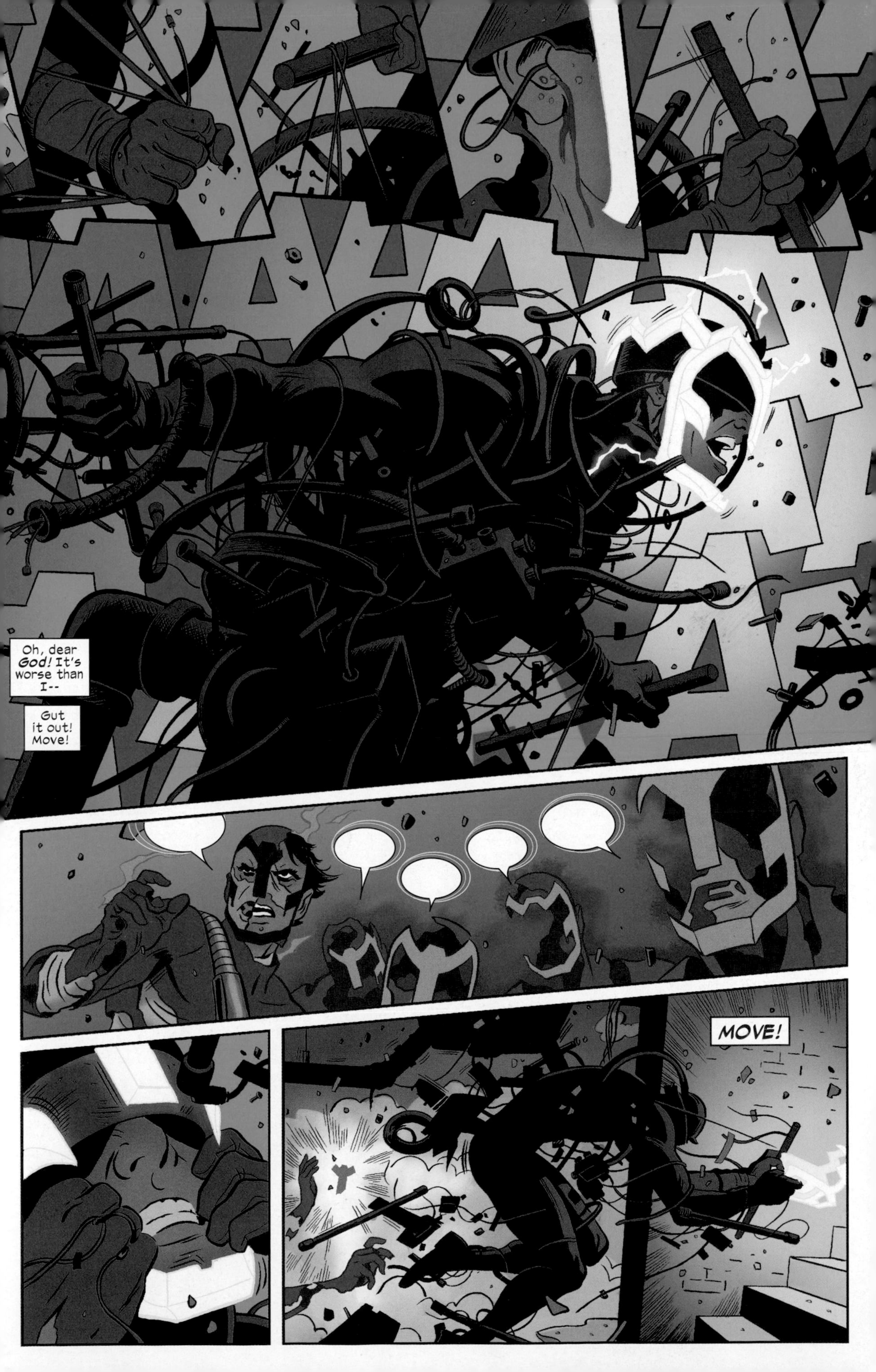

Oh, dear *God!* It's worse than I--
Gut it out! Move!
MOVE!

Where? Doesn't matter. *Away.*

Lost my *grappling line.* Just *run* from the *screaming* before my *brain* explodes--

KLANG

KLANG

--and hope that Klaw's *echodouble* is too weak to *follow.*

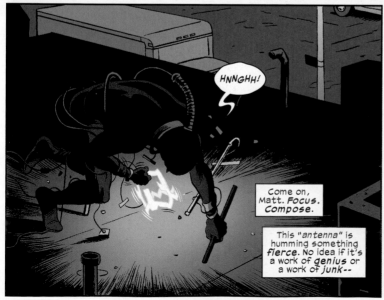

HNNGHH!

Come on, Matt. *Focus. Compose.*

This *"antenna"* is humming something *fierce.* No idea if it's a work of *genius* or a work of *junk*--

--but I'm taking no *chances.*

Wait. Something's *coming*--

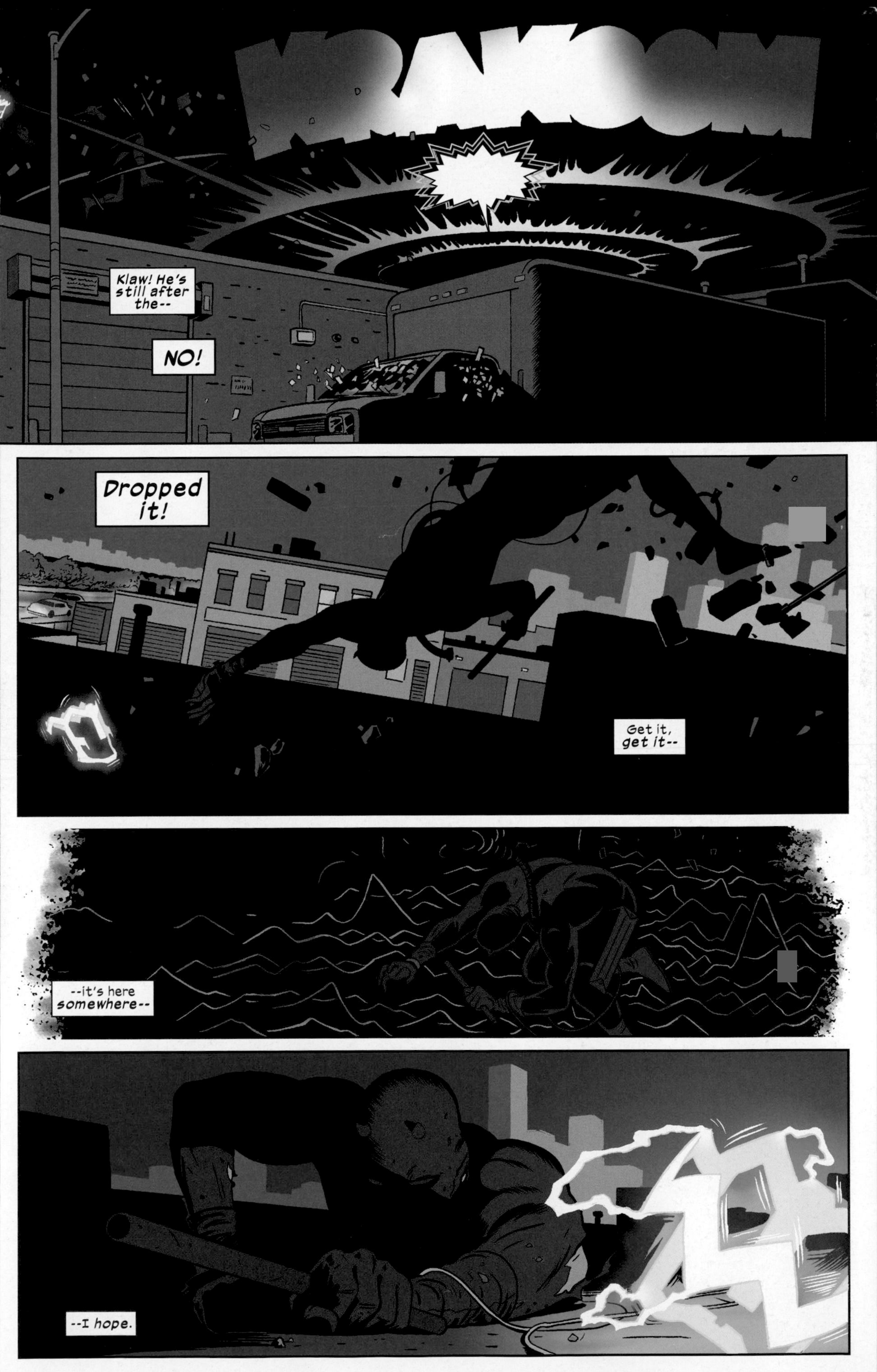
KRAKOOM
Klaw! He's still after the--
NO!
Dropped it!
Get it, get it--
--it's here somewhere--
--I hope.

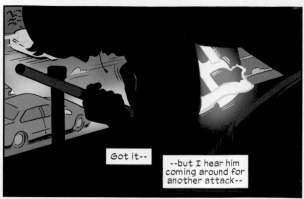

Got it--

--but I hear him coming around for another attack--

KWAM KWAM

GNAAAGH--!

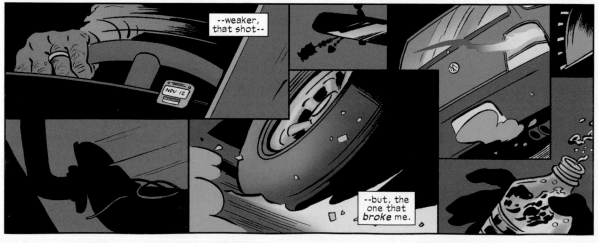

--weaker, that shot--

NOV 12

--but, the one that *broke* me.

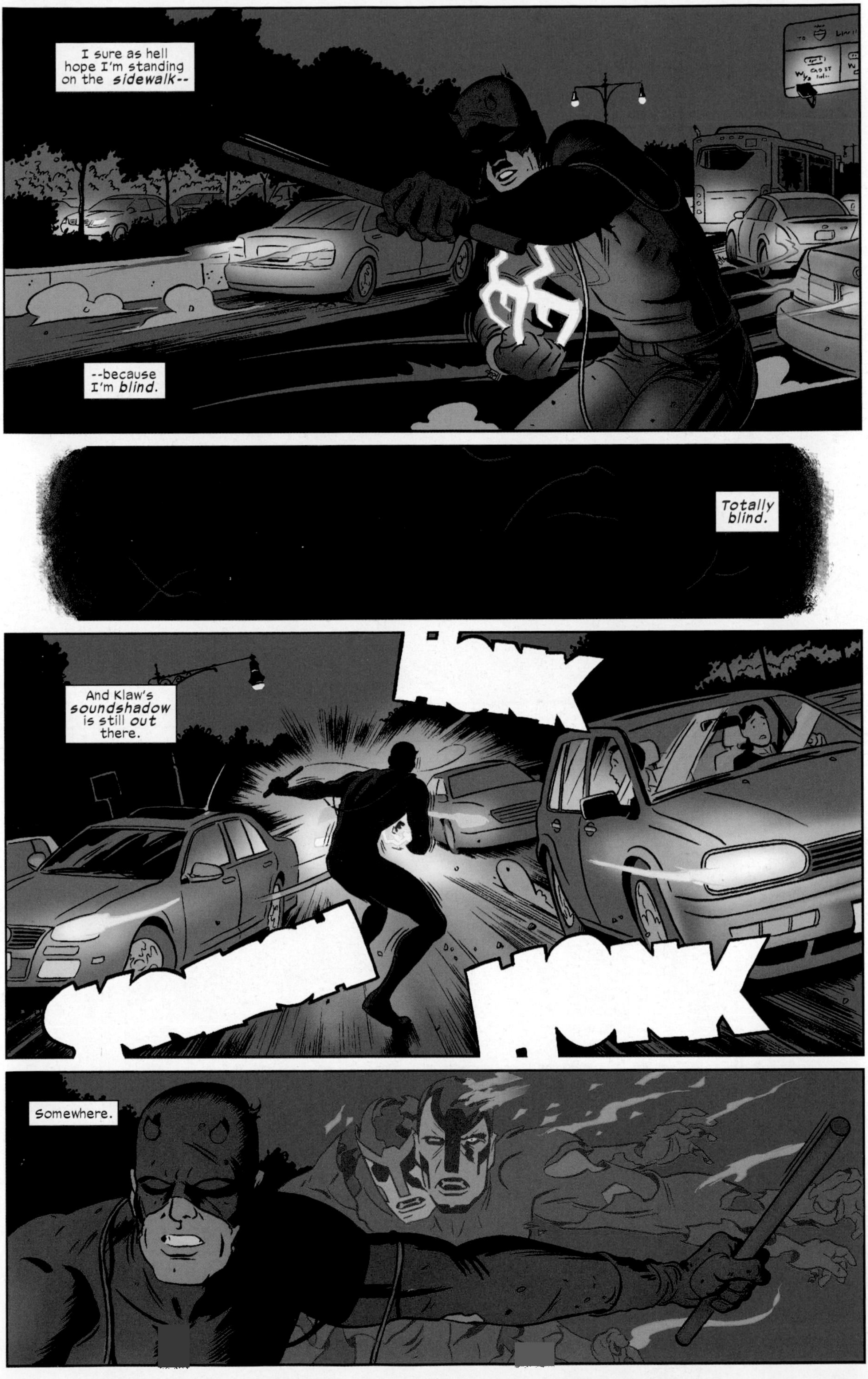

I sure as hell hope I'm standing on the *sidewalk*--
--because I'm *blind*.
Totally blind.
And Klaw's *soundshadow* is still *out* there.
Somewhere.

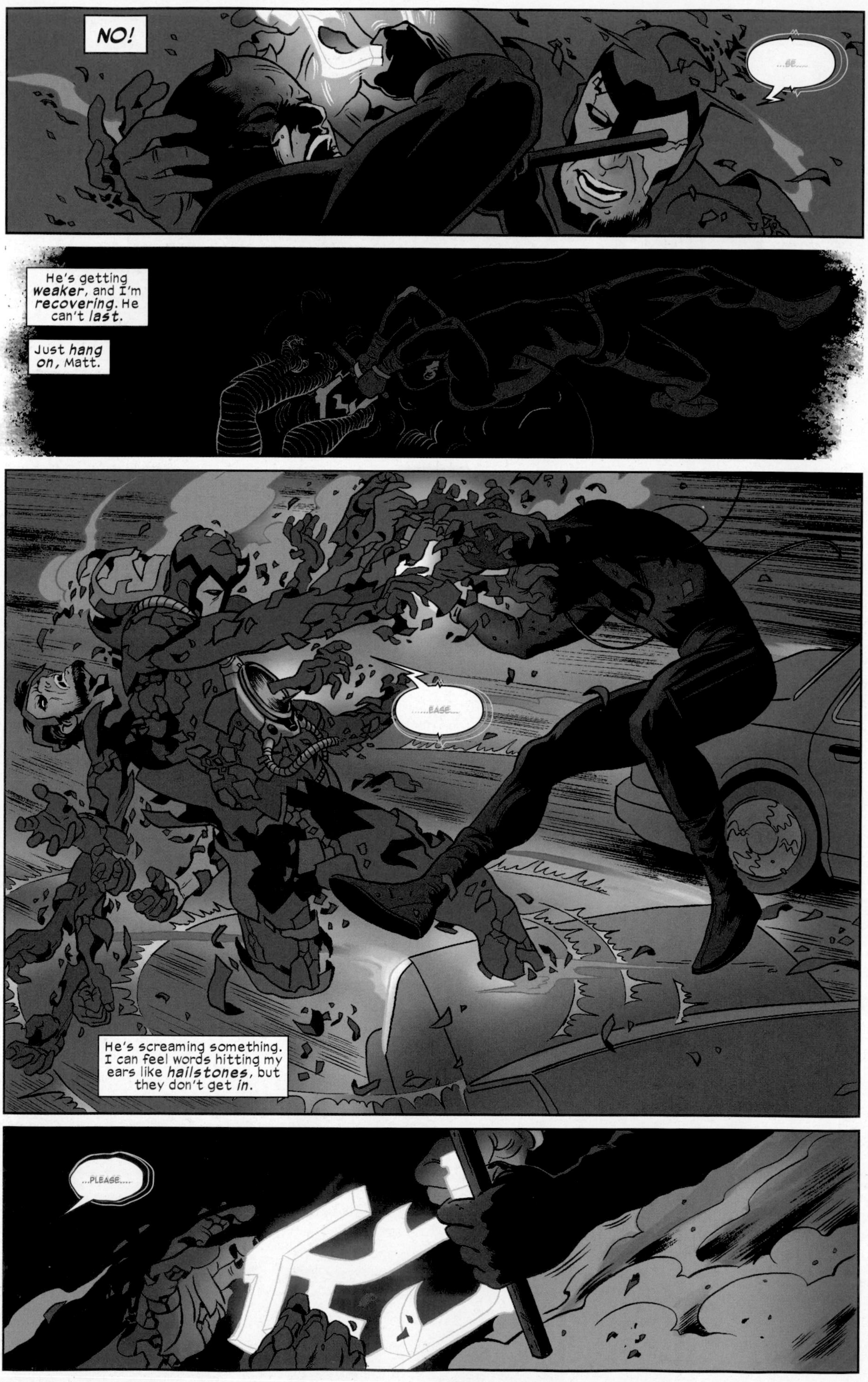
NO!
...SE....
He's getting *weaker*, and I'm *recovering*. He can't *last*.
Just *hang on*, Matt.
......EASE....
He's screaming something. I can feel words hitting my ears like *hailstones*, but they don't get *in*.
...PLEASE.....

SORRY.

DIDN'T *CATCH* THAT.

"OTHERS"! YOU SAID THERE WERE OTHERS WHO HELPED YOU ENGINEER THIS! WHO? *WHO?*

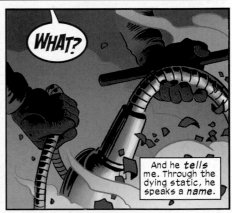

WHAT?

And he *tells* me. Through the dying static, he speaks a *name.*

But I couldn't *hear* it.

And with that, he's gone.

Leaving me with nothing but a deep, deep desire for *cabfare* and a fistful of *aspirin.*

But at least now my client can safely get his day in *court.*

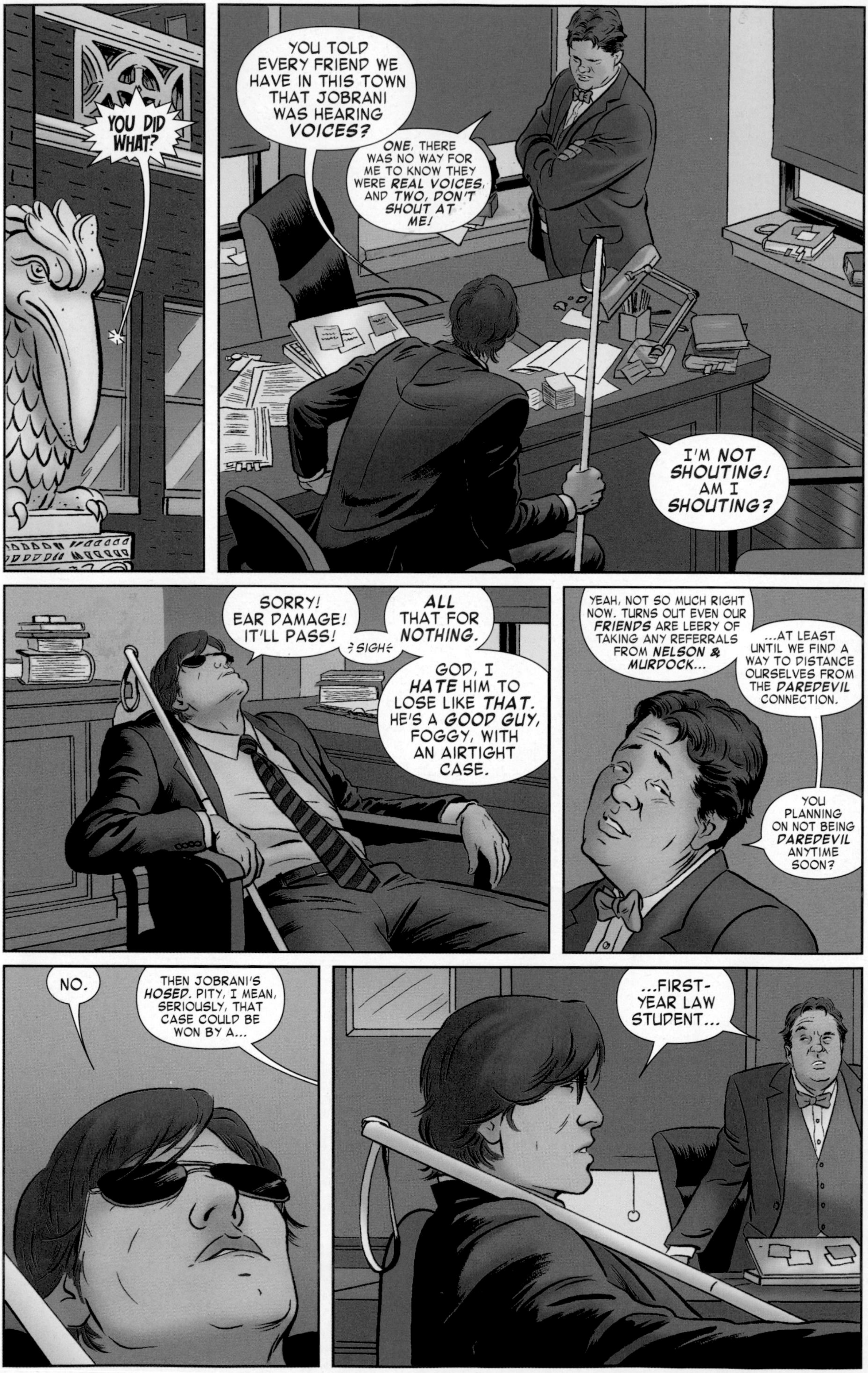
YOU DID WHAT?
YOU TOLD EVERY FRIEND WE HAVE IN THIS TOWN THAT JOBRANI WAS HEARING VOICES?
ONE, THERE WAS NO WAY FOR ME TO KNOW THEY WERE REAL VOICES, AND TWO, DON'T SHOUT AT ME!
I'M NOT SHOUTING! AM I SHOUTING?
SORRY! EAR DAMAGE! IT'LL PASS!
SIGH
ALL THAT FOR NOTHING.
GOD, I HATE HIM TO LOSE LIKE THAT. HE'S A GOOD GUY, FOGGY, WITH AN AIRTIGHT CASE.
YEAH, NOT SO MUCH RIGHT NOW. TURNS OUT EVEN OUR FRIENDS ARE LEERY OF TAKING ANY REFERRALS FROM NELSON & MURDOCK...
...AT LEAST UNTIL WE FIND A WAY TO DISTANCE OURSELVES FROM THE DAREDEVIL CONNECTION.
YOU PLANNING ON NOT BEING DAREDEVIL ANYTIME SOON?
NO.
THEN JOBRANI'S HOSED. PITY, I MEAN, SERIOUSLY, THAT CASE COULD BE WON BY A...
...FIRST-YEAR LAW STUDENT...

THAT'S ABSURD.

AND WHY ARE YOU YELLING AT ME?

IT'S YOUR *BEST SHOT*, MR. JOBRANI.

EAR DAMAGE. IT'LL PASS.

YOU ARE *SMART*. YOU ARE *ARTICULATE*.

JURIES RESPOND WELL TO YOU.

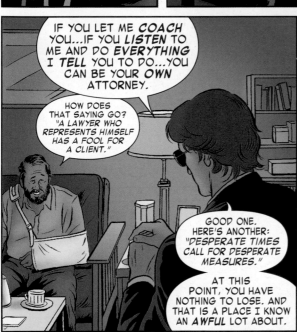

IF YOU LET ME *COACH* YOU...IF YOU *LISTEN* TO ME AND DO *EVERYTHING* I *TELL* YOU TO DO...YOU CAN BE YOUR *OWN* ATTORNEY.

HOW DOES THAT SAYING GO? "A LAWYER WHO REPRESENTS HIMSELF HAS A FOOL FOR A CLIENT."

GOOD ONE. HERE'S ANOTHER: "DESPERATE TIMES CALL FOR DESPERATE MEASURES."

AT THIS POINT, YOU HAVE NOTHING TO LOSE. AND THAT IS A PLACE I KNOW AN *AWFUL* LOT ABOUT.

IF I DON'T, I WALK AWAY *PENNILESS* AND *BULLIED*.

I *WANT* TO TRUST YOU.

BUT STANDING UP...*SPEAKING* IN FRONT OF ALL THOSE PEOPLE...I'D BE SO *NERVOUS*, I COULD NEVER--

MR. JOBRANI, TAKE IT FROM *ME*:

THERE IS *NOTHING* TO BE AFRAID OF.

Big talk. I'm not, by nature, a *teacher*.

But I know how to work a *courtroom*.

In the end, I give Jobrani all the ammo I have and sit back for the ride.

The white-knuckle ride.

He stammers. He fumbles the lingo time and again. I wince so hard and so often that it's a miracle my glasses stay on.

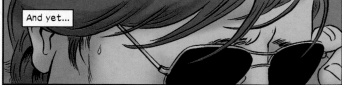

And yet...

...in the end...

...justice *prevails*.

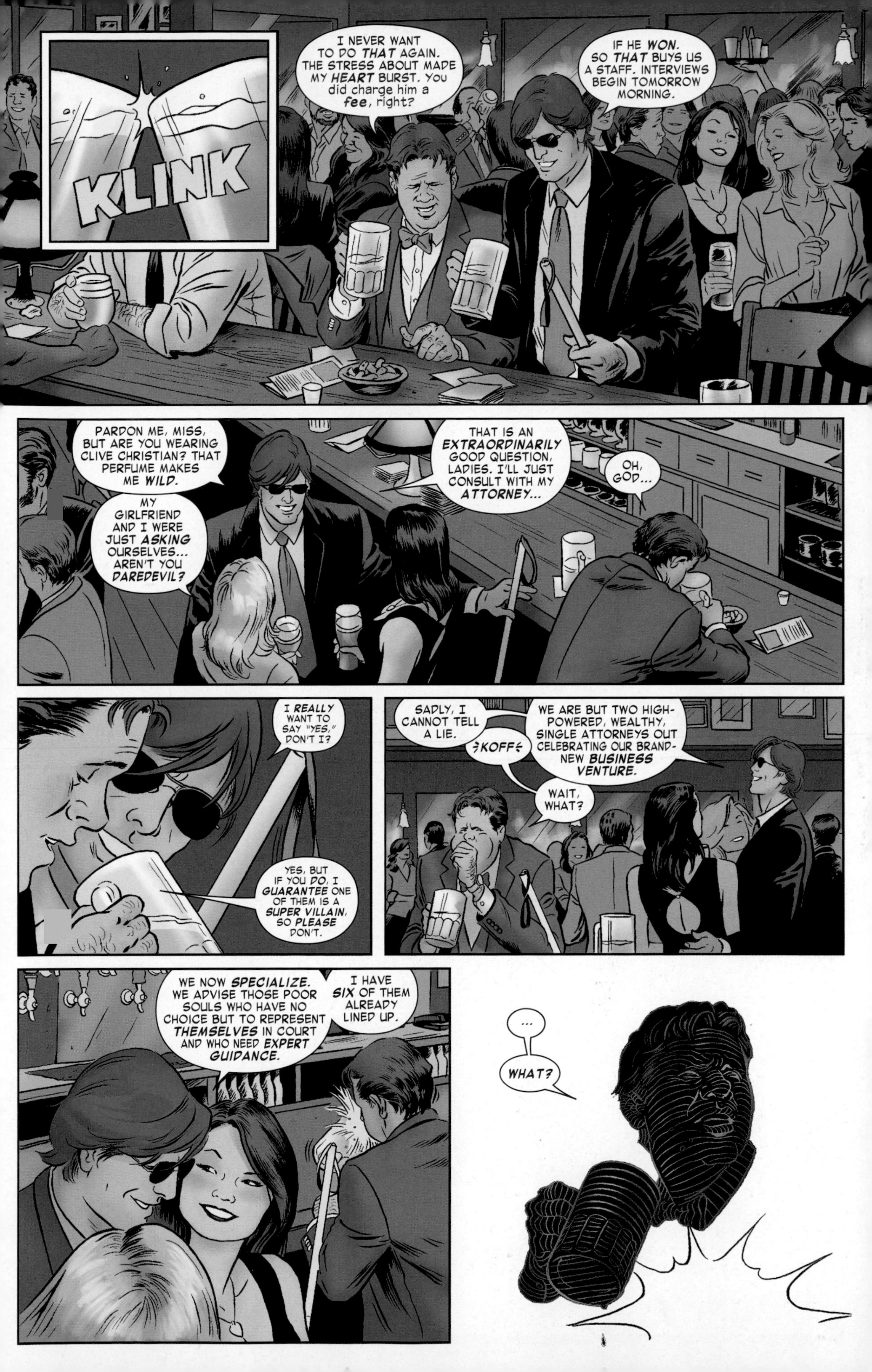
KLINK
I NEVER WANT TO DO THAT AGAIN. THE STRESS ABOUT MADE MY HEART BURST. You did charge him a fee, right?
IF HE WON. SO THAT BUYS US A STAFF. INTERVIEWS BEGIN TOMORROW MORNING.
PARDON ME, MISS, BUT ARE YOU WEARING CLIVE CHRISTIAN? THAT PERFUME MAKES ME WILD.
MY GIRLFRIEND AND I WERE JUST ASKING OURSELVES... AREN'T YOU DAREDEVIL?
THAT IS AN EXTRAORDINARILY GOOD QUESTION, LADIES. I'LL JUST CONSULT WITH MY ATTORNEY...
OH, GOD...
I REALLY WANT TO SAY "YES," DON'T I?
YES, BUT IF YOU DO, I GUARANTEE ONE OF THEM IS A SUPER VILLAIN, SO PLEASE DON'T.
SADLY, I CANNOT TELL A LIE.
WE ARE BUT TWO HIGH-POWERED, WEALTHY, SINGLE ATTORNEYS OUT CELEBRATING OUR BRAND-NEW BUSINESS VENTURE.
KOFF
WAIT, WHAT?
WE NOW SPECIALIZE. WE ADVISE THOSE POOR SOULS WHO HAVE NO CHOICE BUT TO REPRESENT THEMSELVES IN COURT AND WHO NEED EXPERT GUIDANCE.
I HAVE SIX OF THEM ALREADY LINED UP.
...
WHAT?

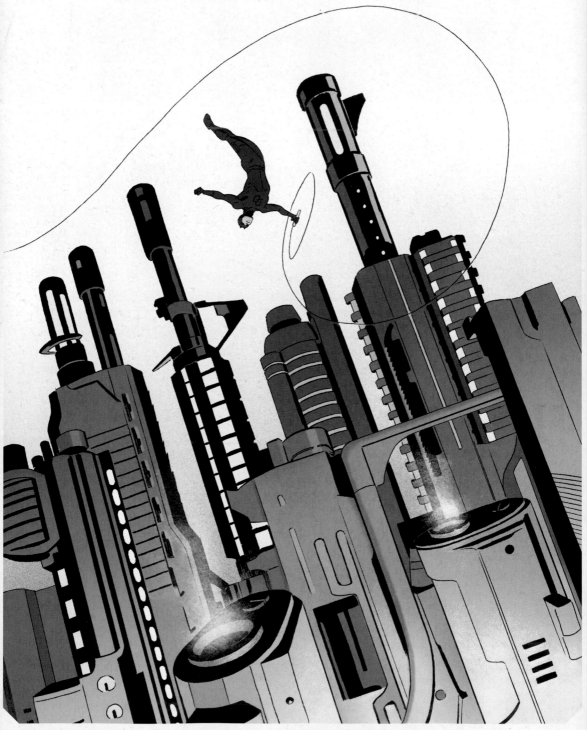

FOUR

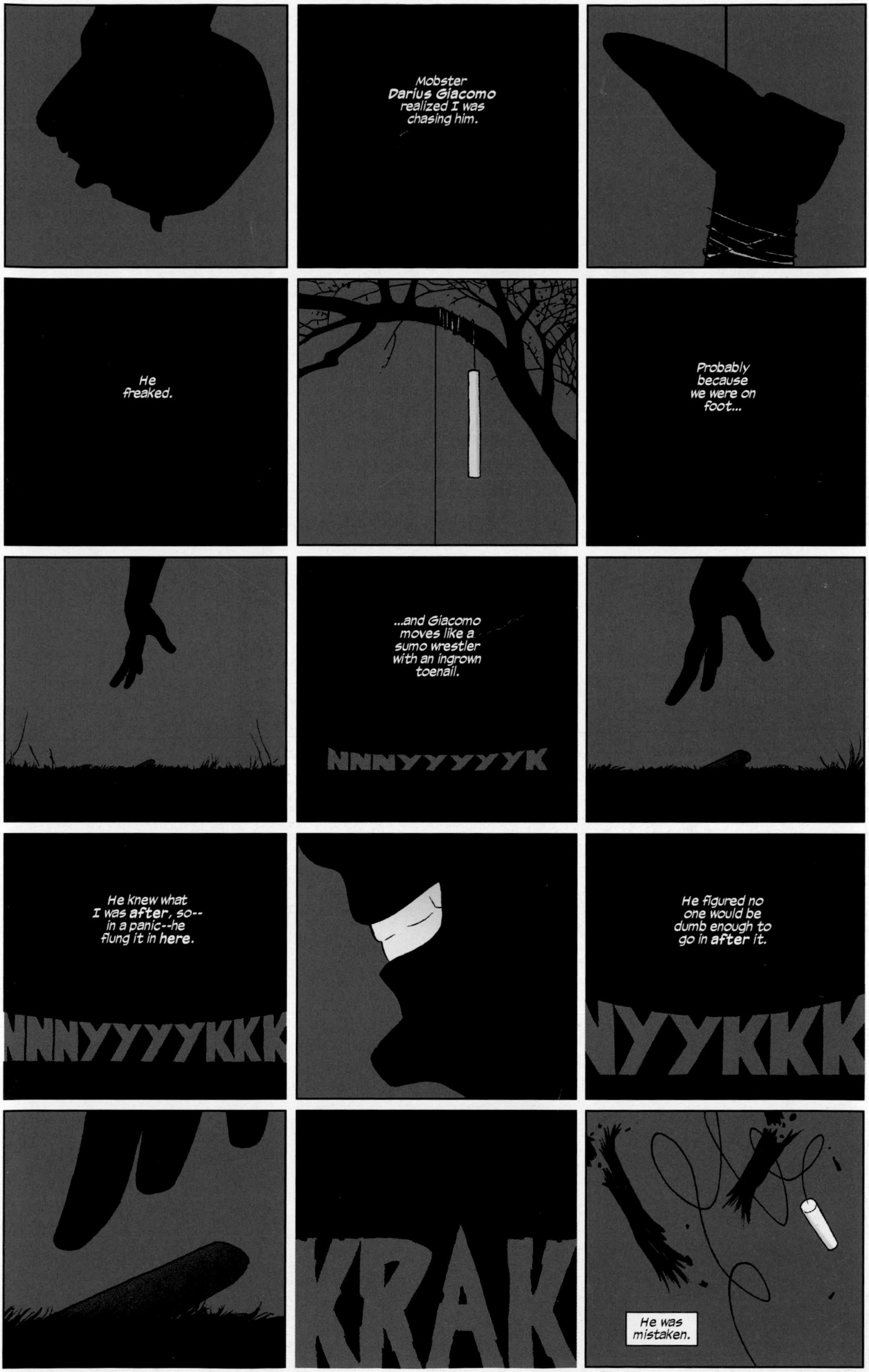
Mobster Darius Giacomo realized I was chasing him.
He freaked.
Probably because we were on foot...
...and Giacomo moves like a sumo wrestler with an ingrown toenail.
NNNYYYYYYK
He knew what I was **after**, so--in a panic--he flung it in **here**.
NNNYYYYKKK
He figured no one would be dumb enough to go in **after** it.
NYYKKK
KRAK
He was mistaken.

So much for the silent approach. To ears as fine as the ones in here, I touch down like a cinderblock.

I can hear their eyelids fluttering as they awaken.

I can smell adrenaline rising...

...mine and theirs.

I can taste the danger in the air.

GRRRRRRRRR

At two a.m., there are a lot of places in New York that a blind man like myself doesn't want to pick a fight.

GRRRRLLL

Exhibit A:

GRRWLL

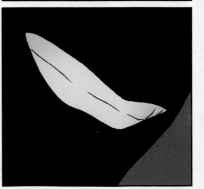

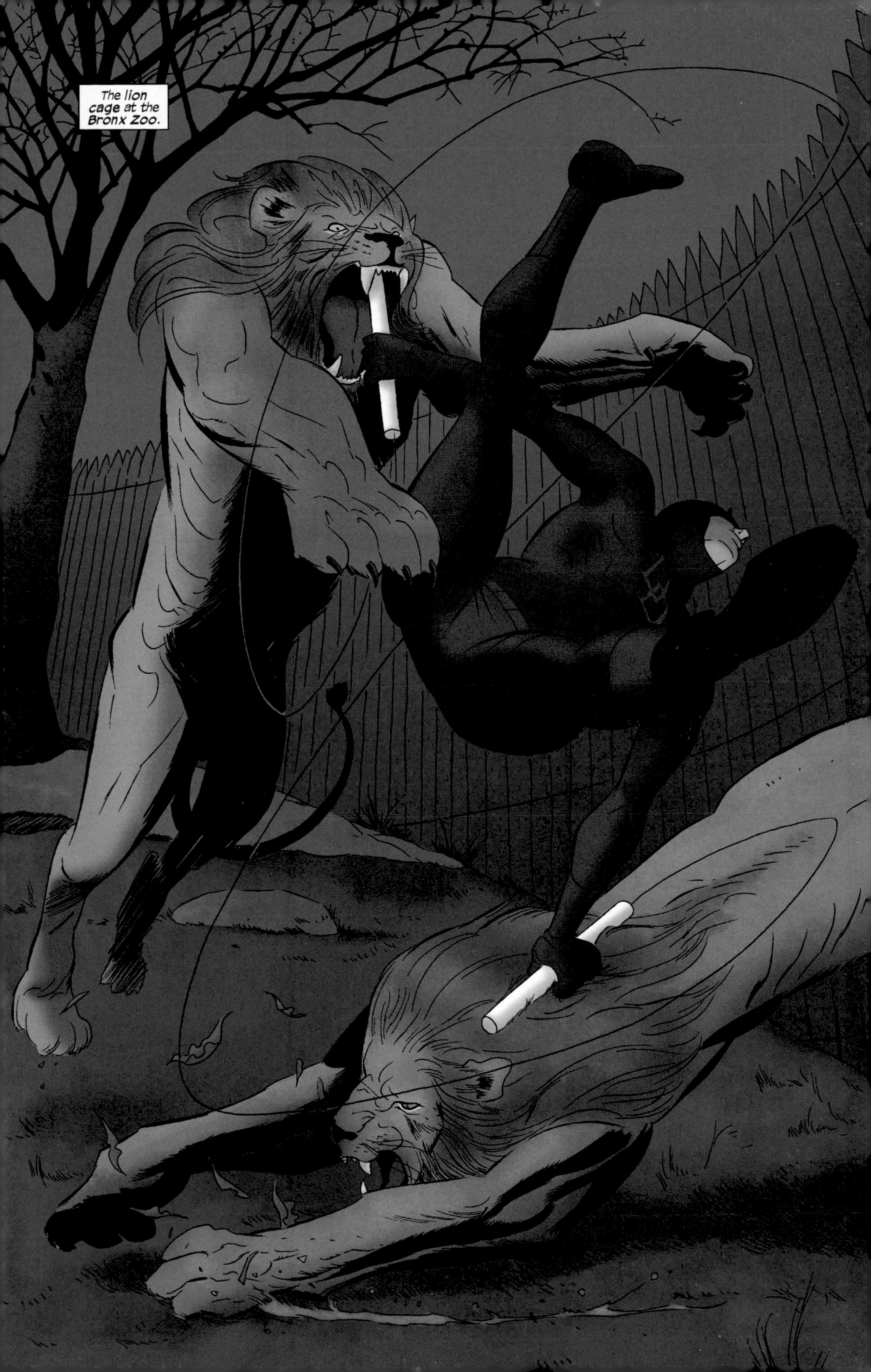
The lion cage at the Bronx Zoo.

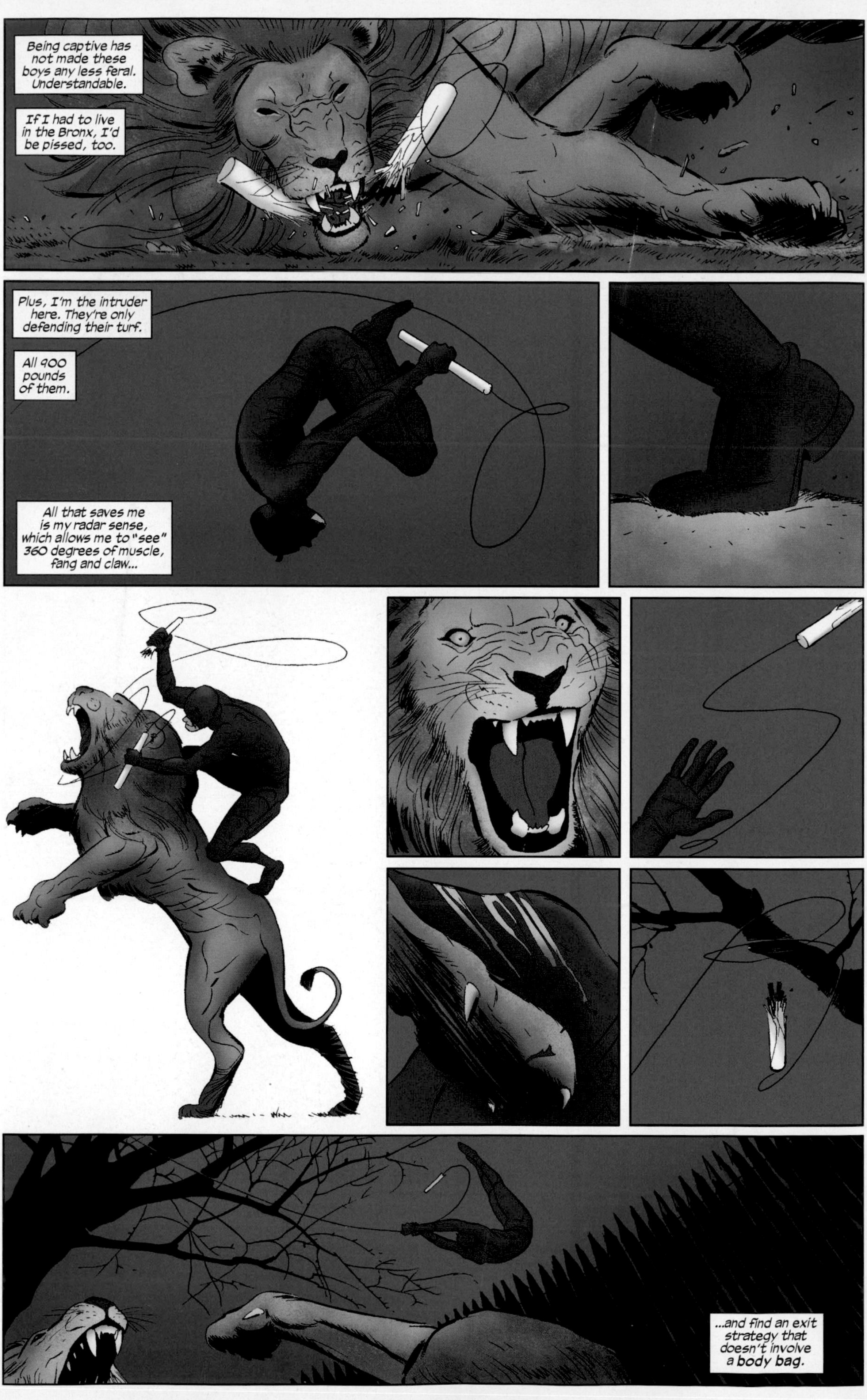
Being captive has not made these boys any less feral. Understandable.
If I had to live in the Bronx, I'd be pissed, too.
Plus, I'm the intruder here. They're only defending their turf.
All 900 pounds of them.
All that saves me is my radar sense, which allows me to "see" 360 degrees of muscle, fang and claw...
...and find an exit strategy that doesn't involve a **body bag**.

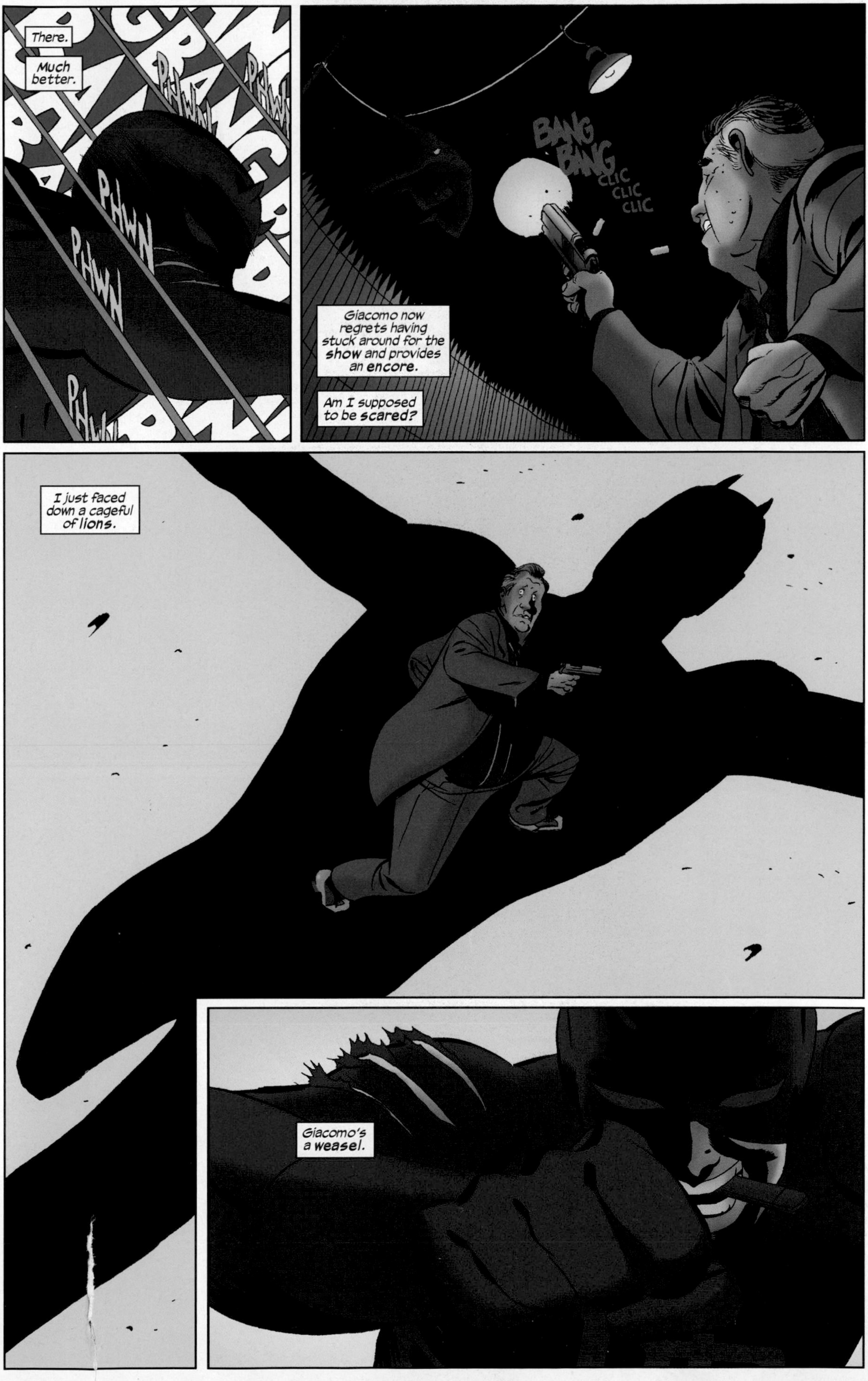

There.
Much better.
PHWN
PHWN
PHWN
PHWN
PHWN
PHWN
Giacomo now regrets having stuck around for the show and provides an encore.
BANG
BANG
CLIC
CLIC
CLIC
Am I supposed to be scared?
I just faced down a cageful of lions.
Giacomo's a weasel.

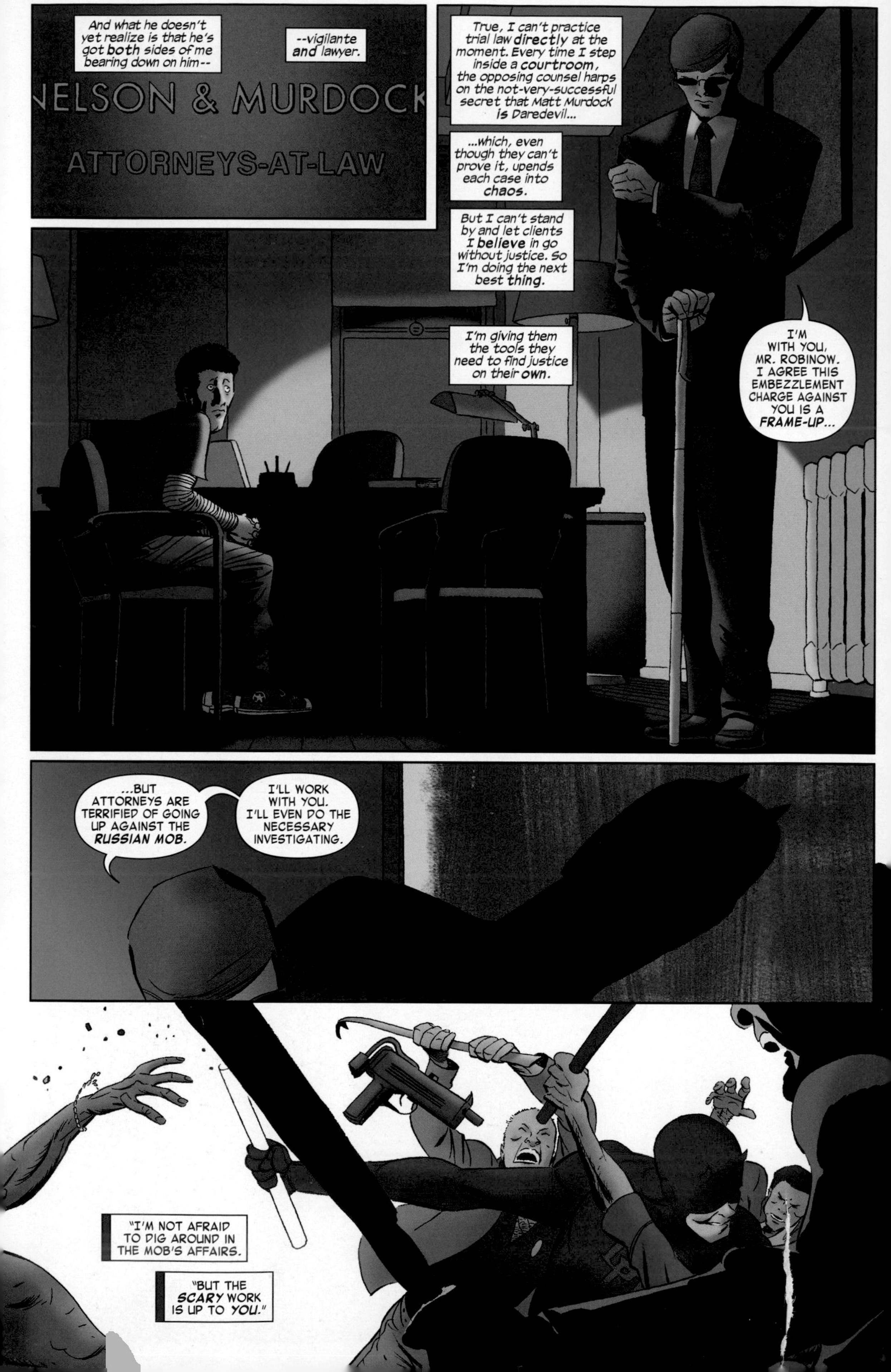

And what he doesn't yet realize is that he's got both sides of me bearing down on him--
--vigilante and lawyer.
NELSON & MURDOCK
ATTORNEYS-AT-LAW
True, I can't practice trial law directly at the moment. Every time I step inside a courtroom, the opposing counsel harps on the not-very-successful secret that Matt Murdock is Daredevil...
...which, even though they can't prove it, upends each case into chaos.
But I can't stand by and let clients I believe in go without justice. So I'm doing the next best thing.
I'm giving them the tools they need to find justice on their own.
I'M WITH YOU, MR. ROBINOW. I AGREE THIS EMBEZZLEMENT CHARGE AGAINST YOU IS A FRAME-UP...
...BUT ATTORNEYS ARE TERRIFIED OF GOING UP AGAINST THE RUSSIAN MOB.
I'LL WORK WITH YOU. I'LL EVEN DO THE NECESSARY INVESTIGATING.
"I'M NOT AFRAID TO DIG AROUND IN THE MOB'S AFFAIRS.
"BUT THE SCARY WORK IS UP TO YOU."

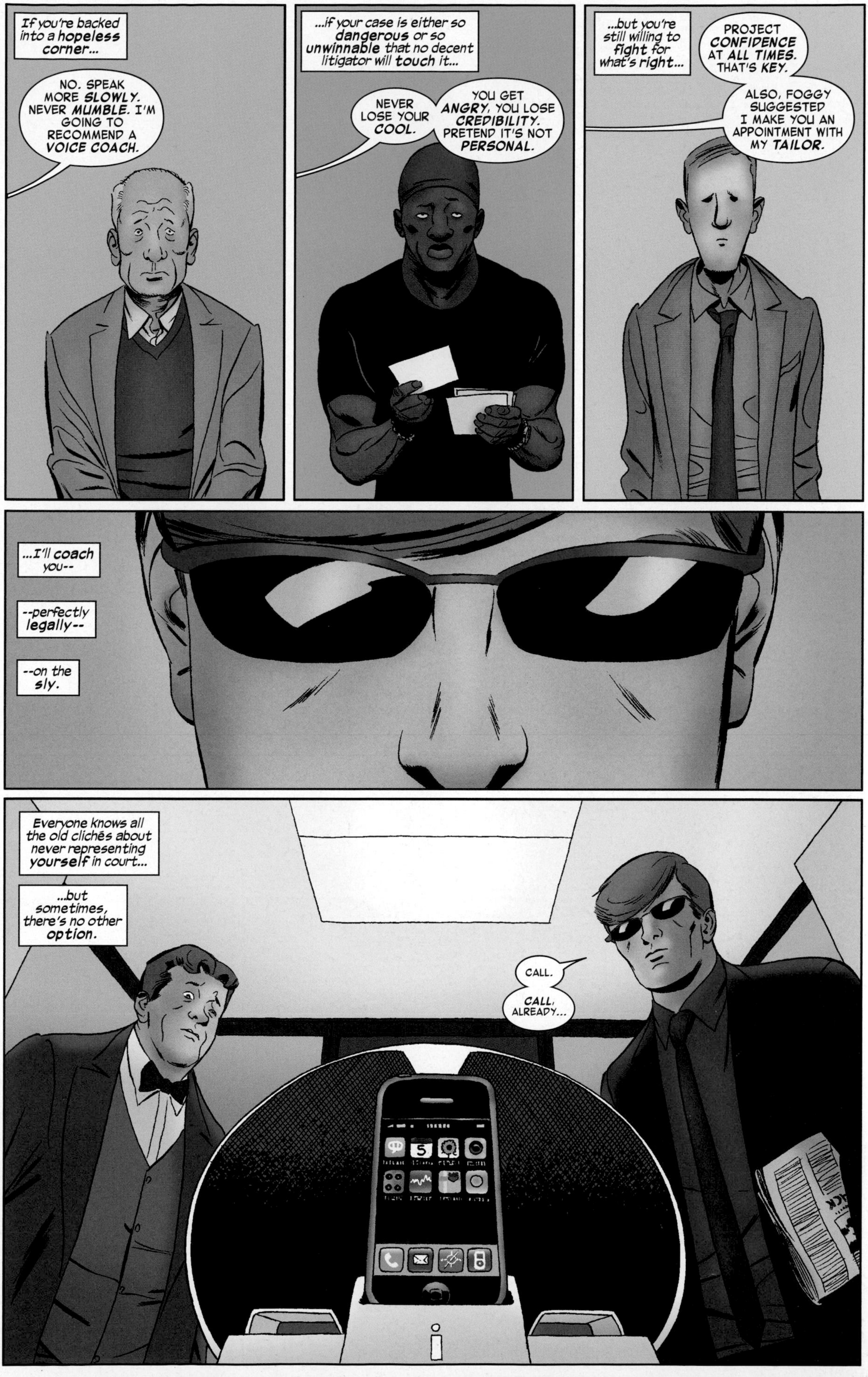

If you're backed into a hopeless corner...
NO. SPEAK MORE SLOWLY. NEVER MUMBLE. I'M GOING TO RECOMMEND A VOICE COACH.
...if your case is either so dangerous or so unwinnable that no decent litigator will touch it...
NEVER LOSE YOUR COOL.
YOU GET ANGRY, YOU LOSE CREDIBILITY. PRETEND IT'S NOT PERSONAL.
...but you're still willing to fight for what's right...
PROJECT CONFIDENCE AT ALL TIMES. THAT'S KEY.
ALSO, FOGGY SUGGESTED I MAKE YOU AN APPOINTMENT WITH MY TAILOR.
...I'll coach you--
--perfectly legally--
--on the sly.
Everyone knows all the old clichés about never representing yourself in court...
...but sometimes, there's no other option.
CALL.
CALL, ALREADY...

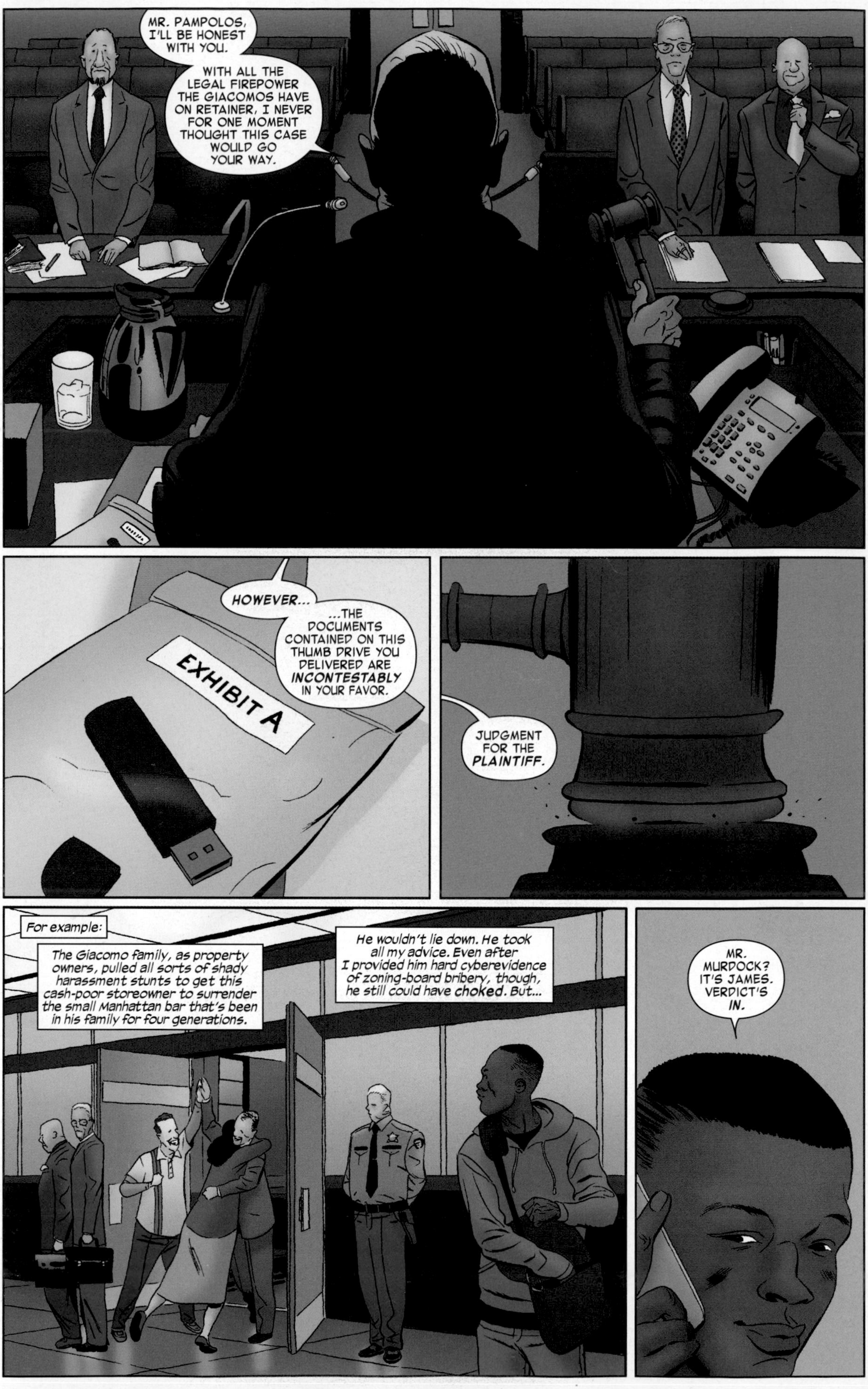
MR. PAMPOLOS, I'LL BE HONEST WITH YOU.
WITH ALL THE LEGAL FIREPOWER THE GIACOMOS HAVE ON RETAINER, I NEVER FOR ONE MOMENT THOUGHT THIS CASE WOULD GO YOUR WAY.
HOWEVER...
...THE DOCUMENTS CONTAINED ON THIS THUMB DRIVE YOU DELIVERED ARE INCONTESTABLY IN YOUR FAVOR.
EXHIBIT A
JUDGMENT FOR THE PLAINTIFF.
For example:
The Giacomo family, as property owners, pulled all sorts of shady harassment stunts to get this cash-poor storeowner to surrender the small Manhattan bar that's been in his family for four generations.
He wouldn't lie down. He took all my advice. Even after I provided him hard cyberevidence of zoning-board bribery, though, he still could have choked. But...
MR. MURDOCK? IT'S JAMES. VERDICT'S IN.

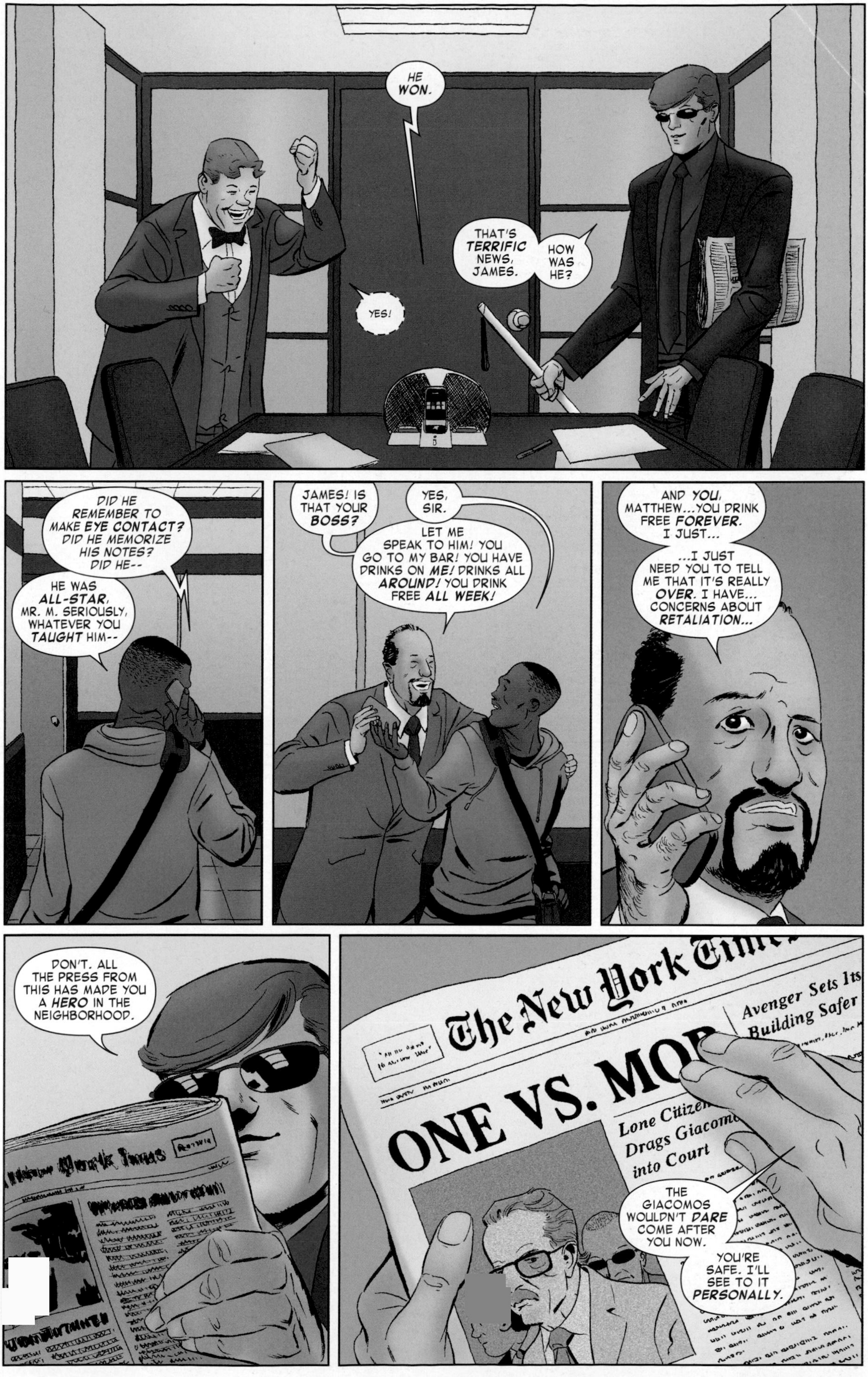
HE WON.
YES!
THAT'S TERRIFIC NEWS, JAMES.
HOW WAS HE?
DID HE REMEMBER TO MAKE EYE CONTACT? DID HE MEMORIZE HIS NOTES? DID HE--
HE WAS ALL-STAR, MR. M. SERIOUSLY, WHATEVER YOU TAUGHT HIM--
JAMES! IS THAT YOUR BOSS?
YES, SIR.
LET ME SPEAK TO HIM! YOU GO TO MY BAR! YOU HAVE DRINKS ON ME! DRINKS ALL AROUND! YOU DRINK FREE ALL WEEK!
AND YOU, MATTHEW...YOU DRINK FREE FOREVER. I JUST...
...I JUST NEED YOU TO TELL ME THAT IT'S REALLY OVER. I HAVE... CONCERNS ABOUT RETALIATION...
DON'T. ALL THE PRESS FROM THIS HAS MADE YOU A HERO IN THE NEIGHBORHOOD.
The New York Times
Avenger Sets Its Building Safer
ONE VS. MOB
Lone Citizen Drags Giacomo into Court
THE GIACOMOS WOULDN'T DARE COME AFTER YOU NOW.
YOU'RE SAFE. I'LL SEE TO IT PERSONALLY.

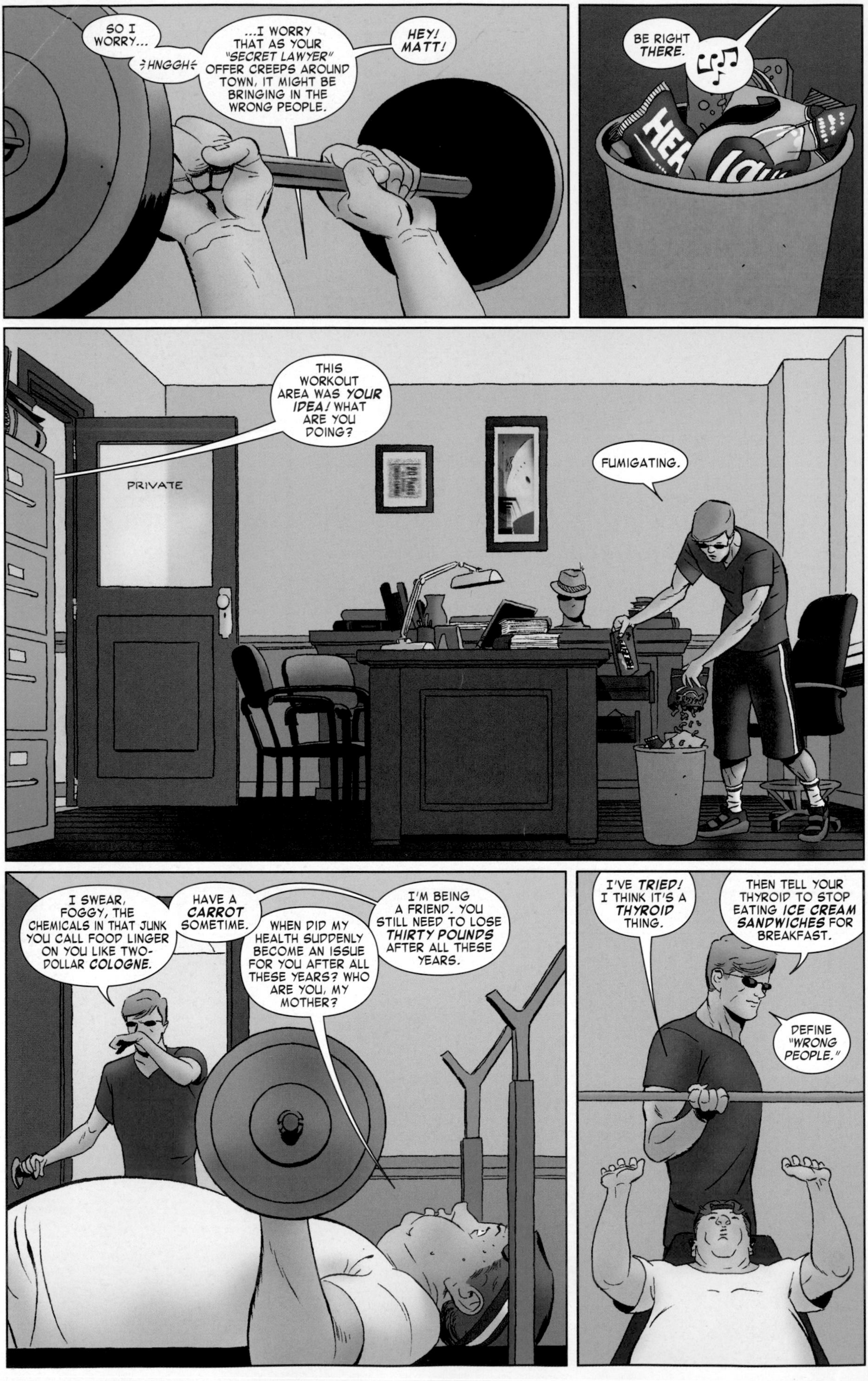
SO I WORRY...
HNGGH
...I WORRY THAT AS YOUR "SECRET LAWYER" OFFER CREEPS AROUND TOWN, IT MIGHT BE BRINGING IN THE WRONG PEOPLE.
HEY! MATT!
BE RIGHT THERE.
THIS WORKOUT AREA WAS YOUR IDEA! WHAT ARE YOU DOING?
PRIVATE
FUMIGATING.
I SWEAR, FOGGY, THE CHEMICALS IN THAT JUNK YOU CALL FOOD LINGER ON YOU LIKE TWO-DOLLAR COLOGNE.
HAVE A CARROT SOMETIME.
WHEN DID MY HEALTH SUDDENLY BECOME AN ISSUE FOR YOU AFTER ALL THESE YEARS? WHO ARE YOU, MY MOTHER?
I'M BEING A FRIEND. YOU STILL NEED TO LOSE THIRTY POUNDS AFTER ALL THESE YEARS.
I'VE TRIED! I THINK IT'S A THYROID THING.
THEN TELL YOUR THYROID TO STOP EATING ICE CREAM SANDWICHES FOR BREAKFAST.
DEFINE "WRONG PEOPLE."

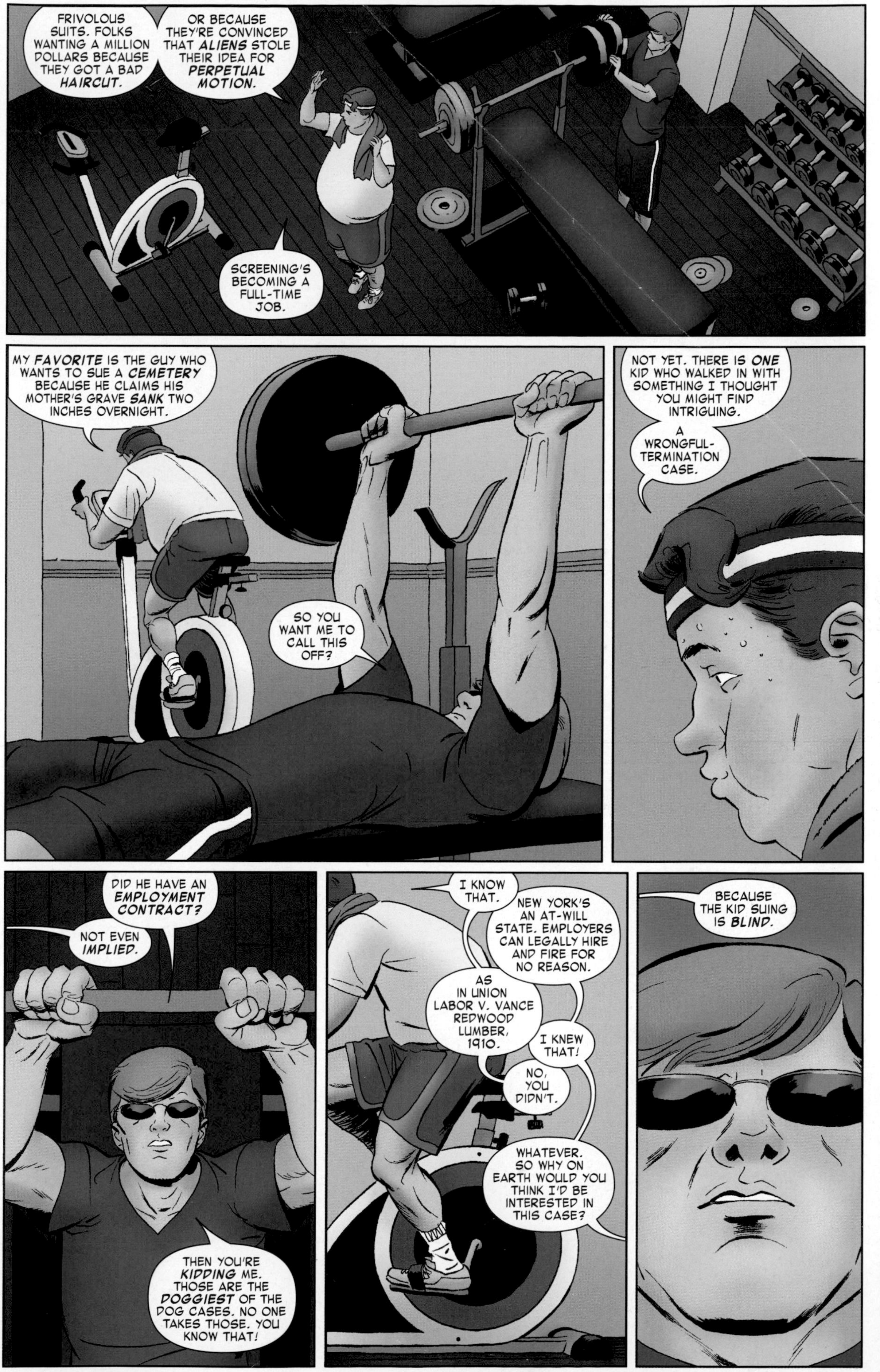
FRIVOLOUS SUITS. FOLKS WANTING A MILLION DOLLARS BECAUSE THEY GOT A BAD HAIRCUT.
OR BECAUSE THEY'RE CONVINCED THAT ALIENS STOLE THEIR IDEA FOR PERPETUAL MOTION.
SCREENING'S BECOMING A FULL-TIME JOB.
MY FAVORITE IS THE GUY WHO WANTS TO SUE A CEMETERY BECAUSE HE CLAIMS HIS MOTHER'S GRAVE SANK TWO INCHES OVERNIGHT.
SO YOU WANT ME TO CALL THIS OFF?
NOT YET. THERE IS ONE KID WHO WALKED IN WITH SOMETHING I THOUGHT YOU MIGHT FIND INTRIGUING.
A WRONGFUL-TERMINATION CASE.
DID HE HAVE AN EMPLOYMENT CONTRACT?
NOT EVEN IMPLIED.
THEN YOU'RE KIDDING ME. THOSE ARE THE DOGGIEST OF THE DOG CASES. NO ONE TAKES THOSE. YOU KNOW THAT!
I KNOW THAT.
NEW YORK'S AN AT-WILL STATE. EMPLOYERS CAN LEGALLY HIRE AND FIRE FOR NO REASON.
AS IN UNION LABOR V. VANCE REDWOOD LUMBER, 1910.
I KNEW THAT!
NO, YOU DIDN'T.
WHATEVER. SO WHY ON EARTH WOULD YOU THINK I'D BE INTERESTED IN THIS CASE?
BECAUSE THE KID SUING IS BLIND.

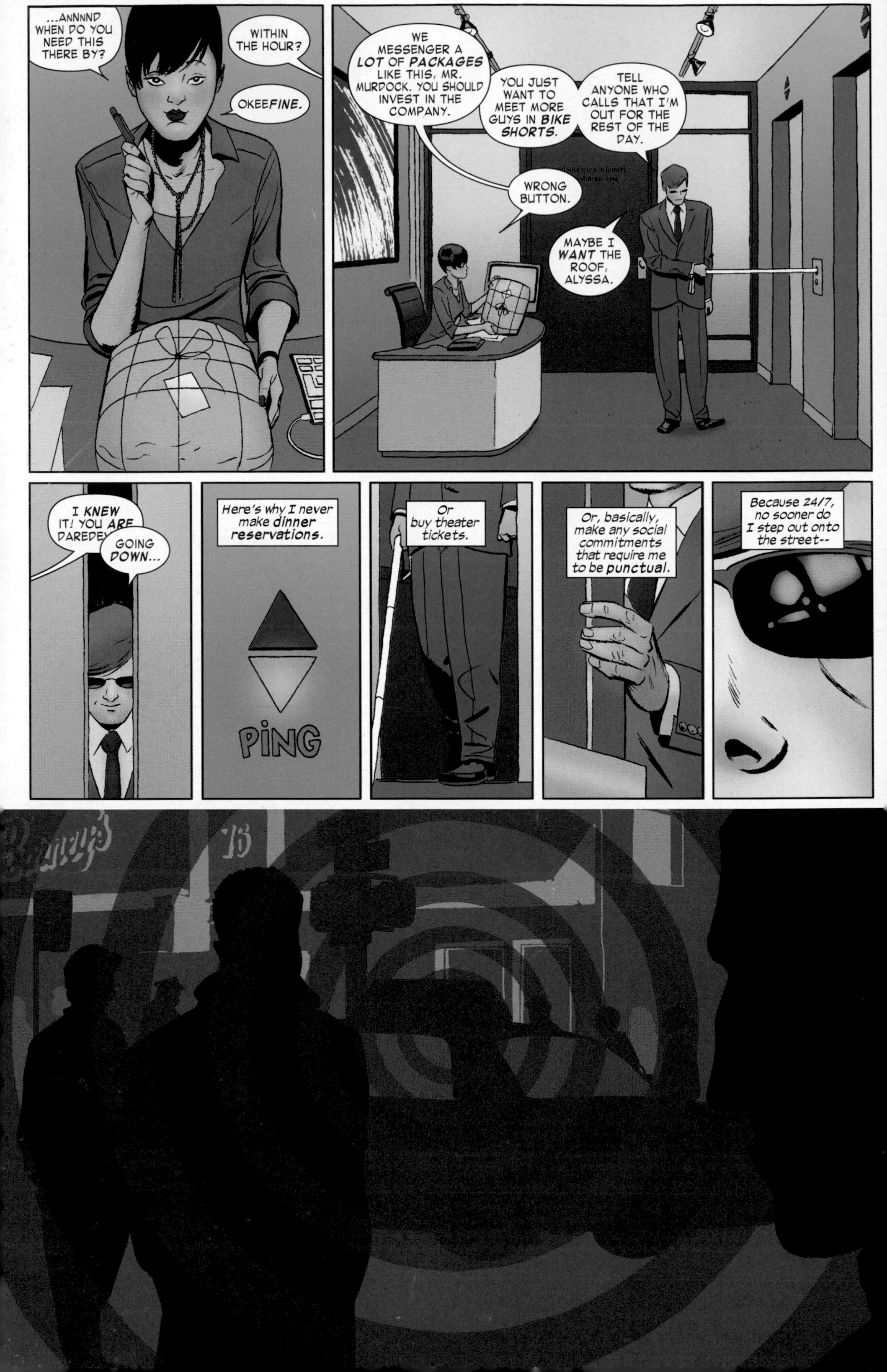

...ANNNND WHEN DO YOU NEED THIS THERE BY?
WITHIN THE HOUR?
OKEEFINE.
WE MESSENGER A LOT OF PACKAGES LIKE THIS, MR. MURDOCK. YOU SHOULD INVEST IN THE COMPANY.
YOU JUST WANT TO MEET MORE GUYS IN BIKE SHORTS.
TELL ANYONE WHO CALLS THAT I'M OUT FOR THE REST OF THE DAY.
WRONG BUTTON.
MAYBE I WANT THE ROOF, ALYSSA.
I KNEW IT! YOU ARE DAREDE
GOING DOWN...
Here's why I never make dinner reservations.
PING
Or buy theater tickets.
Or, basically, make any social commitments that require me to be punctual.
Because 24/7, no sooner do I step out onto the street--

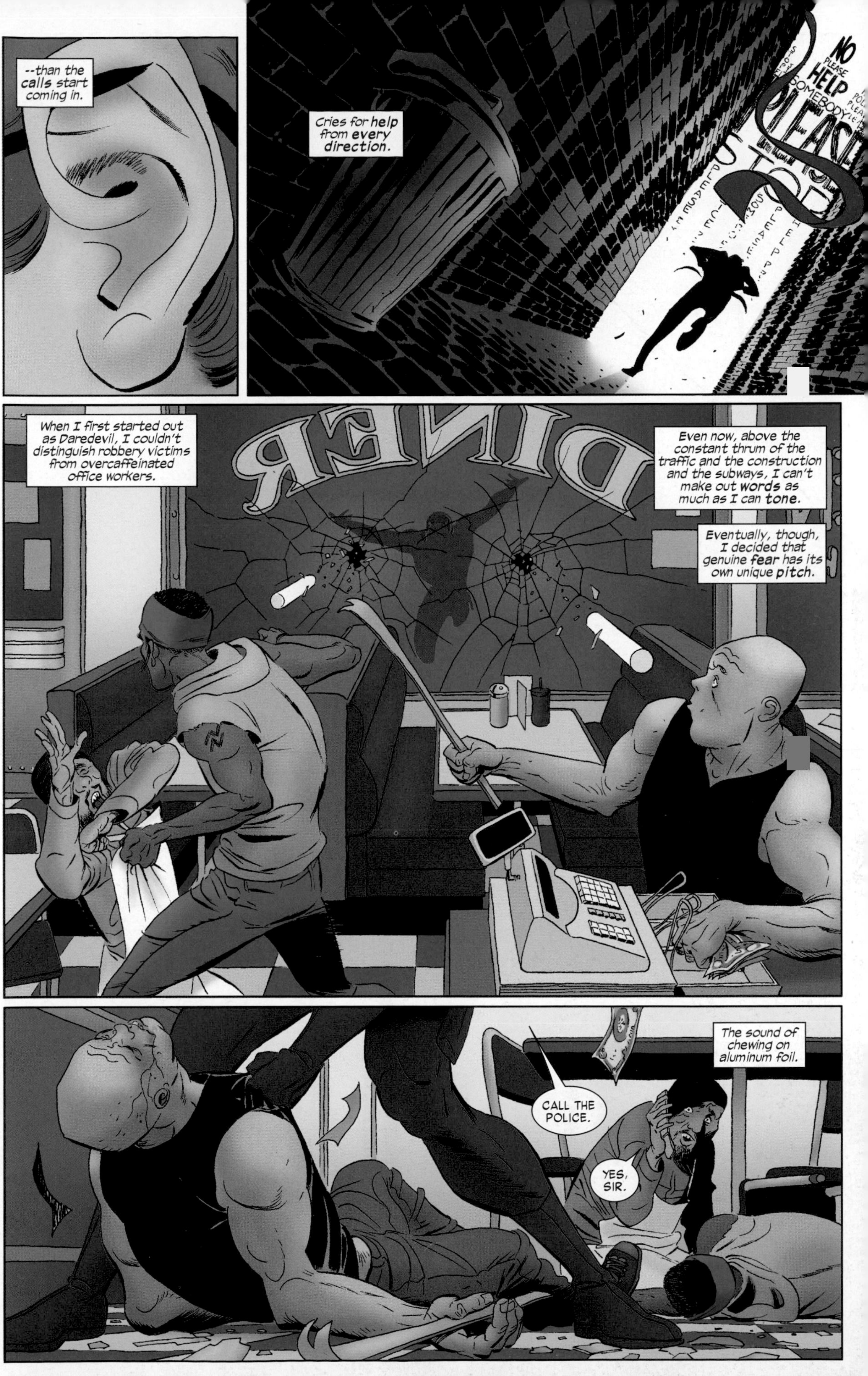
--than the calls start coming in.
Cries for help from every direction.
NO
PLEASE
HELP
SOMEBODY
When I first started out as Daredevil, I couldn't distinguish robbery victims from overcaffeinated office workers.
DINER
Even now, above the constant thrum of the traffic and the construction and the subways, I can't make out words as much as I can tone.
Eventually, though, I decided that genuine fear has its own unique pitch.
The sound of chewing on aluminum foil.
CALL THE POLICE.
YES, SIR.

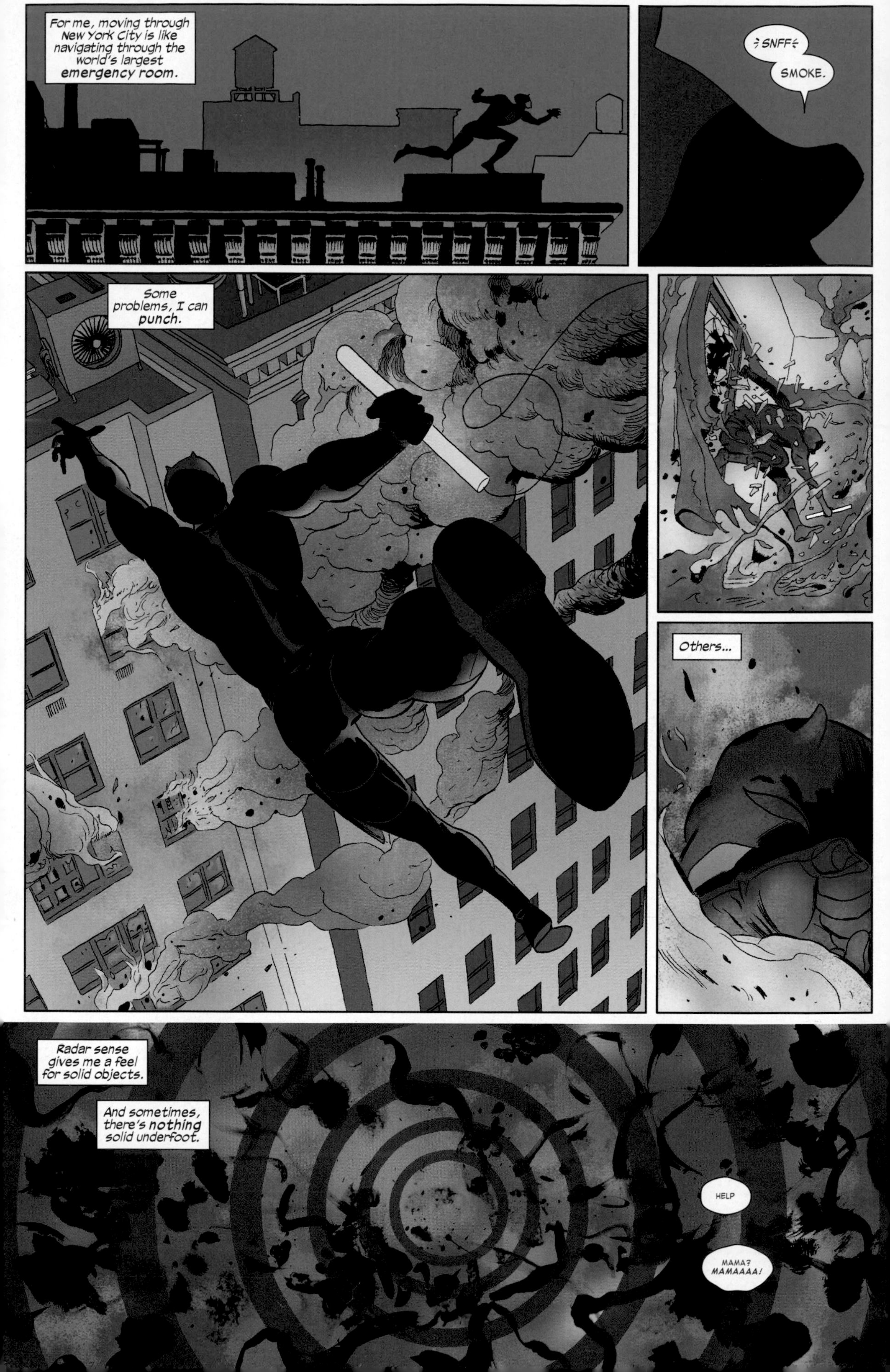
For me, moving through New York City is like navigating through the world's largest emergency room.
SNFF
SMOKE.
Some problems, I can punch.
Others...
Radar sense gives me a feel for solid objects.
And sometimes, there's nothing solid underfoot.
HELP
MAMA? MAMAAAA!

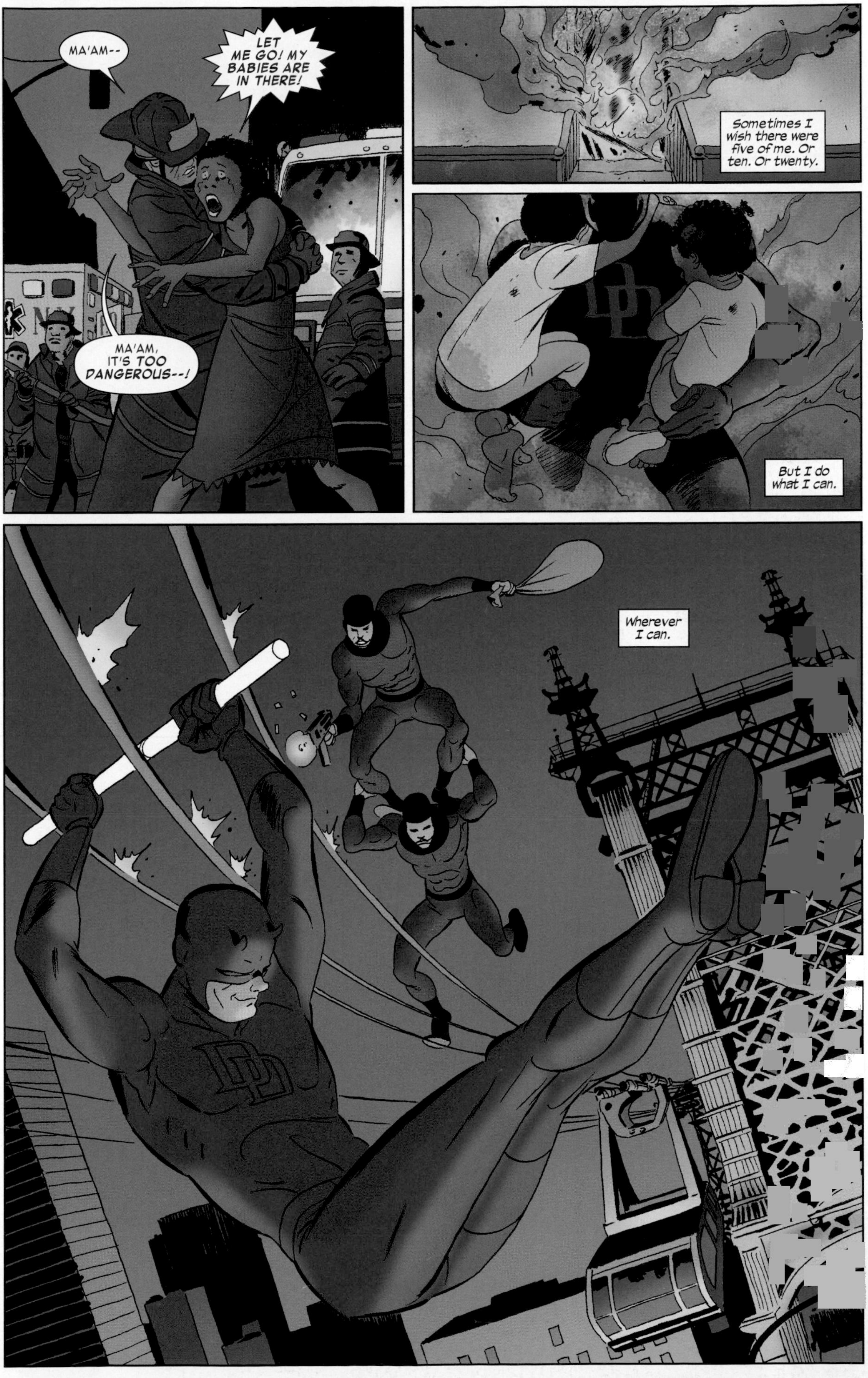
MA'AM--
LET ME GO! MY BABIES ARE IN THERE!
MA'AM, IT'S TOO DANGEROUS--!
Sometimes I wish there were five of me. Or ten. Or twenty.
But I do what I can.
Wherever I can.

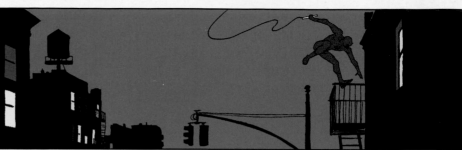

In summation, whenever Matt Murdock hits the pavement, *Daredevil* almost always ends up pinballing randomly across town from crisis to crisis--

--miles from wherever I had to leave my street clothes, which have almost *always* been stolen by the time I double back.

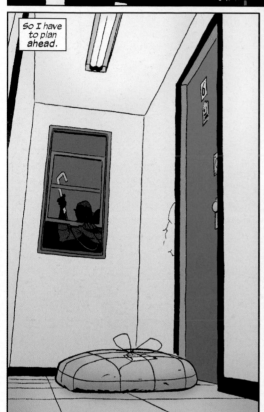

So I have to plan ahead.

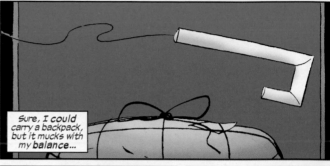

Sure, I could carry a backpack, but it mucks with my *balance*...

...and besides...

...you don't stuff a *Jay Kos* suit into a *backpack.*

KNOCK KNOCK

If I could itemize crimefighting expenses on my taxes, I'd be a millionaire.

MR. CAO? THIS IS *MATT MURDOCK.*

MR. AUSTIN CAO?

'S ME.

C'MON IN.

ANYONE ELSE WITH YOU?

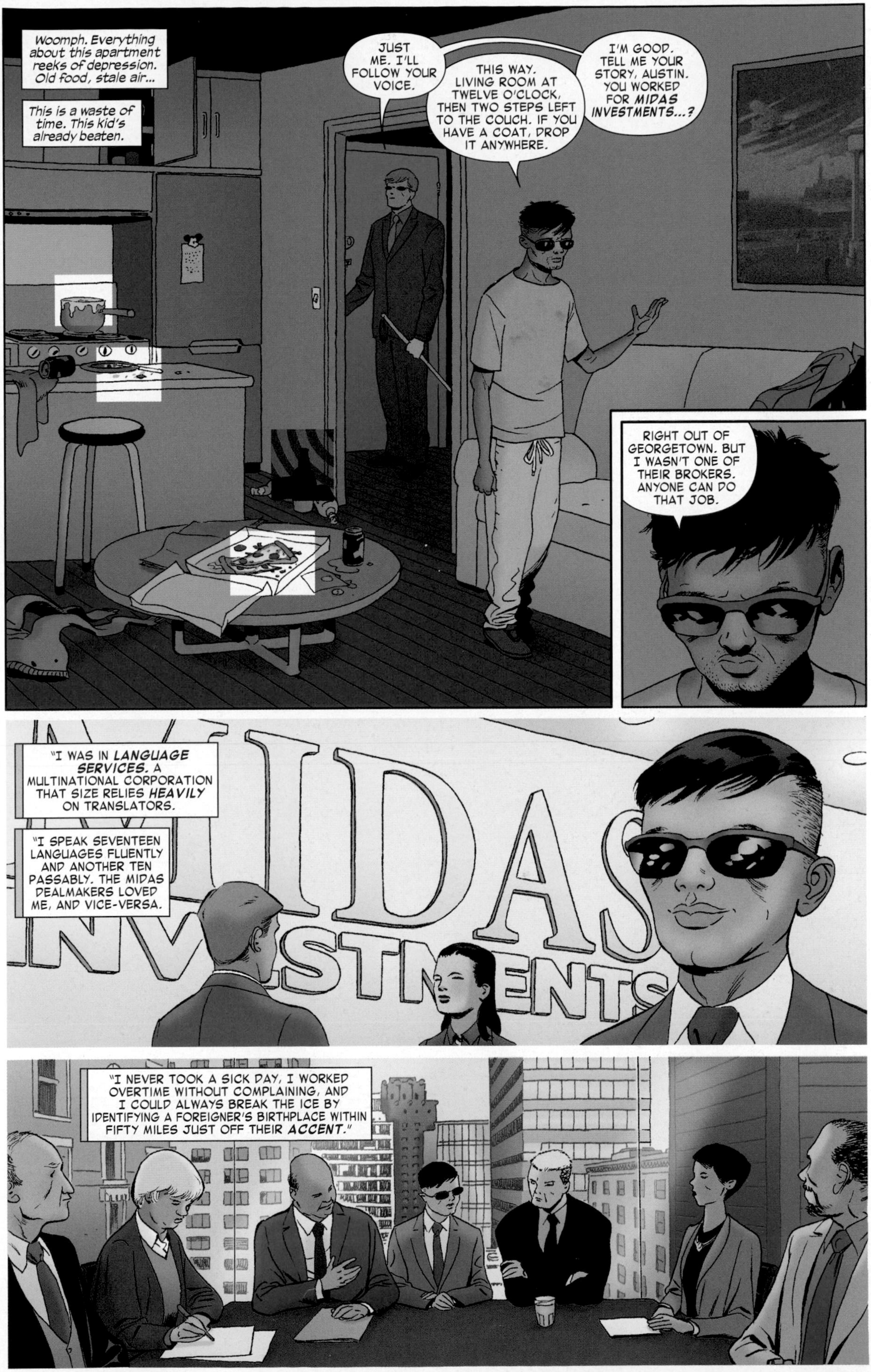
Woomph. Everything about this apartment reeks of depression. Old food, stale air...
This is a waste of time. This kid's already beaten.
JUST ME. I'LL FOLLOW YOUR VOICE.
THIS WAY. LIVING ROOM AT TWELVE O'CLOCK, THEN TWO STEPS LEFT TO THE COUCH. IF YOU HAVE A COAT, DROP IT ANYWHERE.
I'M GOOD. TELL ME YOUR STORY, AUSTIN. YOU WORKED FOR MIDAS INVESTMENTS...?
RIGHT OUT OF GEORGETOWN. BUT I WASN'T ONE OF THEIR BROKERS. ANYONE CAN DO THAT JOB.
"I WAS IN LANGUAGE SERVICES. A MULTINATIONAL CORPORATION THAT SIZE RELIES HEAVILY ON TRANSLATORS.
"I SPEAK SEVENTEEN LANGUAGES FLUENTLY AND ANOTHER TEN PASSABLY. THE MIDAS DEALMAKERS LOVED ME, AND VICE-VERSA.
"I NEVER TOOK A SICK DAY, I WORKED OVERTIME WITHOUT COMPLAINING, AND I COULD ALWAYS BREAK THE ICE BY IDENTIFYING A FOREIGNER'S BIRTHPLACE WITHIN FIFTY MILES JUST OFF THEIR ACCENT."

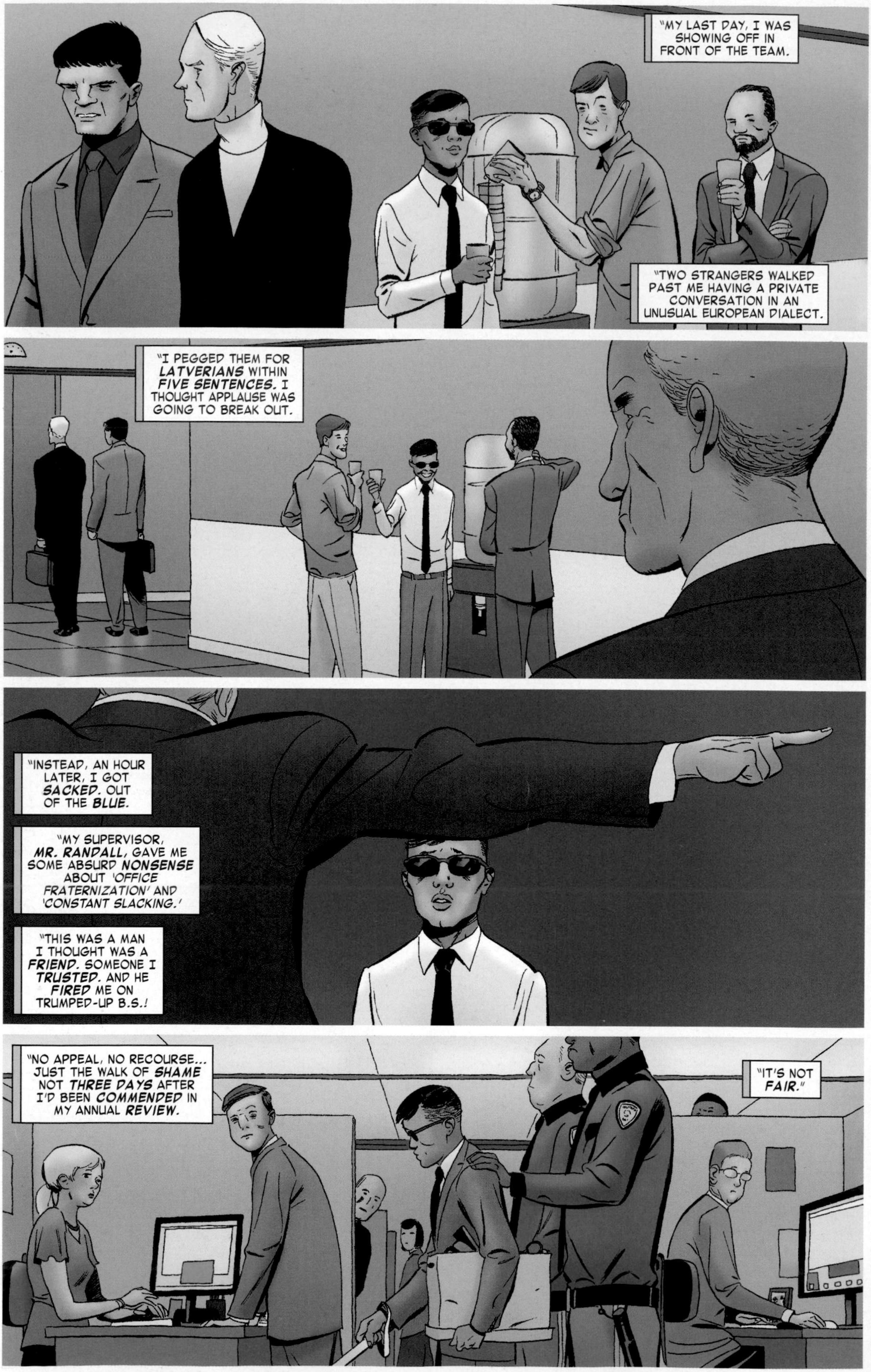
"MY LAST DAY, I WAS SHOWING OFF IN FRONT OF THE TEAM.
"TWO STRANGERS WALKED PAST ME HAVING A PRIVATE CONVERSATION IN AN UNUSUAL EUROPEAN DIALECT.
"I PEGGED THEM FOR LATVERIANS WITHIN FIVE SENTENCES. I THOUGHT APPLAUSE WAS GOING TO BREAK OUT.
"INSTEAD, AN HOUR LATER, I GOT SACKED. OUT OF THE BLUE.
"MY SUPERVISOR, MR. RANDALL, GAVE ME SOME ABSURD NONSENSE ABOUT 'OFFICE FRATERNIZATION' AND 'CONSTANT SLACKING.'
"THIS WAS A MAN I THOUGHT WAS A FRIEND. SOMEONE I TRUSTED. AND HE FIRED ME ON TRUMPED-UP B.S.!
"NO APPEAL, NO RECOURSE... JUST THE WALK OF SHAME NOT THREE DAYS AFTER I'D BEEN COMMENDED IN MY ANNUAL REVIEW.
"IT'S NOT FAIR."

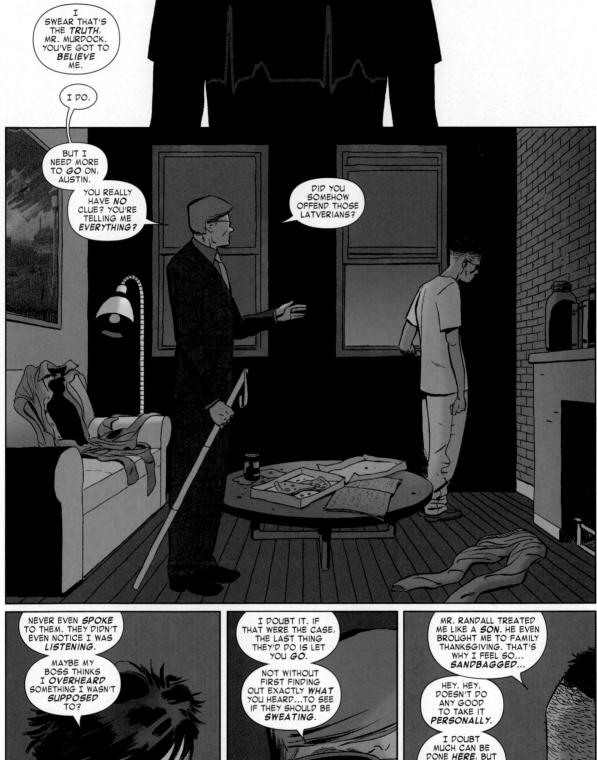

I SWEAR THAT'S THE *TRUTH*, MR. MURDOCK. YOU'VE GOT TO *BELIEVE* ME.

I DO.

BUT I NEED MORE TO *GO* ON, AUSTIN.

YOU REALLY HAVE *NO* CLUE? YOU'RE TELLING ME *EVERYTHING*?

DID YOU SOMEHOW OFFEND THOSE LATVERIANS?

NEVER EVEN *SPOKE* TO THEM. THEY DIDN'T EVEN NOTICE I WAS *LISTENING*.

MAYBE MY BOSS THINKS I *OVERHEARD* SOMETHING I WASN'T *SUPPOSED* TO?

I DOUBT IT. IF THAT WERE THE CASE, THE LAST THING THEY'D DO IS LET YOU *GO*.

NOT WITHOUT FIRST FINDING OUT EXACTLY *WHAT* YOU HEARD...TO SEE IF THEY SHOULD BE *SWEATING*.

THIS MR. RANDALL...DID HE EVER SAY ANYTHING DISPARAGING ABOUT YOUR BLINDNESS? BECAUSE THAT WOULD AT LEAST GIVE US A *FINGERHOLD*--

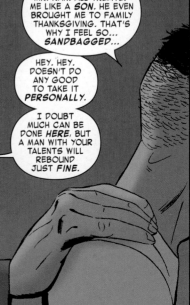

MR. RANDALL TREATED ME LIKE A *SON*. HE EVEN BROUGHT ME TO FAMILY THANKSGIVING. THAT'S WHY I FEEL SO... *SANDBAGGED*...

HEY. HEY. DOESN'T DO ANY GOOD TO TAKE IT *PERSONALLY*.

I DOUBT MUCH CAN BE DONE *HERE*, BUT A MAN WITH YOUR TALENTS WILL REBOUND JUST *FINE*.

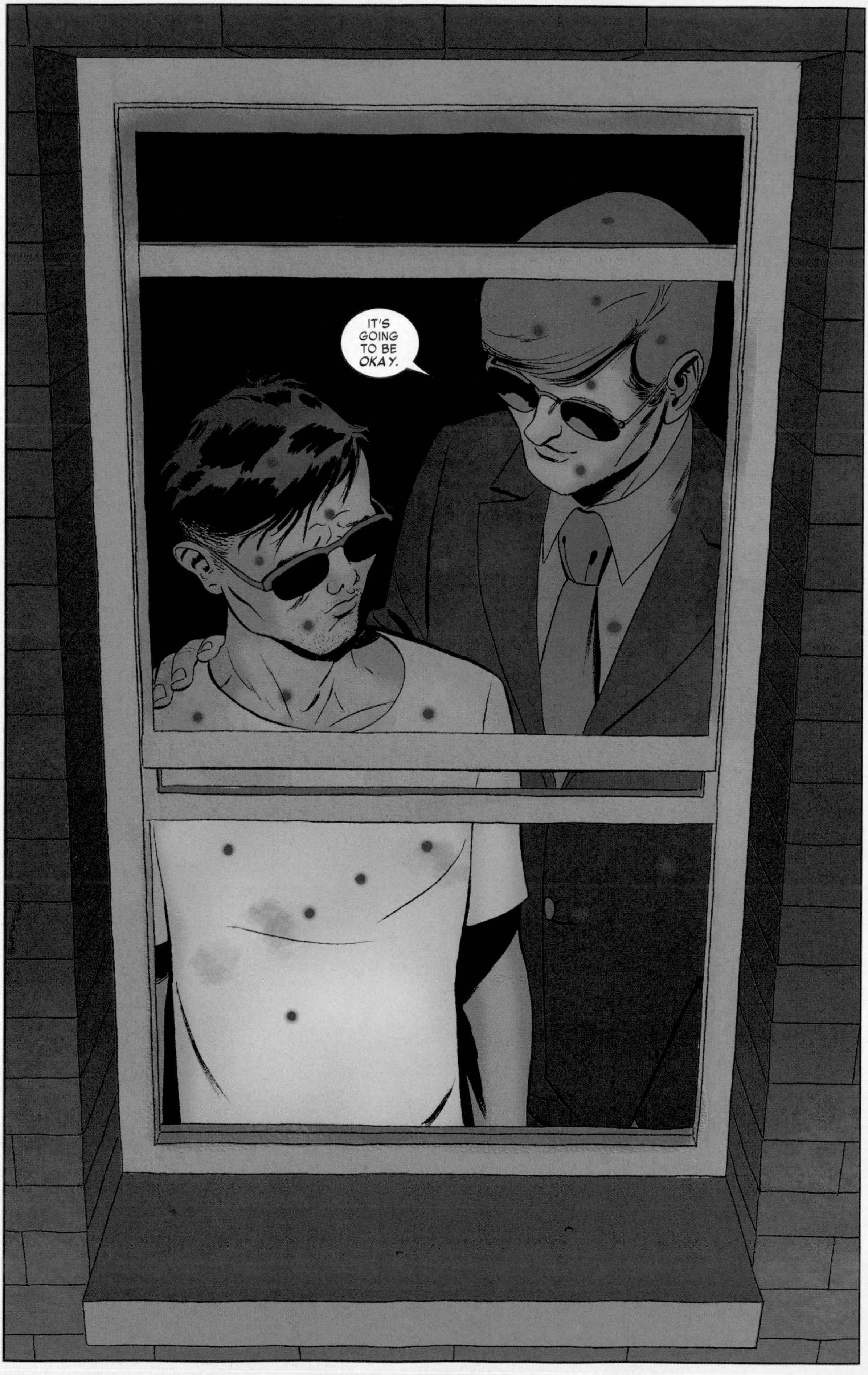
IT'S GOING TO BE OKAY.

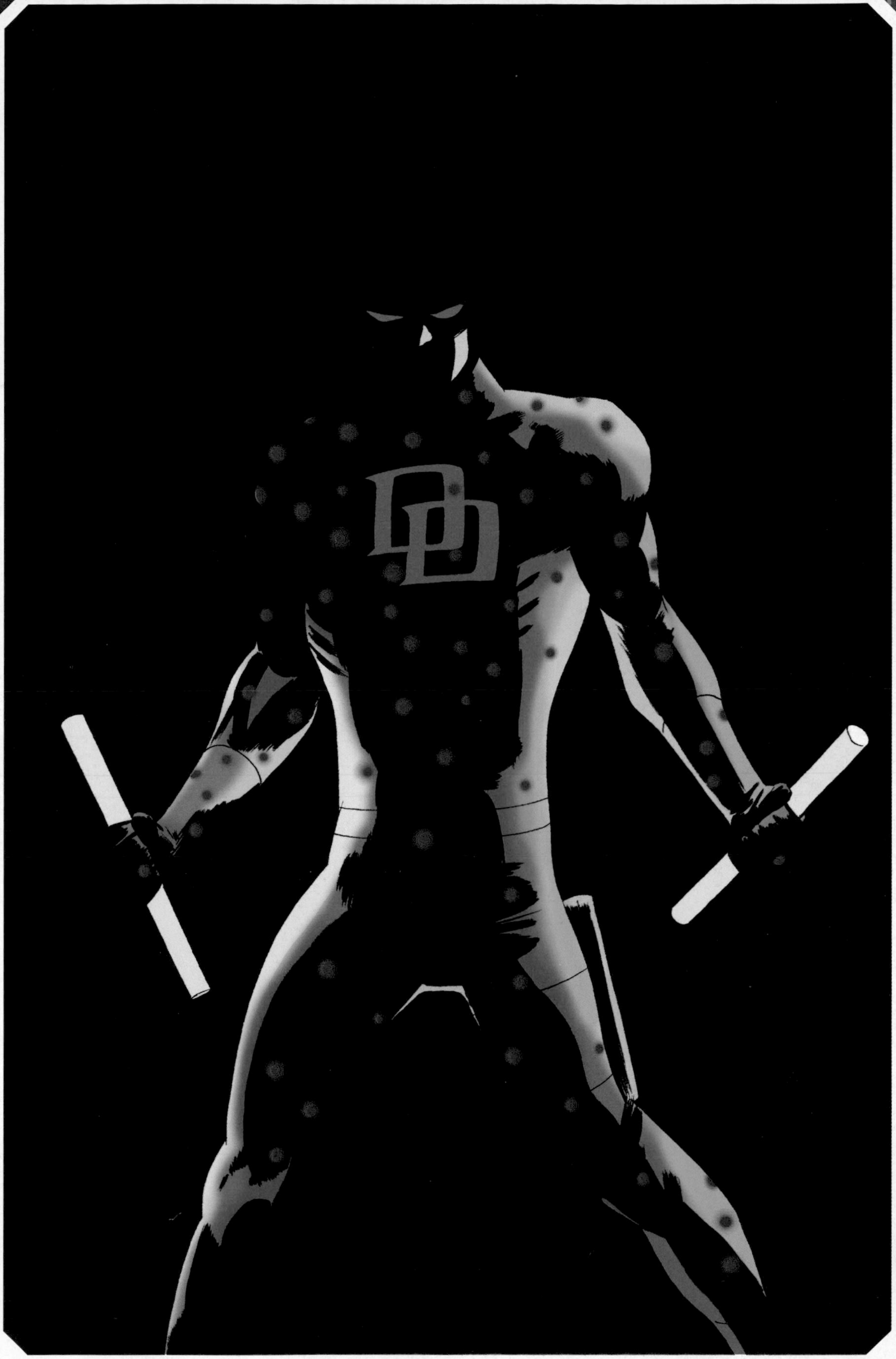

FIVE

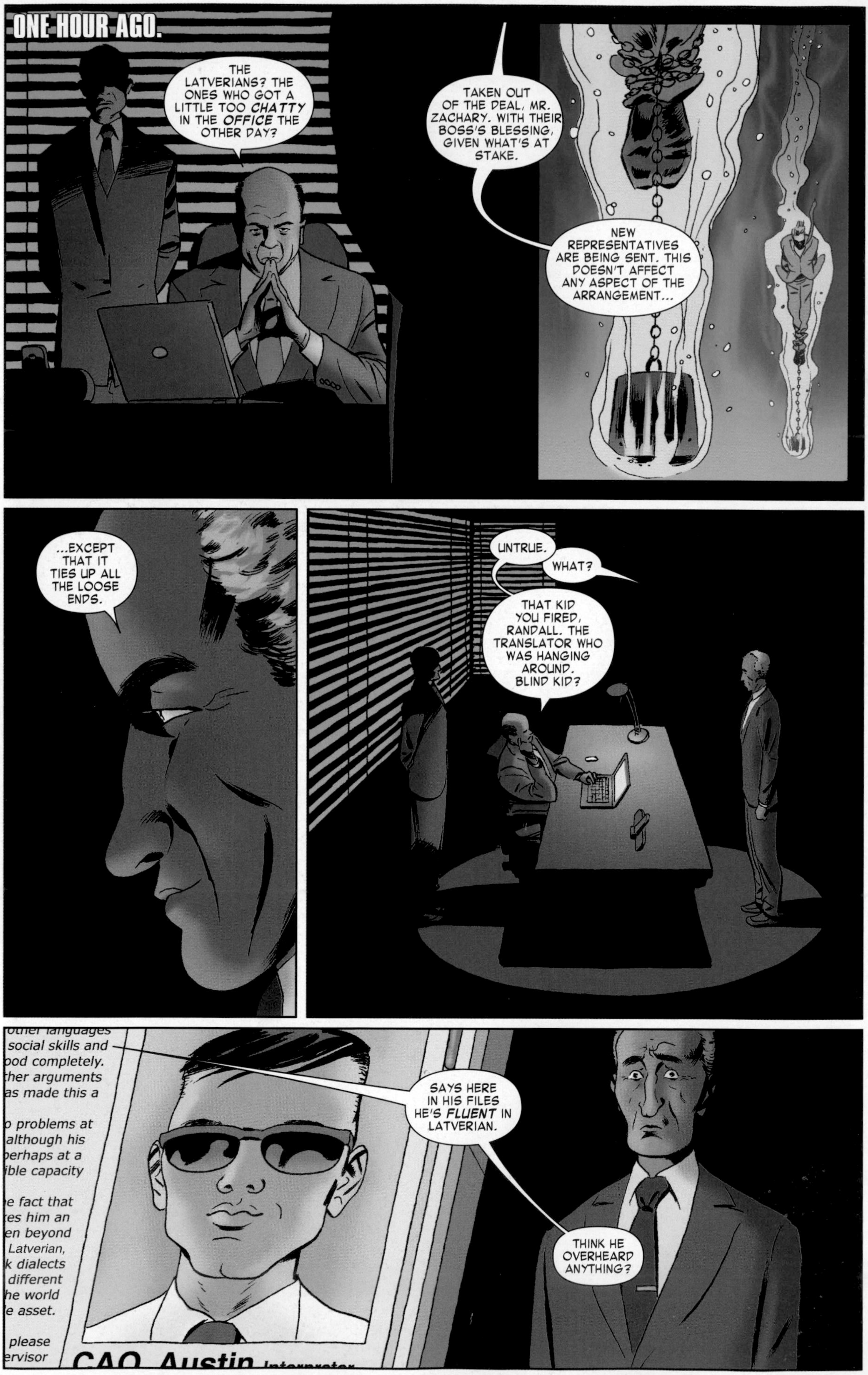
ONE HOUR AGO.
THE LATVERIANS? THE ONES WHO GOT A LITTLE TOO CHATTY IN THE OFFICE THE OTHER DAY?
TAKEN OUT OF THE DEAL, MR. ZACHARY. WITH THEIR BOSS'S BLESSING, GIVEN WHAT'S AT STAKE.
NEW REPRESENTATIVES ARE BEING SENT. THIS DOESN'T AFFECT ANY ASPECT OF THE ARRANGEMENT...
...EXCEPT THAT IT TIES UP ALL THE LOOSE ENDS.
UNTRUE.
WHAT?
THAT KID YOU FIRED, RANDALL. THE TRANSLATOR WHO WAS HANGING AROUND. BLIND KID?
social skills and
ood completely.
ther arguments
as made this a
o problems at
although his
perhaps at a
ible capacity
e fact that
es him an
en beyond
Latverian,
k dialects
different
he world
e asset.
please
ervisor
SAYS HERE IN HIS FILES HE'S FLUENT IN LATVERIAN.
THINK HE OVERHEARD ANYTHING?

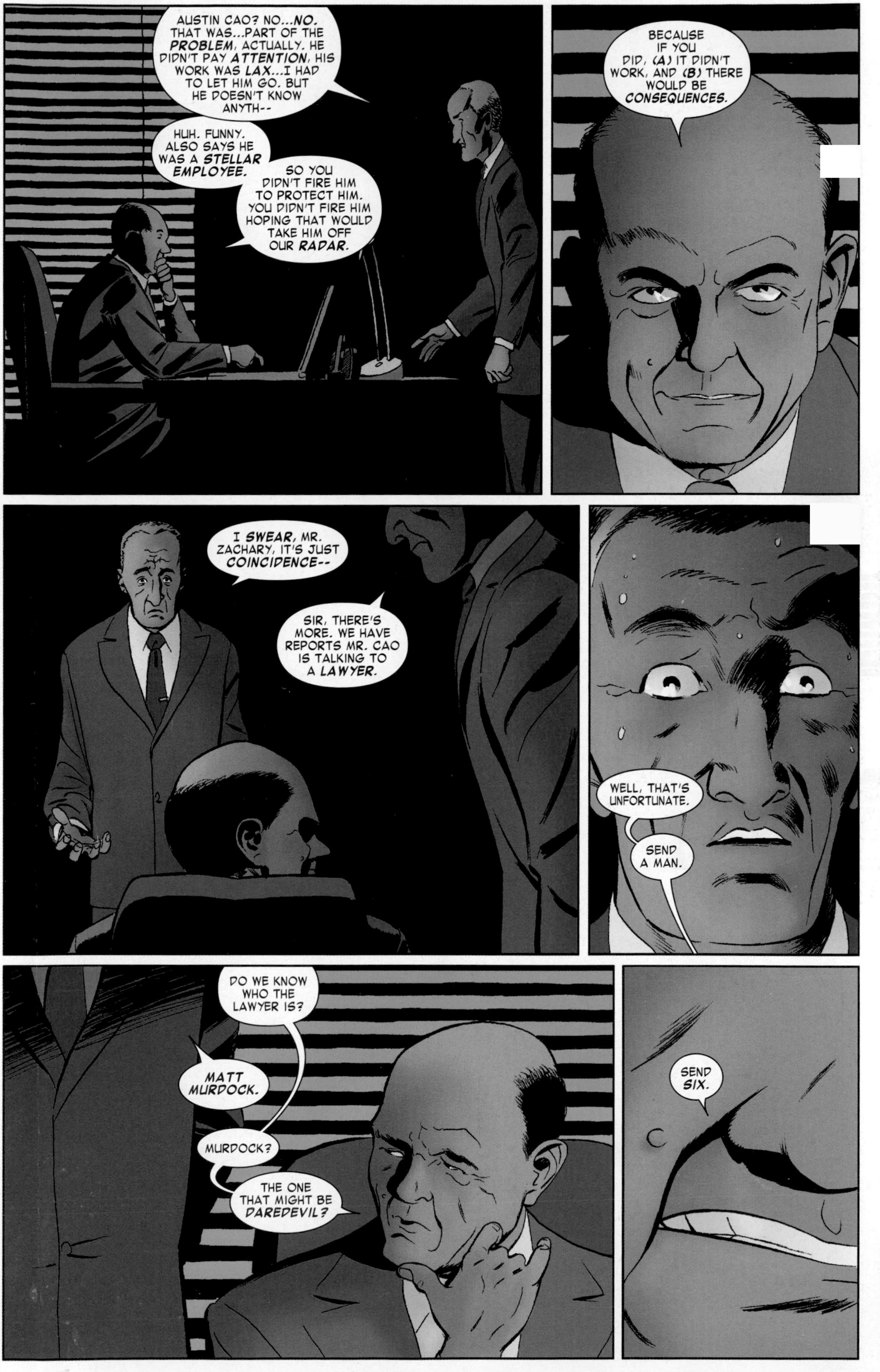
AUSTIN CAO? NO...NO. THAT WAS...PART OF THE PROBLEM, ACTUALLY. HE DIDN'T PAY ATTENTION, HIS WORK WAS LAX...I HAD TO LET HIM GO. BUT HE DOESN'T KNOW ANYTH--
HUH. FUNNY. ALSO SAYS HE WAS A STELLAR EMPLOYEE.
SO YOU DIDN'T FIRE HIM TO PROTECT HIM. YOU DIDN'T FIRE HIM HOPING THAT WOULD TAKE HIM OFF OUR RADAR.
BECAUSE IF YOU DID, (A) IT DIDN'T WORK, AND (B) THERE WOULD BE CONSEQUENCES.
I SWEAR, MR. ZACHARY, IT'S JUST COINCIDENCE--
SIR, THERE'S MORE. WE HAVE REPORTS MR. CAO IS TALKING TO A LAWYER.
WELL, THAT'S UNFORTUNATE.
SEND A MAN.
DO WE KNOW WHO THE LAWYER IS?
MATT MURDOCK.
MURDOCK?
THE ONE THAT MIGHT BE DAREDEVIL?
SEND SIX.

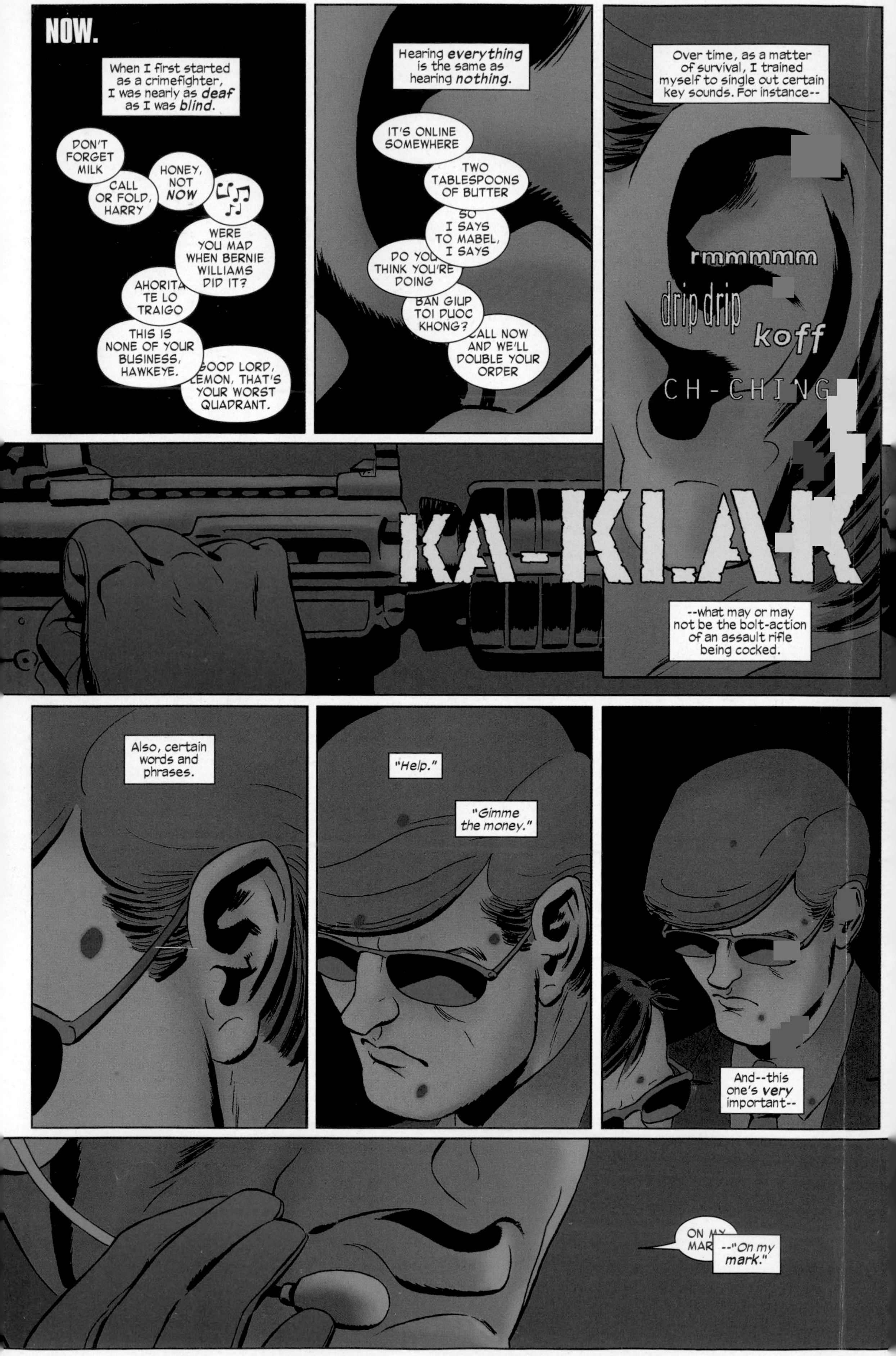

NOW.
When I first started as a crimefighter, I was nearly as deaf as I was blind.
DON'T FORGET MILK
CALL OR FOLD, HARRY
HONEY, NOT NOW
WERE YOU MAD WHEN BERNIE WILLIAMS DID IT?
AHORITA TE LO TRAIGO
THIS IS NONE OF YOUR BUSINESS, HAWKEYE.
GOOD LORD, LEMON, THAT'S YOUR WORST QUADRANT.
Hearing everything is the same as hearing nothing.
IT'S ONLINE SOMEWHERE
TWO TABLESPOONS OF BUTTER
SO I SAYS TO MABEL, I SAYS
DO YOU THINK YOU'RE DOING
BAN GIUP TOI DUOC KHONG?
CALL NOW AND WE'LL DOUBLE YOUR ORDER
Over time, as a matter of survival, I trained myself to single out certain key sounds. For instance--
rmmmmmm
drip drip
koff
CH-CHING
KA-KLAK
--what may or may not be the bolt-action of an assault rifle being cocked.
Also, certain words and phrases.
"Help."
"Gimme the money."
And--this one's very important--
ON MY MARK
--"On my mark."

AAAAAAH!

BUDDABUDDABUDDABUDDA...

WHAT WAS THAT? WHAT'S HAPPENING? WHAT--

STAY ON THE FLOOR. DON'T MOVE, DON'T MAKE A SOUND.

APARTMENT'S DARK. THAT GIVES US THE ADVANTAGE. ELIMINATE CAO AND MURDOCK BOTH.

Five sets of feet, maybe six. And the dental-drill whine of night-vision goggles.

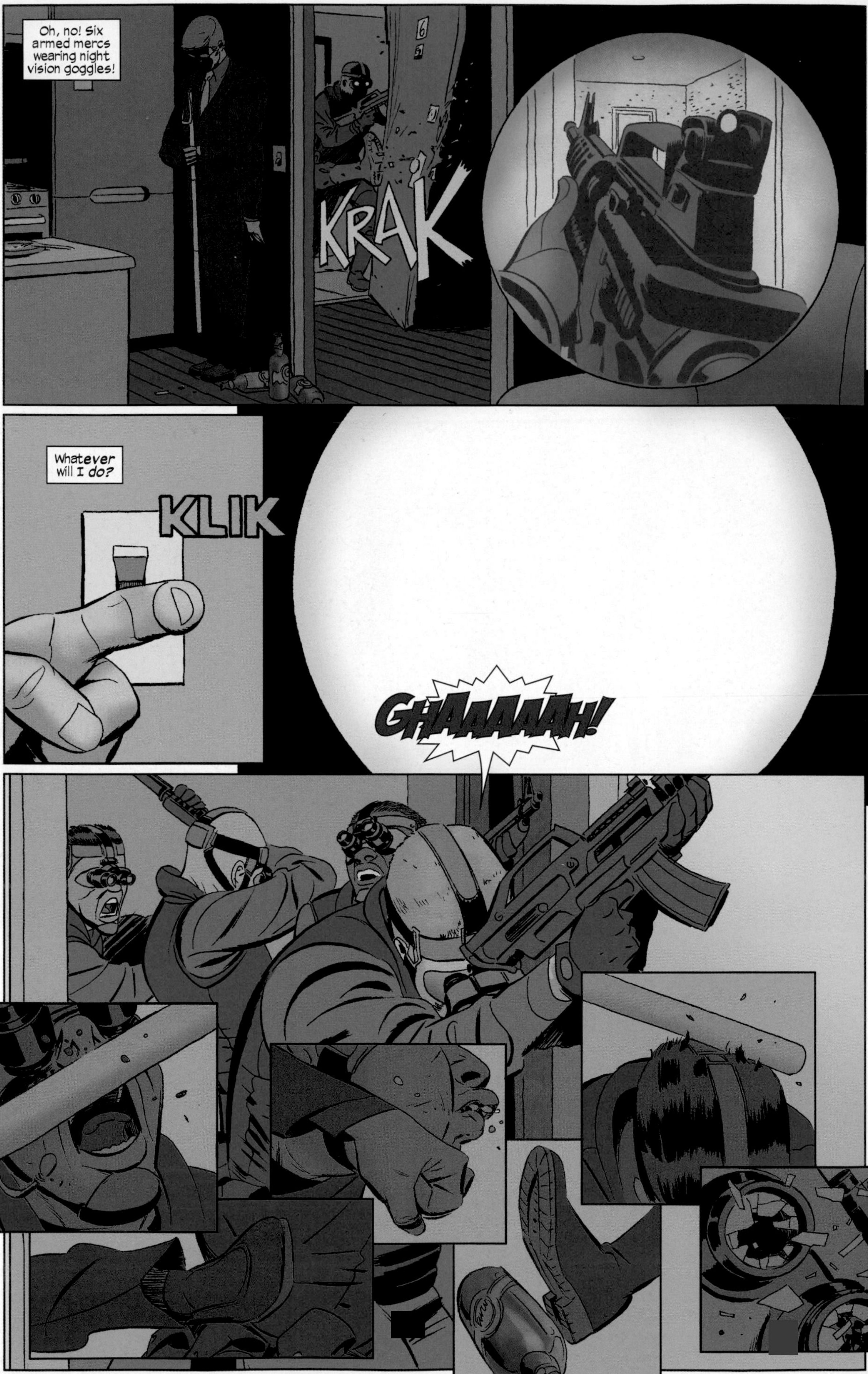

Oh, no! Six armed mercs wearing night vision goggles!
KRAK
Whatever will I do?
KLIK
GHAAAAAH!

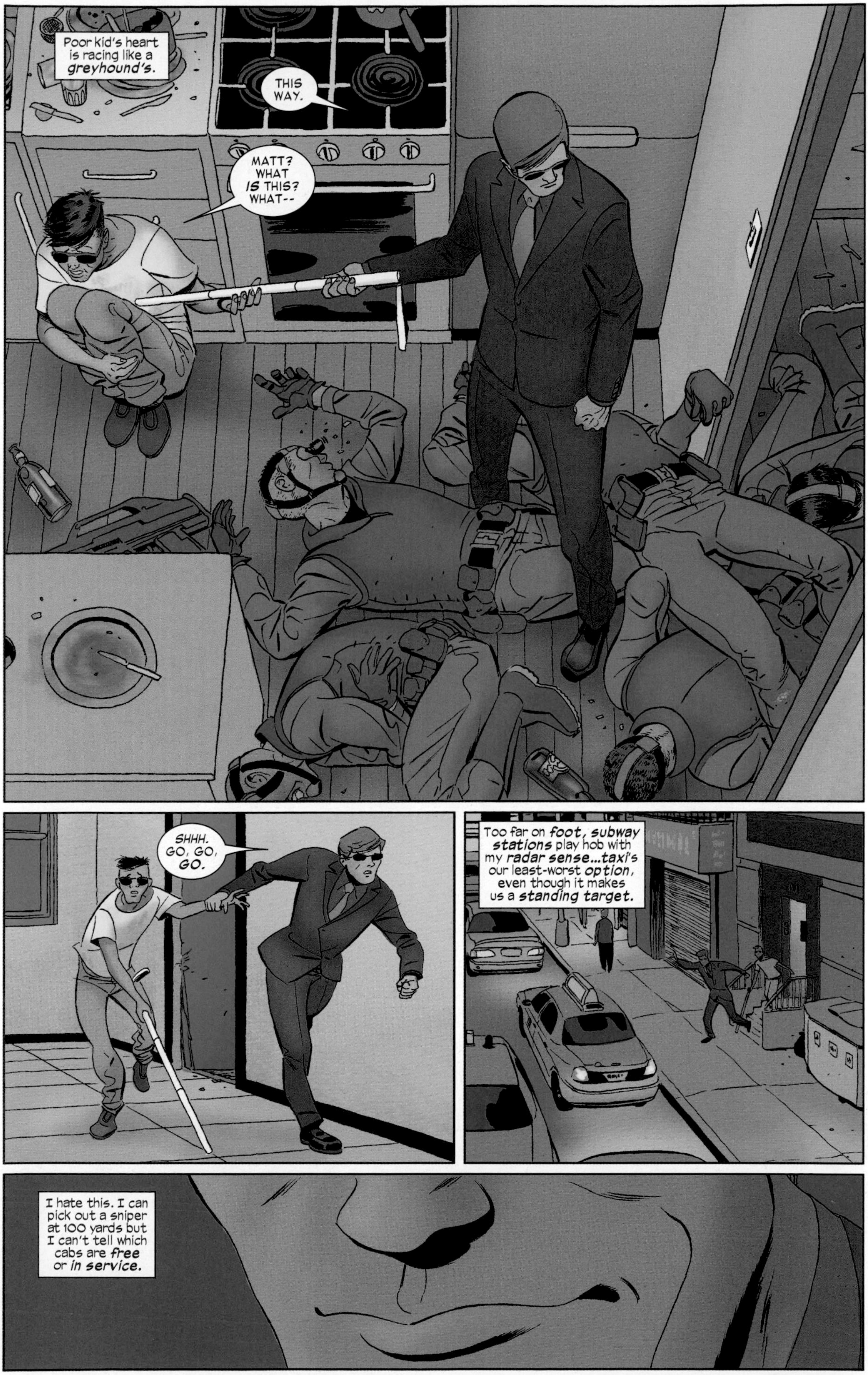

Poor kid's heart is racing like a *greyhound's.*
THIS WAY.
MATT? WHAT *IS* THIS? WHAT--
SHHH. GO, GO, *GO.*
Too far on *foot, subway stations* play hob with my *radar sense...taxi's* our least-worst *option*, even though it makes us a *standing target.*
I hate this. I can pick out a sniper at 100 yards but I can't tell which cabs are *free* or *in service.*

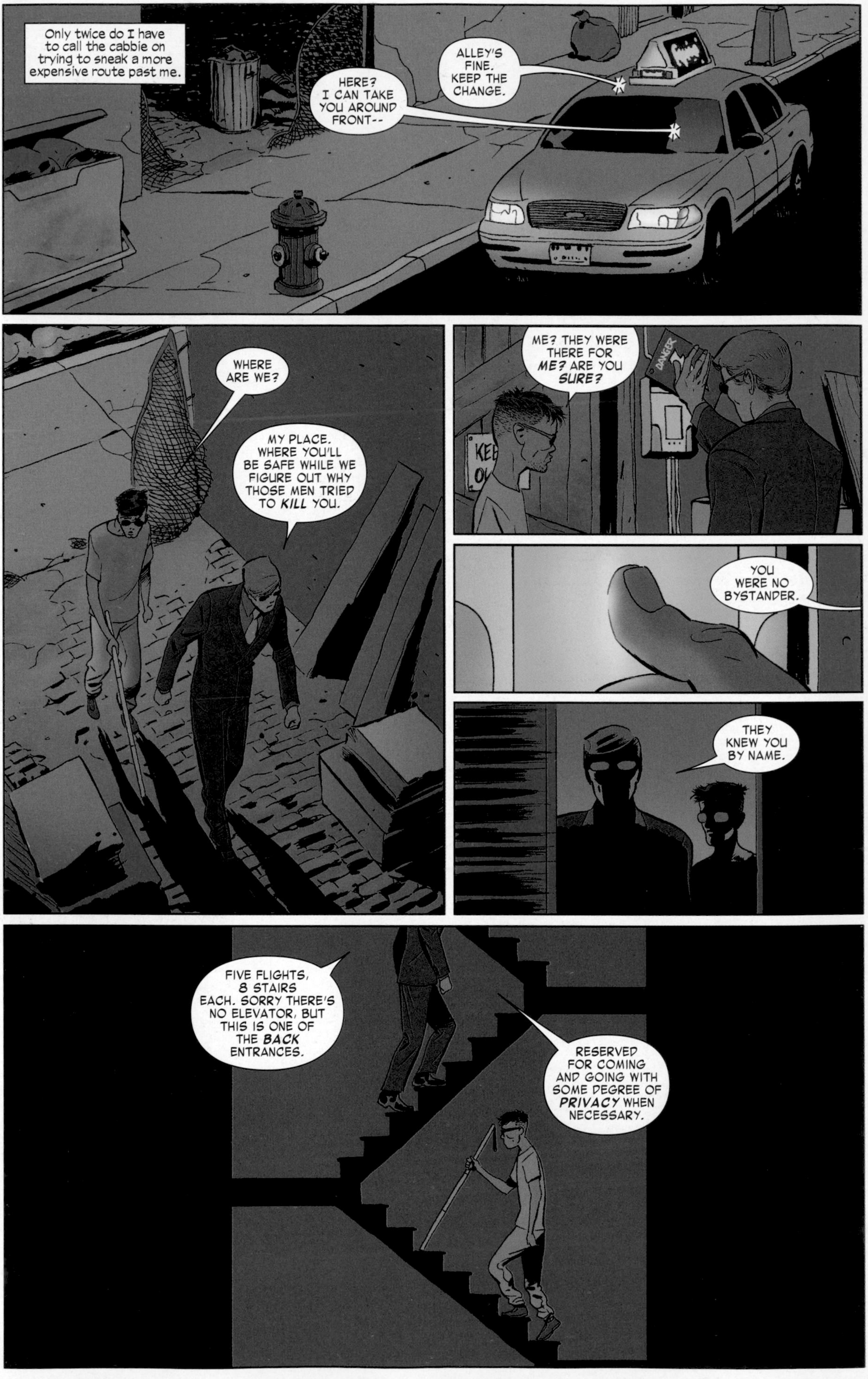
Only twice do I have to call the cabbie on trying to sneak a more expensive route past me.
HERE? I CAN TAKE YOU AROUND FRONT--
ALLEY'S FINE. KEEP THE CHANGE.
WHERE ARE WE?
MY PLACE. WHERE YOU'LL BE SAFE WHILE WE FIGURE OUT WHY THOSE MEN TRIED TO KILL YOU.
ME? THEY WERE THERE FOR ME? ARE YOU SURE?
DANGER
YOU WERE NO BYSTANDER.
THEY KNEW YOU BY NAME.
FIVE FLIGHTS, 8 STAIRS EACH. SORRY THERE'S NO ELEVATOR, BUT THIS IS ONE OF THE BACK ENTRANCES.
RESERVED FOR COMING AND GOING WITH SOME DEGREE OF PRIVACY WHEN NECESSARY.

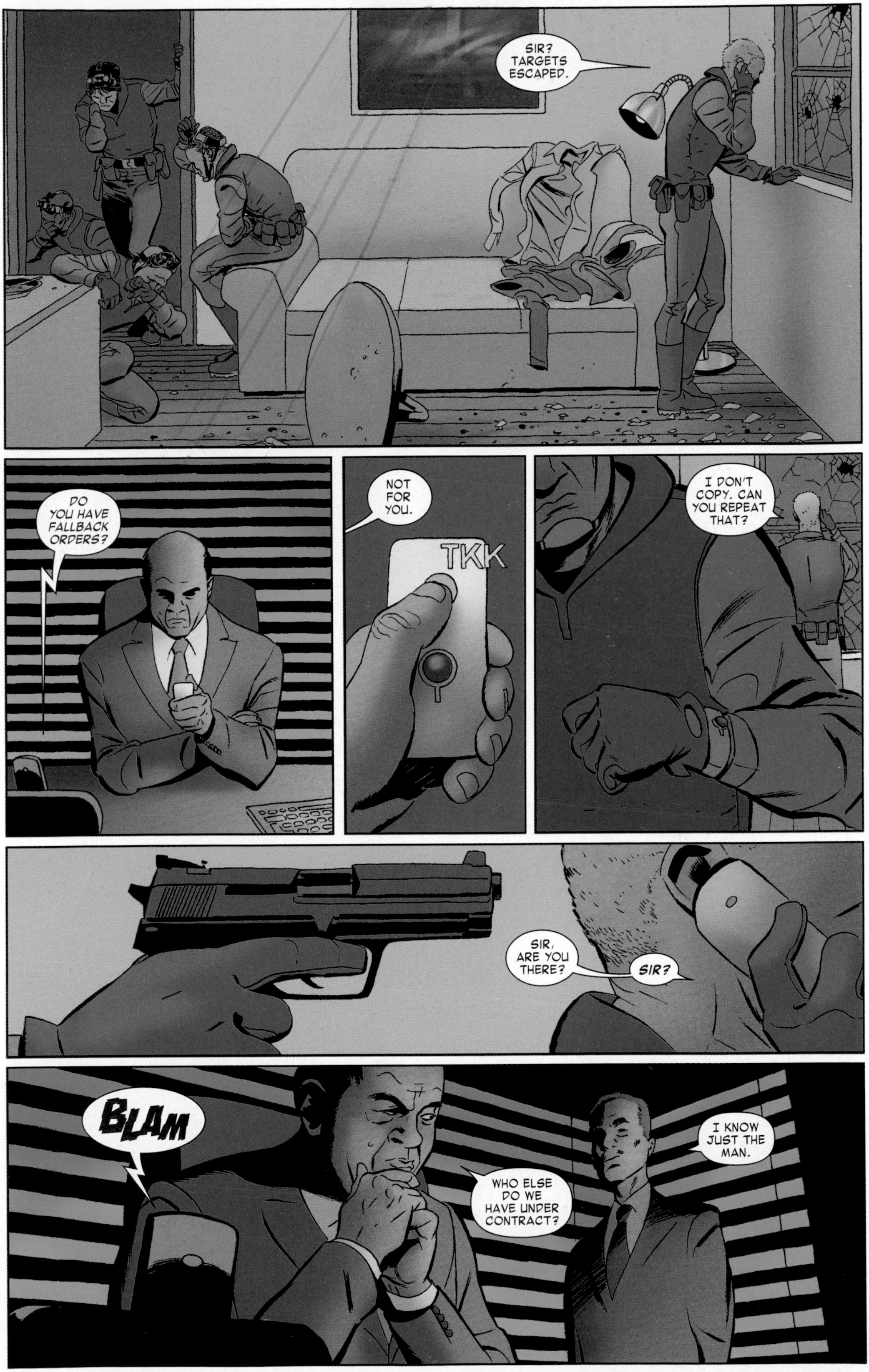
SIR? TARGETS ESCAPED.
DO YOU HAVE FALLBACK ORDERS?
NOT FOR YOU.
TKK
I DON'T COPY. CAN YOU REPEAT THAT?
SIR, ARE YOU THERE?
SIR?
BLAM
WHO ELSE DO WE HAVE UNDER CONTRACT?
I KNOW JUST THE MAN.

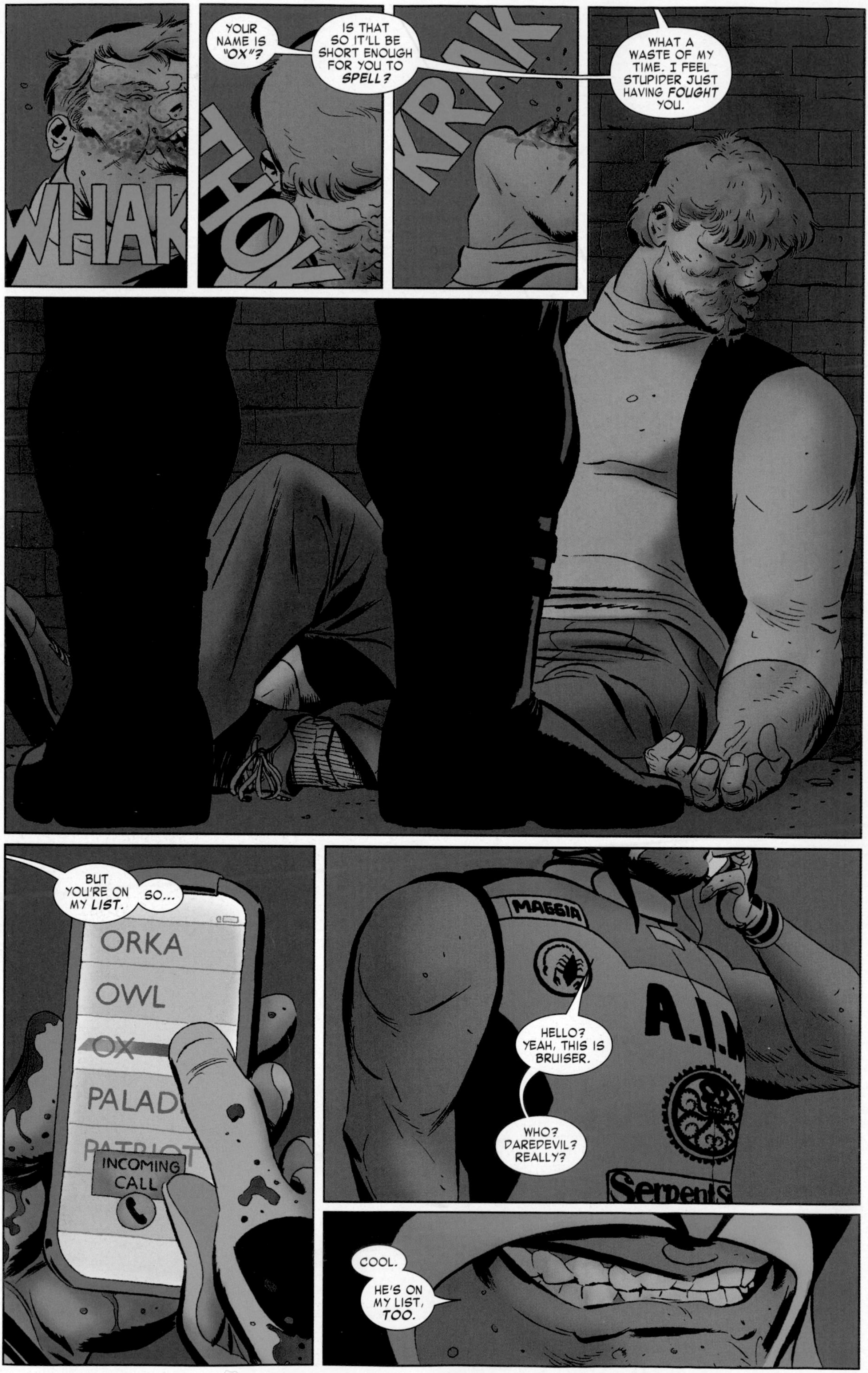
WHAK
YOUR NAME IS "OX"?
THOK
IS THAT SO IT'LL BE SHORT ENOUGH FOR YOU TO SPELL?
KRAK
WHAT A WASTE OF MY TIME. I FEEL STUPIDER JUST HAVING FOUGHT YOU.
BUT YOU'RE ON MY LIST.
SO...
ORKA
OWL
OX
INCOMING CALL
MAGGIA
A.I.M
HELLO? YEAH, THIS IS BRUISER.
WHO? DAREDEVIL? REALLY?
COOL.
HE'S ON MY LIST, TOO.

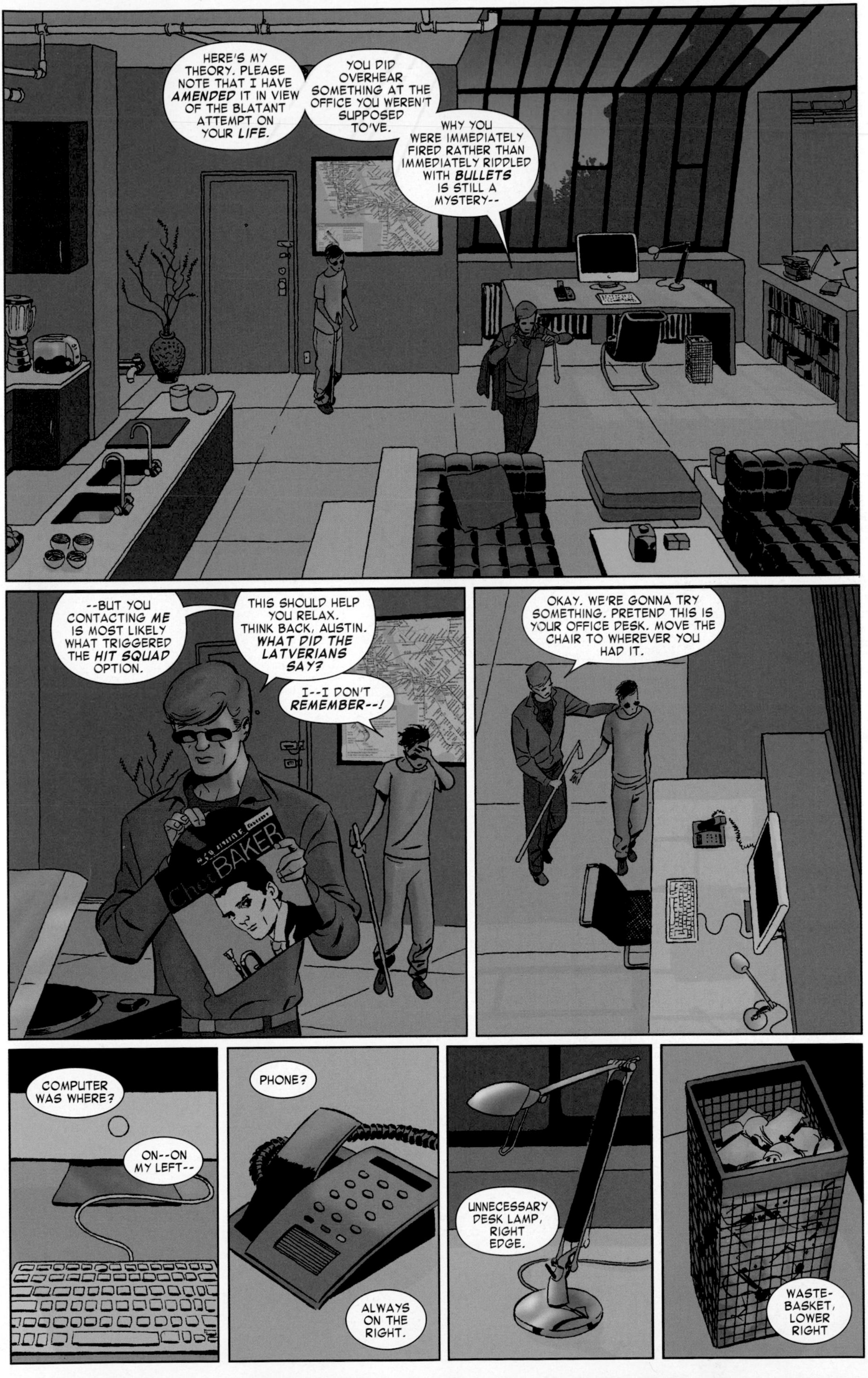
HERE'S MY THEORY. PLEASE NOTE THAT I HAVE AMENDED IT IN VIEW OF THE BLATANT ATTEMPT ON YOUR LIFE.
YOU DID OVERHEAR SOMETHING AT THE OFFICE YOU WEREN'T SUPPOSED TO'VE.
WHY YOU WERE IMMEDIATELY FIRED RATHER THAN IMMEDIATELY RIDDLED WITH BULLETS IS STILL A MYSTERY--
--BUT YOU CONTACTING ME IS MOST LIKELY WHAT TRIGGERED THE HIT SQUAD OPTION.
THIS SHOULD HELP YOU RELAX. THINK BACK, AUSTIN. WHAT DID THE LATVERIANS SAY?
I--I DON'T REMEMBER--!
Chet BAKER
OKAY. WE'RE GONNA TRY SOMETHING. PRETEND THIS IS YOUR OFFICE DESK. MOVE THE CHAIR TO WHEREVER YOU HAD IT.
COMPUTER WAS WHERE?
ON--ON MY LEFT--
PHONE?
ALWAYS ON THE RIGHT.
UNNECESSARY DESK LAMP, RIGHT EDGE.
WASTE-BASKET, LOWER RIGHT

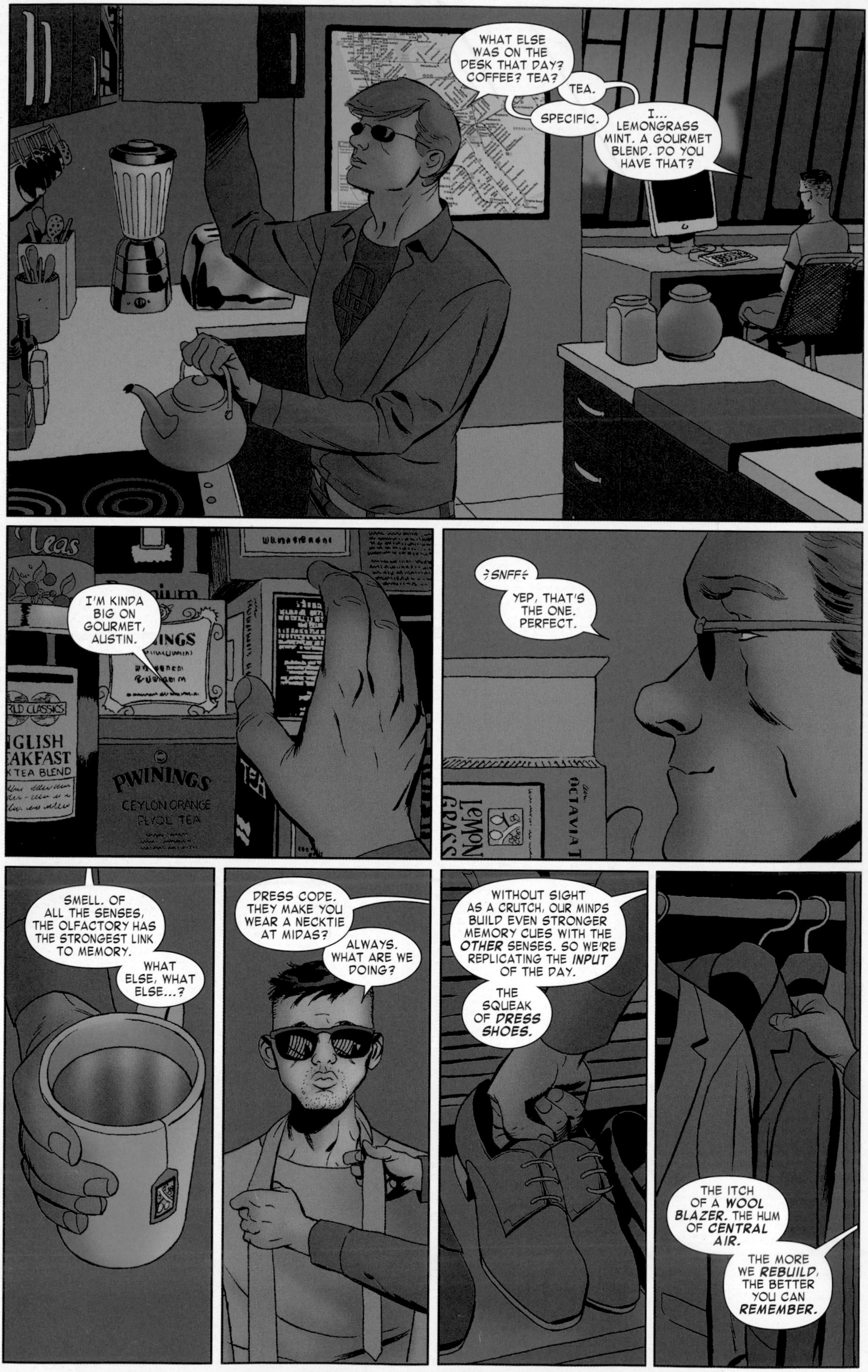
WHAT ELSE WAS ON THE DESK THAT DAY? COFFEE? TEA?
TEA.
SPECIFIC.
I... LEMONGRASS MINT. A GOURMET BLEND. DO YOU HAVE THAT?
I'M KINDA BIG ON GOURMET, AUSTIN.
TWININGS
WORLD CLASSICS
ENGLISH BREAKFAST
TWININGS
CEYLON ORANGE PEKOE TEA
SNFF
YEP, THAT'S THE ONE. PERFECT.
LEMON GRASS
OCTAVIA T
SMELL. OF ALL THE SENSES, THE OLFACTORY HAS THE STRONGEST LINK TO MEMORY.
WHAT ELSE, WHAT ELSE...?
DRESS CODE. THEY MAKE YOU WEAR A NECKTIE AT MIDAS?
ALWAYS. WHAT ARE WE DOING?
WITHOUT SIGHT AS A CRUTCH, OUR MINDS BUILD EVEN STRONGER MEMORY CUES WITH THE OTHER SENSES. SO WE'RE REPLICATING THE INPUT OF THE DAY.
THE SQUEAK OF DRESS SHOES.
THE ITCH OF A WOOL BLAZER. THE HUM OF CENTRAL AIR.
THE MORE WE REBUILD, THE BETTER YOU CAN REMEMBER.

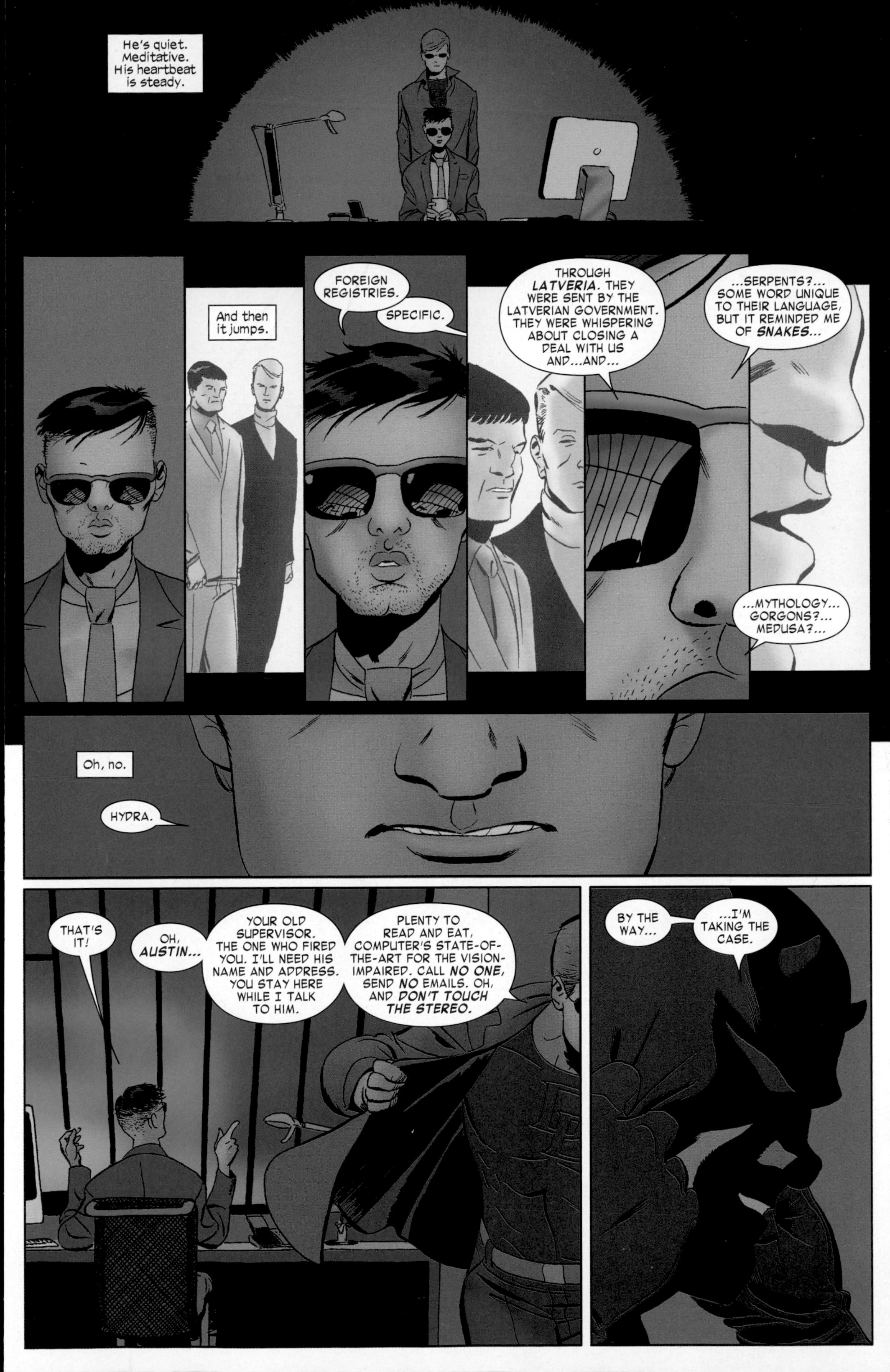
He's quiet. Meditative. His heartbeat is steady.
And then it jumps.
FOREIGN REGISTRIES.
SPECIFIC.
THROUGH LATVERIA. THEY WERE SENT BY THE LATVERIAN GOVERNMENT. THEY WERE WHISPERING ABOUT CLOSING A DEAL WITH US AND...AND...
...SERPENTS?... SOME WORD UNIQUE TO THEIR LANGUAGE, BUT IT REMINDED ME OF SNAKES...
...MYTHOLOGY... GORGONS?... MEDUSA?...
Oh, no.
HYDRA.
THAT'S IT!
OH, AUSTIN...
YOUR OLD SUPERVISOR. THE ONE WHO FIRED YOU. I'LL NEED HIS NAME AND ADDRESS. YOU STAY HERE WHILE I TALK TO HIM.
PLENTY TO READ AND EAT, COMPUTER'S STATE-OF-THE-ART FOR THE VISION-IMPAIRED. CALL NO ONE, SEND NO EMAILS. OH, AND DON'T TOUCH THE STEREO.
BY THE WAY...
...I'M TAKING THE CASE.

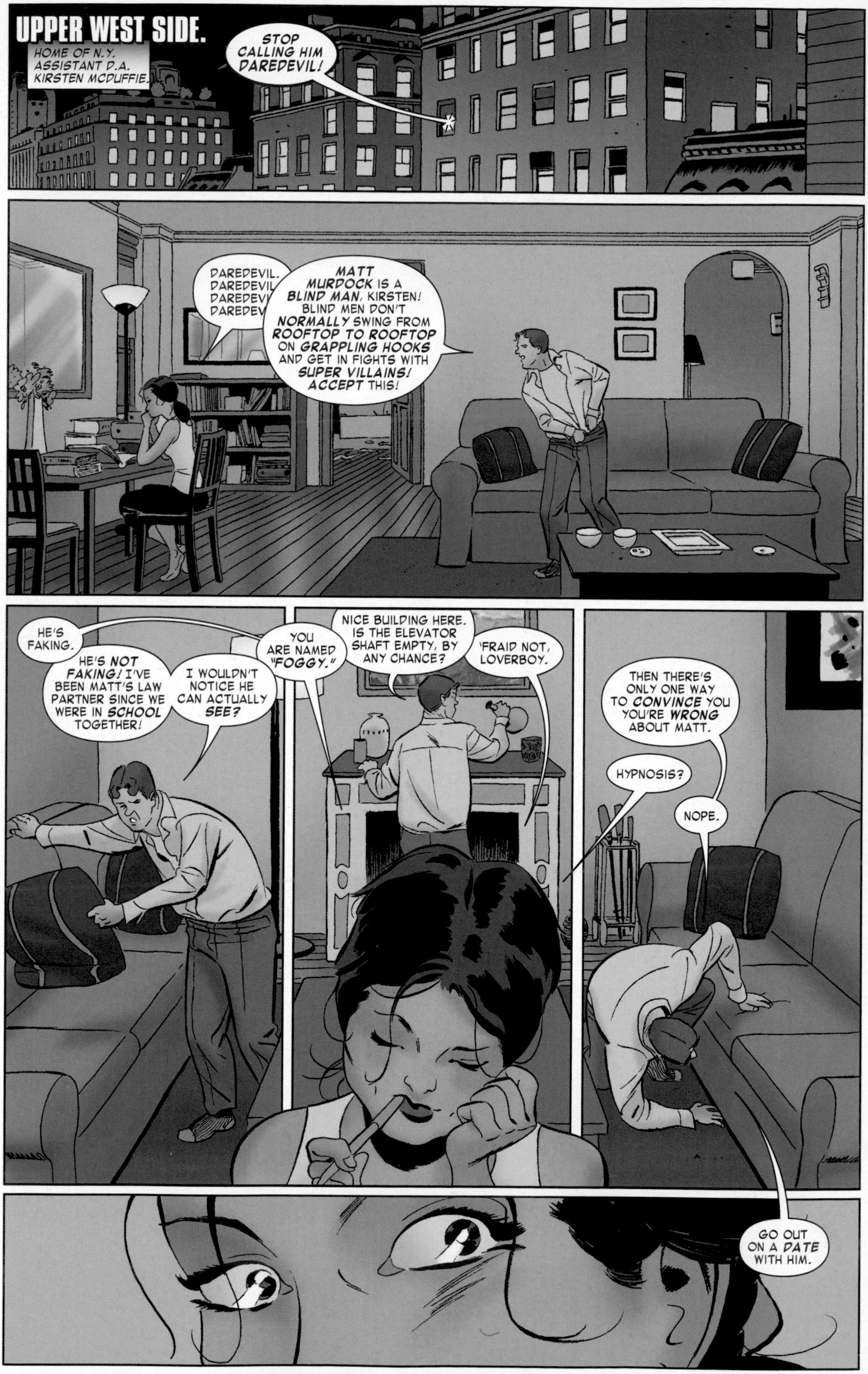
UPPER WEST SIDE.
HOME OF N.Y. ASSISTANT D.A. KIRSTEN MCDUFFIE.
STOP CALLING HIM DAREDEVIL!
DAREDEVIL. DAREDEVIL. DAREDEVIL. DAREDEVIL.
MATT MURDOCK IS A BLIND MAN, KIRSTEN! BLIND MEN DON'T NORMALLY SWING FROM ROOFTOP TO ROOFTOP ON GRAPPLING HOOKS AND GET IN FIGHTS WITH SUPER VILLAINS! ACCEPT THIS!
HE'S FAKING.
HE'S NOT FAKING! I'VE BEEN MATT'S LAW PARTNER SINCE WE WERE IN SCHOOL TOGETHER!
I WOULDN'T NOTICE HE CAN ACTUALLY SEE?
YOU ARE NAMED "FOGGY."
NICE BUILDING HERE. IS THE ELEVATOR SHAFT EMPTY, BY ANY CHANCE?
'FRAID NOT, LOVERBOY.
THEN THERE'S ONLY ONE WAY TO CONVINCE YOU YOU'RE WRONG ABOUT MATT.
HYPNOSIS?
NOPE.
GO OUT ON A DATE WITH HIM.

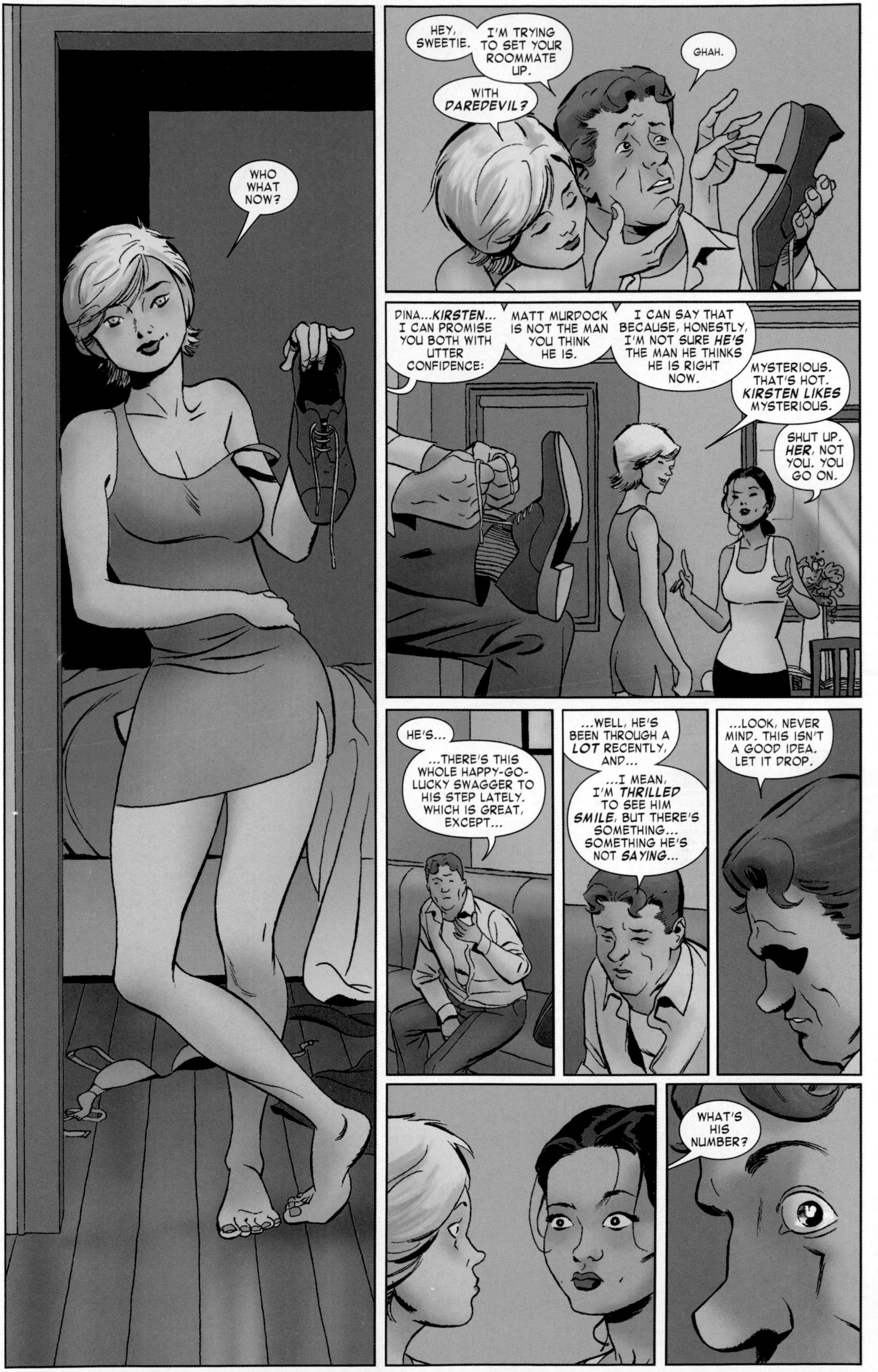
WHO WHAT NOW?
HEY, SWEETIE.
I'M TRYING TO SET YOUR ROOMMATE UP.
WITH DAREDEVIL?
GHAH.
DINA...KIRSTEN... I CAN PROMISE YOU BOTH WITH UTTER CONFIDENCE:
MATT MURDOCK IS NOT THE MAN YOU THINK HE IS.
I CAN SAY THAT BECAUSE, HONESTLY, I'M NOT SURE HE'S THE MAN HE THINKS HE IS RIGHT NOW.
MYSTERIOUS. THAT'S HOT. KIRSTEN LIKES MYSTERIOUS.
SHUT UP. HER, NOT YOU. YOU GO ON.
HE'S...
...THERE'S THIS WHOLE HAPPY-GO-LUCKY SWAGGER TO HIS STEP LATELY. WHICH IS GREAT, EXCEPT...
...WELL, HE'S BEEN THROUGH A LOT RECENTLY, AND...
...I MEAN, I'M THRILLED TO SEE HIM SMILE, BUT THERE'S SOMETHING... SOMETHING HE'S NOT SAYING...
...LOOK, NEVER MIND. THIS ISN'T A GOOD IDEA. LET IT DROP.
WHAT'S HIS NUMBER?

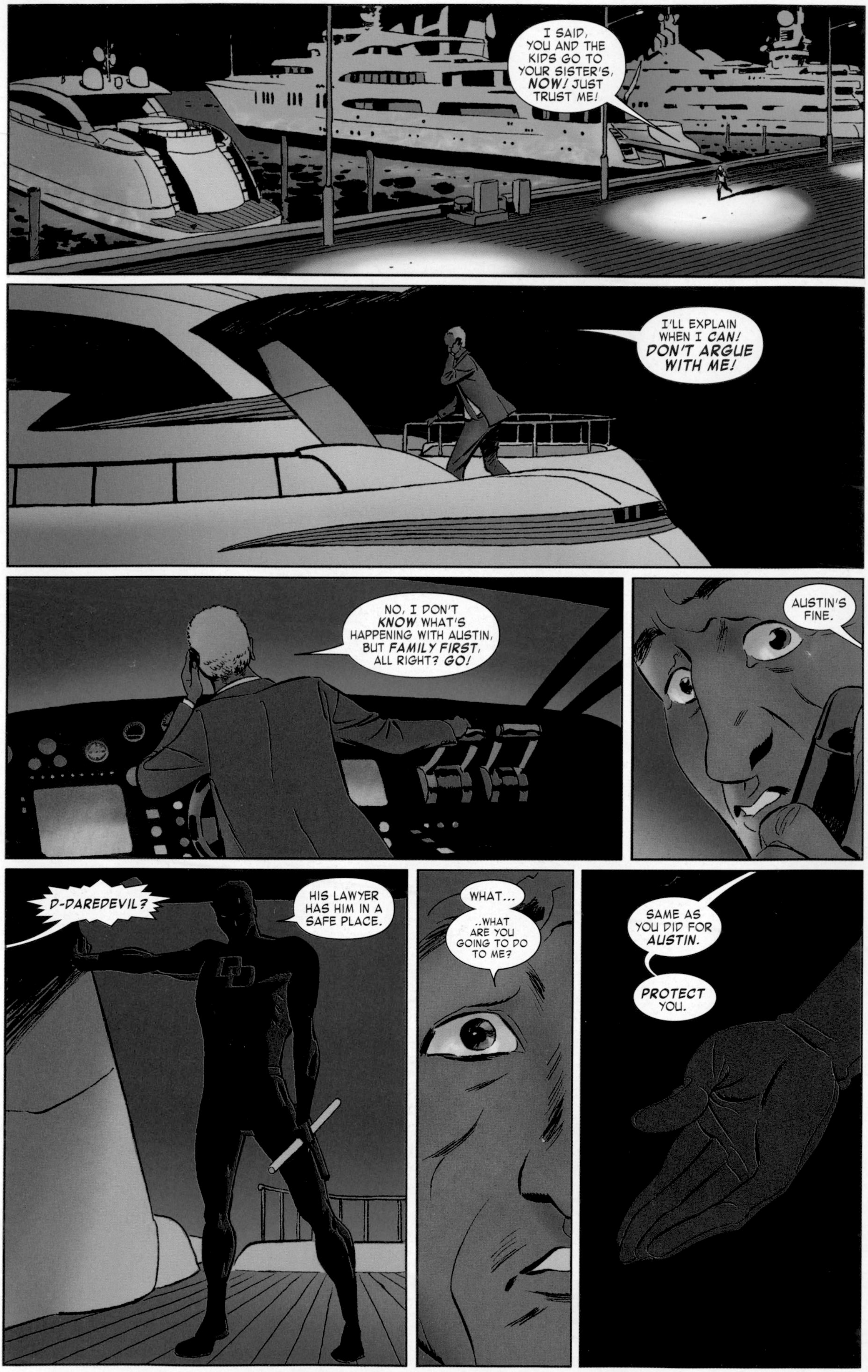
I SAID, YOU AND THE KIDS GO TO YOUR SISTER'S, NOW! JUST TRUST ME!
I'LL EXPLAIN WHEN I CAN! DON'T ARGUE WITH ME!
NO, I DON'T KNOW WHAT'S HAPPENING WITH AUSTIN, BUT FAMILY FIRST, ALL RIGHT? GO!
AUSTIN'S FINE.
HIS LAWYER HAS HIM IN A SAFE PLACE.
D-DAREDEVIL?
WHAT...
..WHAT ARE YOU GOING TO DO TO ME?
SAME AS YOU DID FOR AUSTIN.
PROTECT YOU.

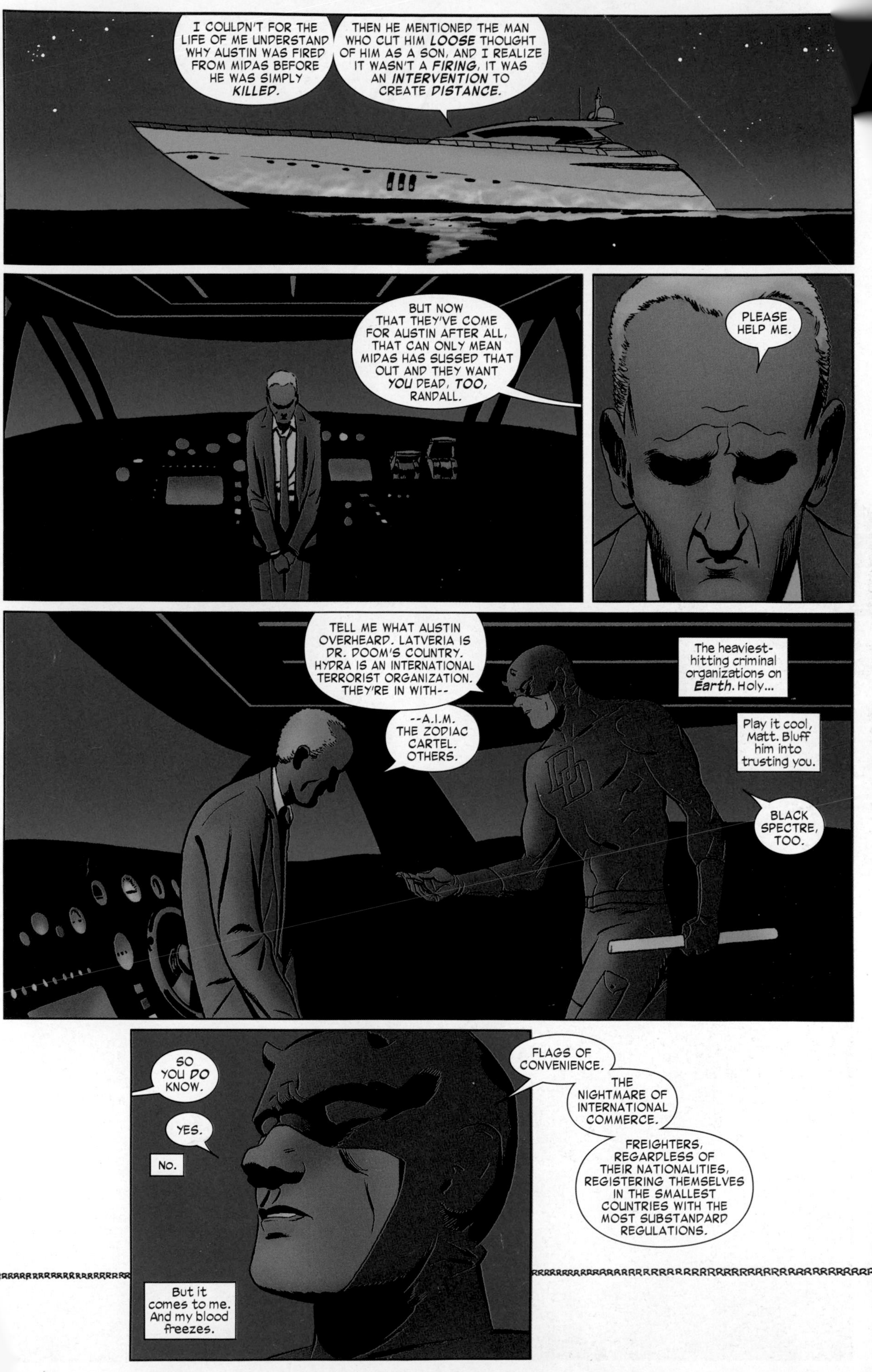
I COULDN'T FOR THE LIFE OF ME UNDERSTAND WHY AUSTIN WAS FIRED FROM MIDAS BEFORE HE WAS SIMPLY KILLED.
THEN HE MENTIONED THE MAN WHO CUT HIM LOOSE THOUGHT OF HIM AS A SON, AND I REALIZE IT WASN'T A FIRING, IT WAS AN INTERVENTION TO CREATE DISTANCE.
BUT NOW THAT THEY'VE COME FOR AUSTIN AFTER ALL, THAT CAN ONLY MEAN MIDAS HAS SUSSED THAT OUT AND THEY WANT YOU DEAD, TOO, RANDALL.
PLEASE HELP ME.
TELL ME WHAT AUSTIN OVERHEARD. LATVERIA IS DR. DOOM'S COUNTRY. HYDRA IS AN INTERNATIONAL TERRORIST ORGANIZATION. THEY'RE IN WITH--
--A.I.M. THE ZODIAC CARTEL. OTHERS.
The heaviest-hitting criminal organizations on Earth. Holy...
Play it cool, Matt. Bluff him into trusting you.
BLACK SPECTRE, TOO.
SO YOU DO KNOW.
YES.
No.
FLAGS OF CONVENIENCE.
THE NIGHTMARE OF INTERNATIONAL COMMERCE.
FREIGHTERS, REGARDLESS OF THEIR NATIONALITIES, REGISTERING THEMSELVES IN THE SMALLEST COUNTRIES WITH THE MOST SUBSTANDARD REGULATIONS.
RRRRRRRRRRRRRRRRRRRRRRRRRRRRRRRRRRRRRRRRRRRRRRRRRRRRRRRR
But it comes to me. And my blood freezes.

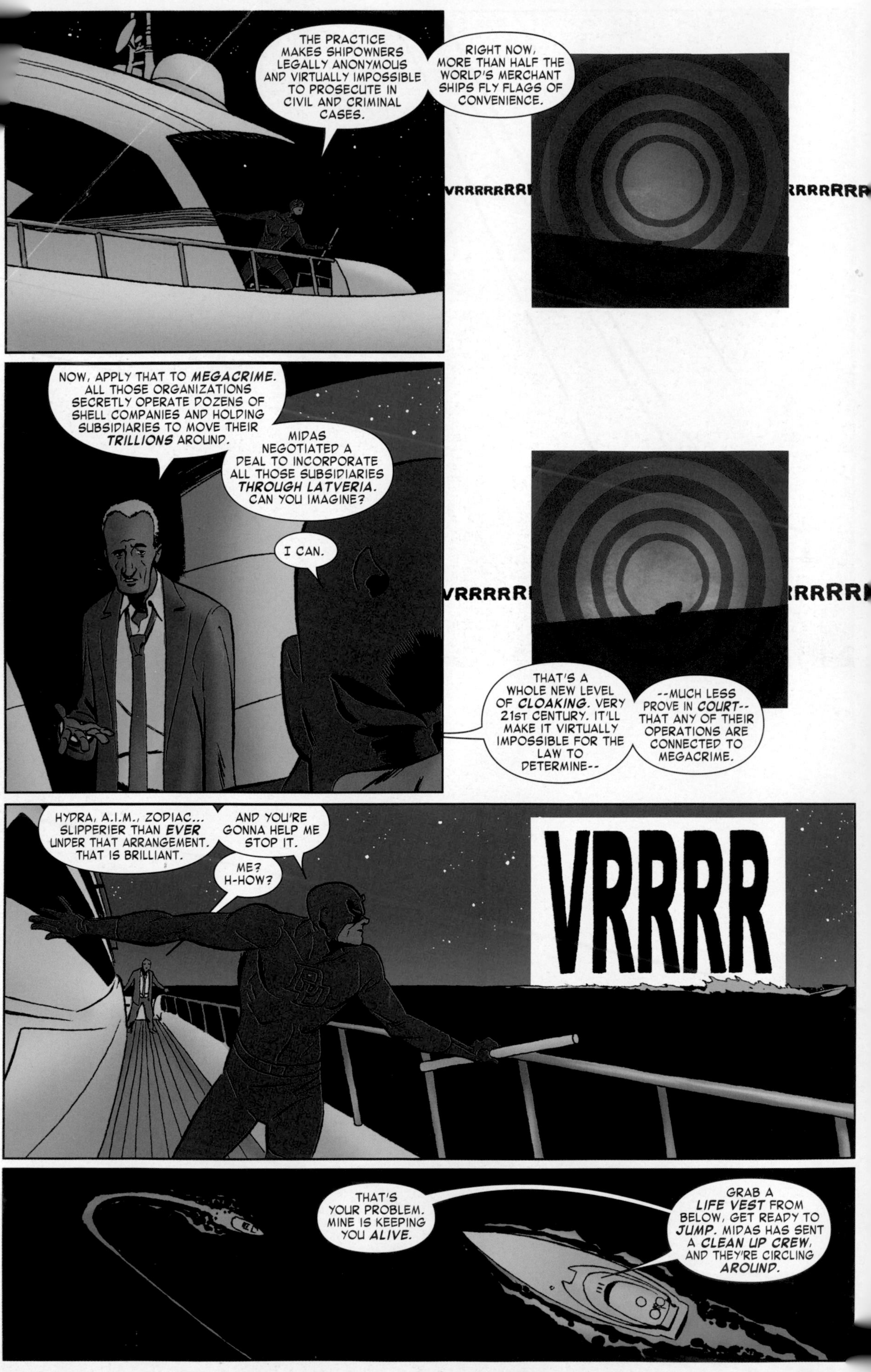
THE PRACTICE MAKES SHIPOWNERS LEGALLY ANONYMOUS AND VIRTUALLY IMPOSSIBLE TO PROSECUTE IN CIVIL AND CRIMINAL CASES.
RIGHT NOW, MORE THAN HALF THE WORLD'S MERCHANT SHIPS FLY FLAGS OF CONVENIENCE.
VRRRRRRRRRRRRRRRRRR
NOW, APPLY THAT TO *MEGACRIME.* ALL THOSE ORGANIZATIONS SECRETLY OPERATE DOZENS OF SHELL COMPANIES AND HOLDING SUBSIDIARIES TO MOVE THEIR *TRILLIONS* AROUND.
MIDAS NEGOTIATED A DEAL TO INCORPORATE ALL THOSE SUBSIDIARIES *THROUGH LATVERIA.* CAN YOU IMAGINE?
I CAN.
VRRRRRRRRRRR
THAT'S A WHOLE NEW LEVEL OF *CLOAKING.* VERY 21ST CENTURY. IT'LL MAKE IT VIRTUALLY IMPOSSIBLE FOR THE LAW TO DETERMINE--
--MUCH LESS PROVE IN *COURT*-- THAT ANY OF THEIR OPERATIONS ARE CONNECTED TO MEGACRIME.
HYDRA, A.I.M., ZODIAC... SLIPPERIER THAN *EVER* UNDER THAT ARRANGEMENT. THAT IS BRILLIANT.
AND YOU'RE GONNA HELP ME STOP IT.
ME? H-HOW?
VRRRR
THAT'S YOUR PROBLEM. MINE IS KEEPING YOU *ALIVE.*
GRAB A *LIFE VEST* FROM BELOW, GET READY TO *JUMP.* MIDAS HAS SENT A *CLEAN UP CREW,* AND THEY'RE CIRCLING *AROUND.*

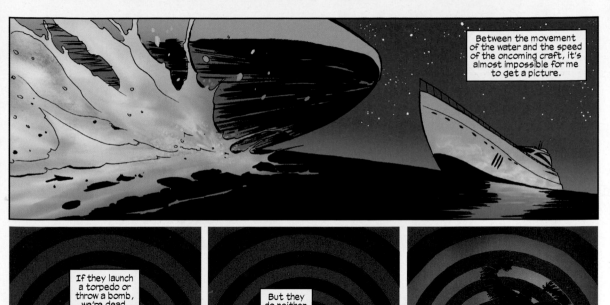

Between the movement of the water and the speed of the oncoming craft, it's almost impossible for me to get a picture.

If they launch a torpedo or throw a bomb, we're dead.

But they do neither.

Frankly, I don't know *what's* coming at us--

FATHOOM

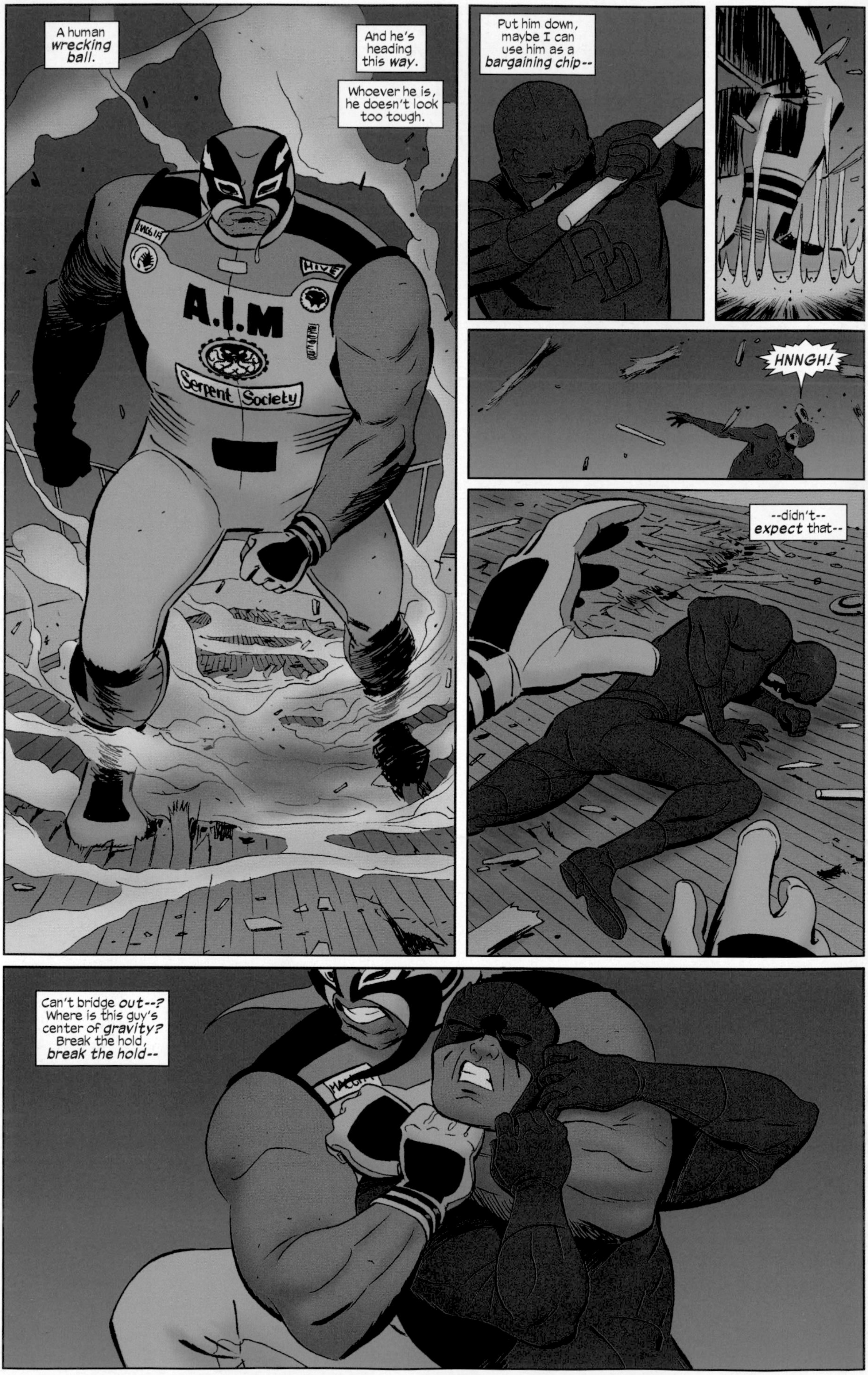

A human *wrecking* ball.
And he's heading this *way*.
Whoever he is, he doesn't look too tough.
A.I.M
HIVE
Serpent Society
Put him down, maybe I can use him as a *bargaining chip*--
HNNGH!
--didn't-- *expect* that--
Can't bridge *out*--? Where is this guy's center of *gravity*? Break the hold, *break the hold*--

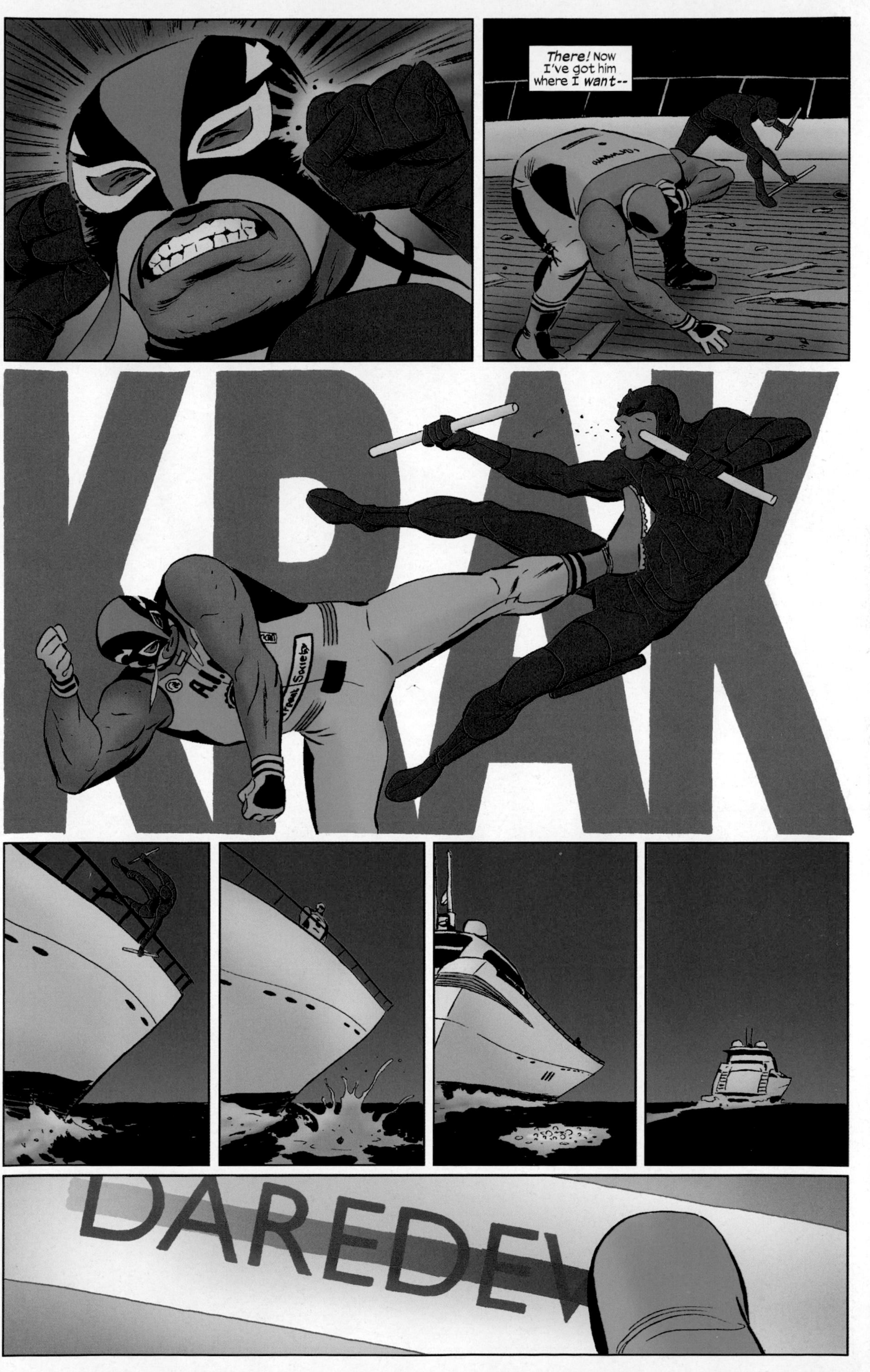
There! Now I've got him where I want--
KRAK
DAREDEV

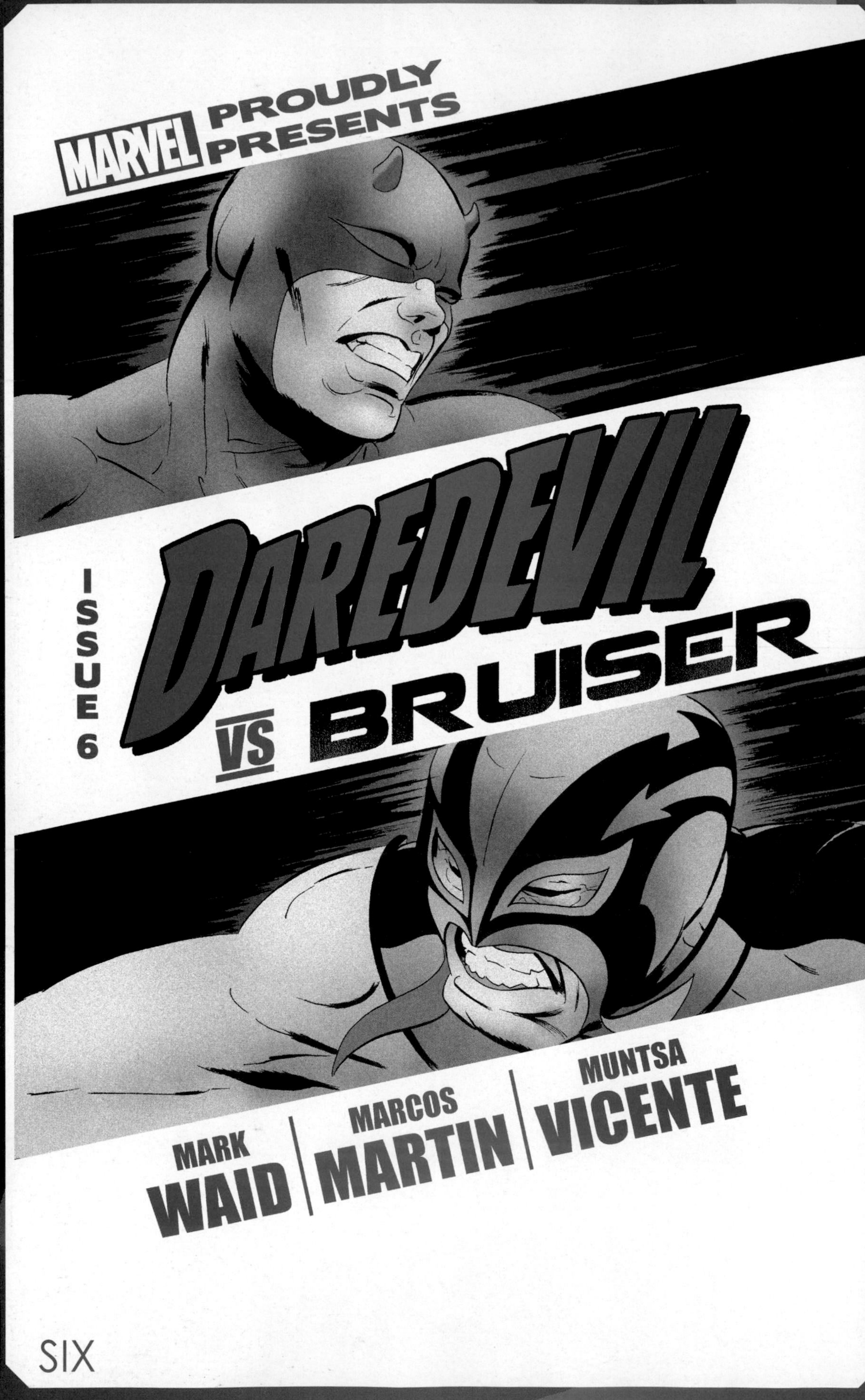
MARVEL PROUDLY PRESENTS
DAREDEVIL
VS BRUISER
ISSUE 6
MARK WAID
MARCOS MARTIN
MUNTSA VICENTE
SIX

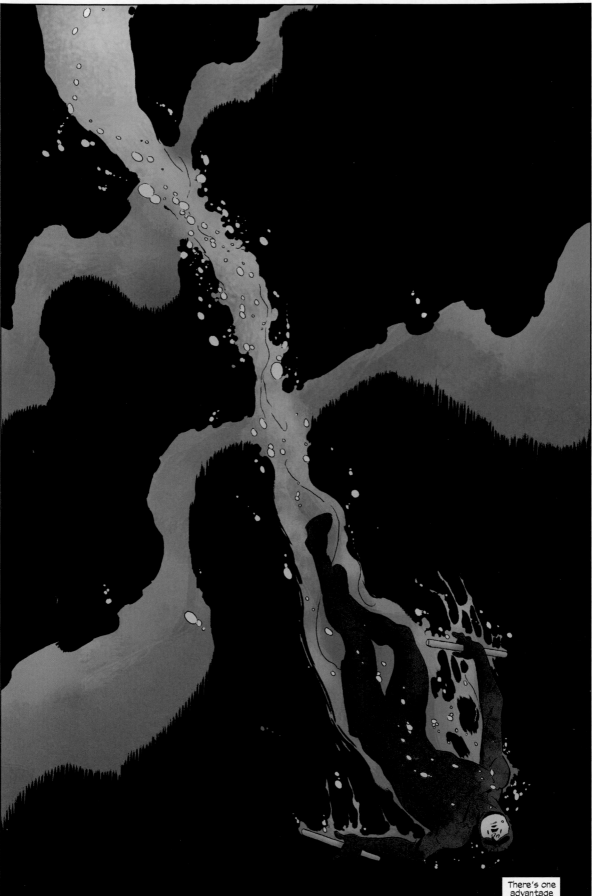

There's one advantage to being underwater.

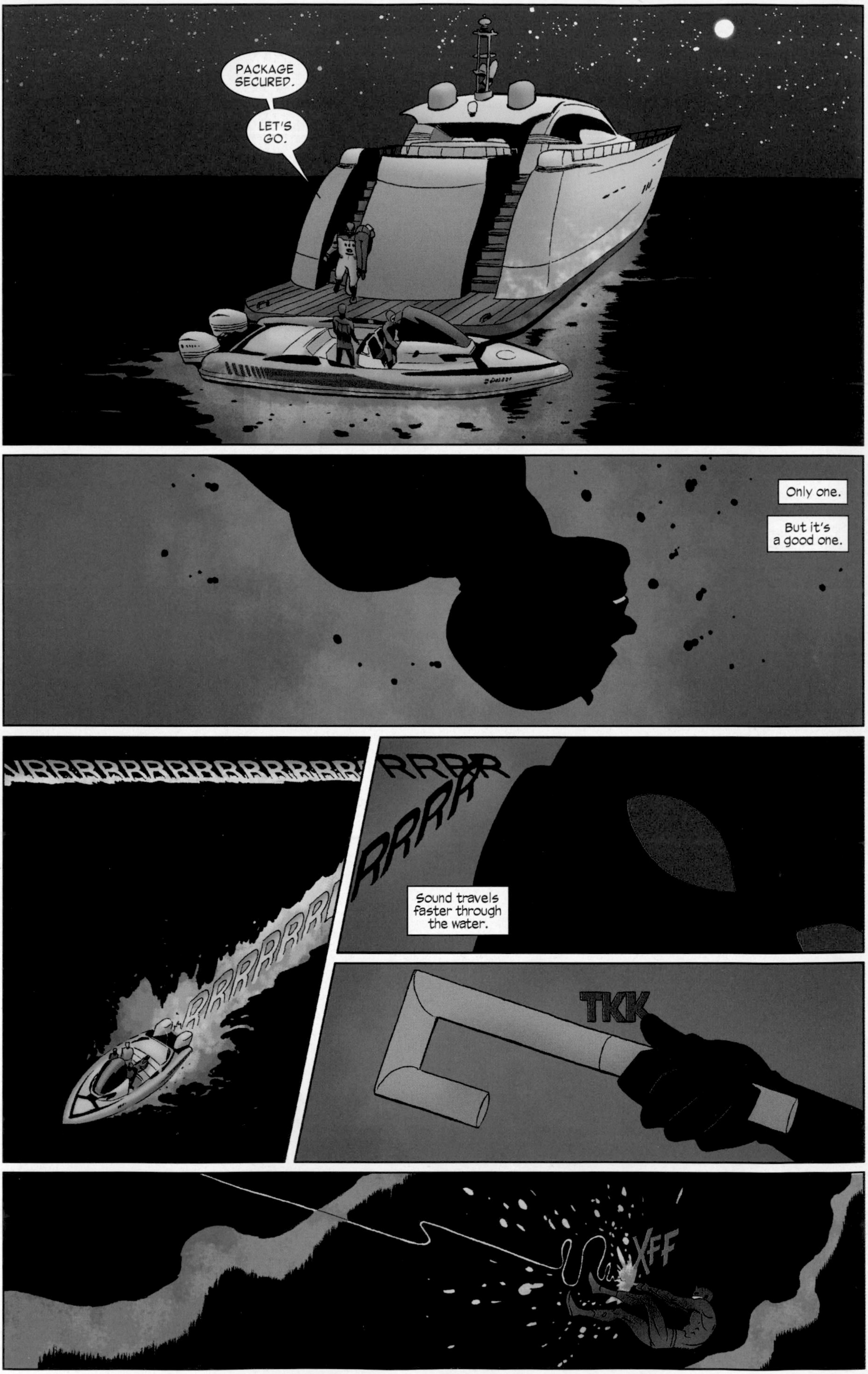
PACKAGE SECURED.
LET'S GO.
Only one.
But it's a good one.
VRRRRRRRRRRRRRRRRRRRRRRR
RRRR
RRRR
RRRRRRRRR
Sound travels faster through the water.
TKK
XFF

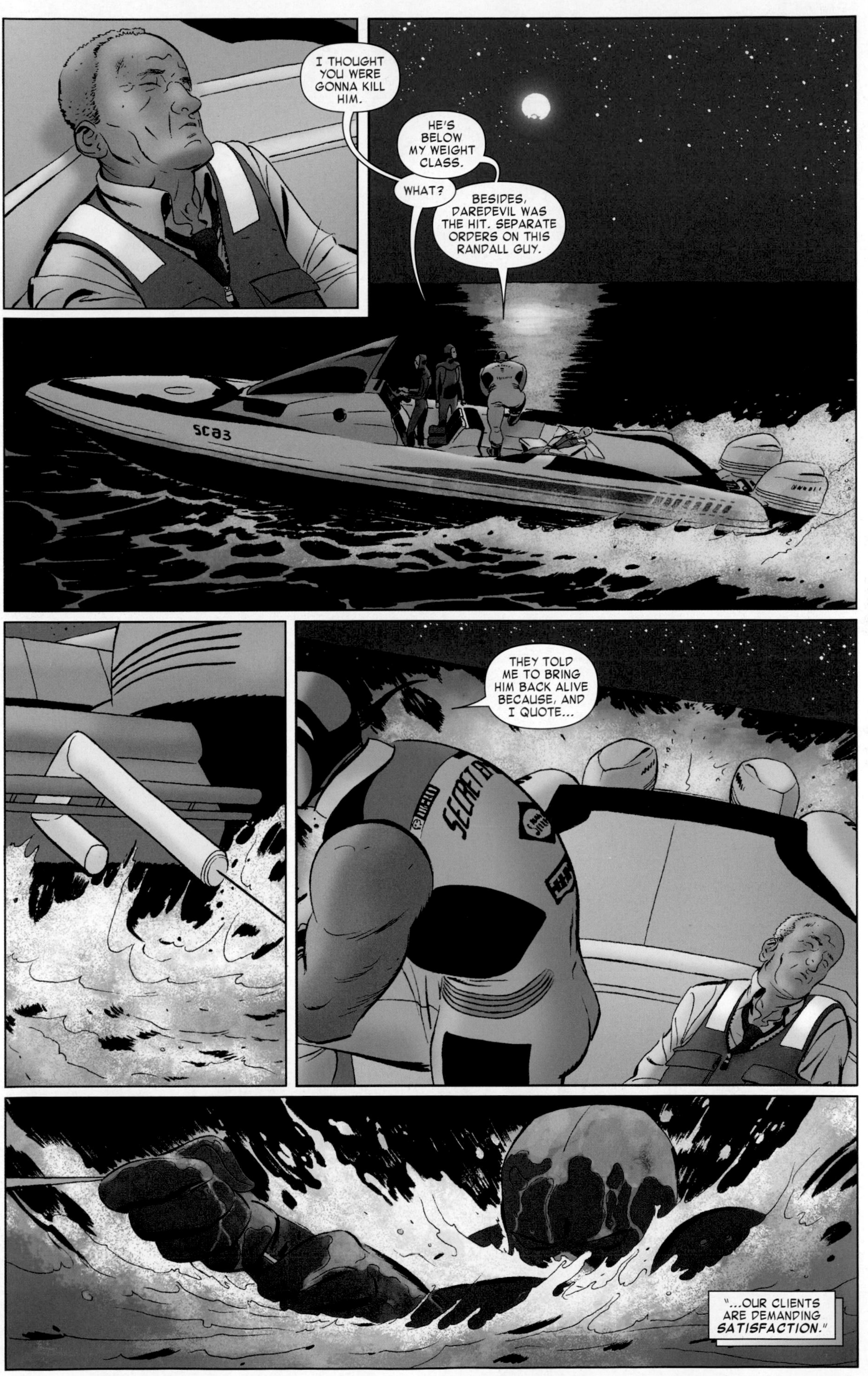
I THOUGHT YOU WERE GONNA KILL HIM.
HE'S BELOW MY WEIGHT CLASS.
WHAT?
BESIDES, DAREDEVIL WAS THE HIT. SEPARATE ORDERS ON THIS RANDALL GUY.
SC83
THEY TOLD ME TO BRING HIM BACK ALIVE BECAUSE, AND I QUOTE...
"...OUR CLIENTS ARE DEMANDING *SATISFACTION*."

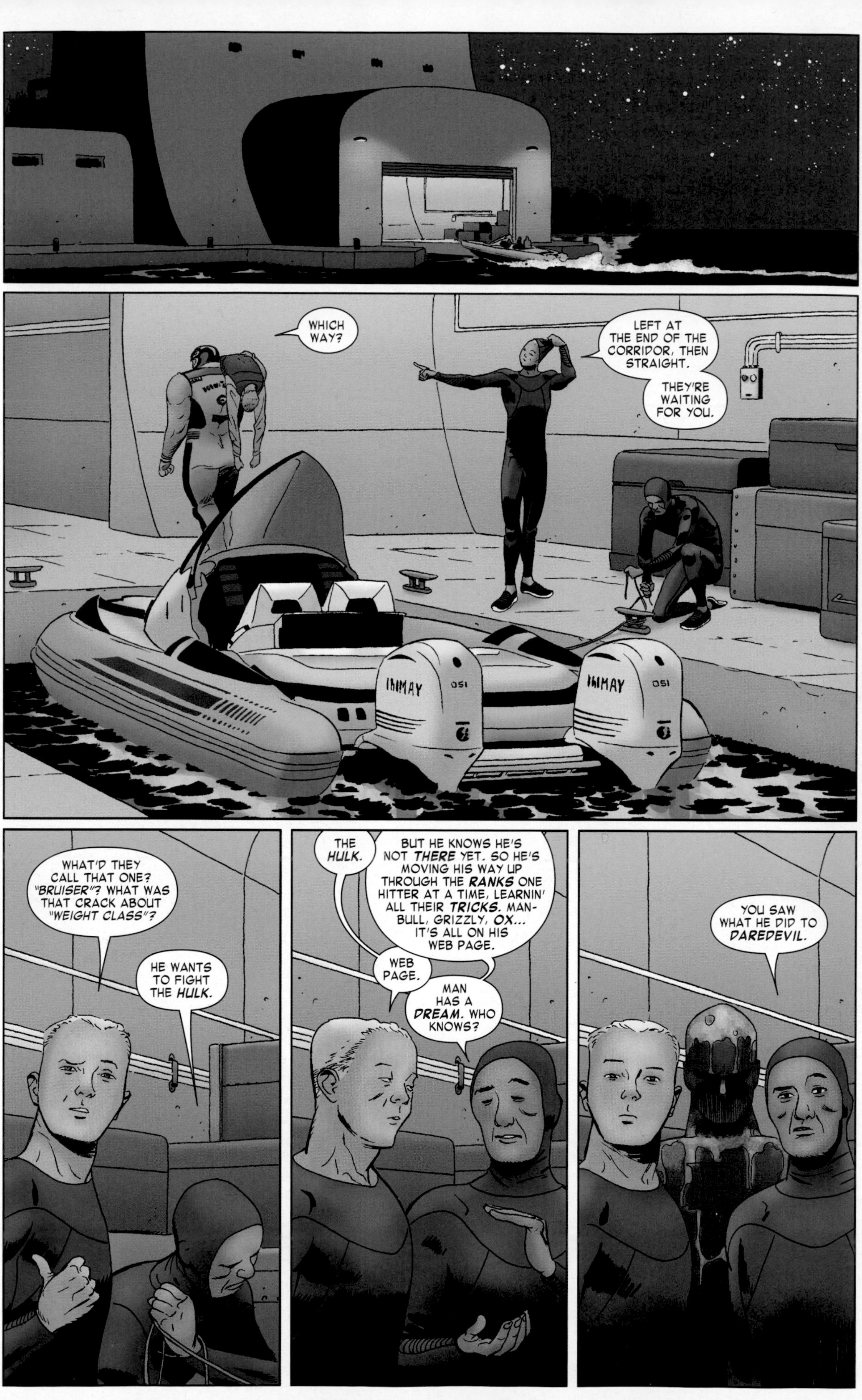
WHICH WAY?
LEFT AT THE END OF THE CORRIDOR, THEN STRAIGHT.
THEY'RE WAITING FOR YOU.
WHAT'D THEY CALL THAT ONE? "*BRUISER*"? WHAT WAS THAT CRACK ABOUT "*WEIGHT CLASS*"?
HE WANTS TO FIGHT THE *HULK.*
THE *HULK.*
BUT HE KNOWS HE'S NOT *THERE* YET. SO HE'S MOVING HIS WAY UP THROUGH THE *RANKS* ONE HITTER AT A TIME, LEARNIN' ALL THEIR *TRICKS.* MAN-BULL, GRIZZLY, *OX...* IT'S ALL ON HIS WEB PAGE.
WEB PAGE.
MAN HAS A *DREAM.* WHO KNOWS?
YOU SAW WHAT HE DID TO *DAREDEVIL.*

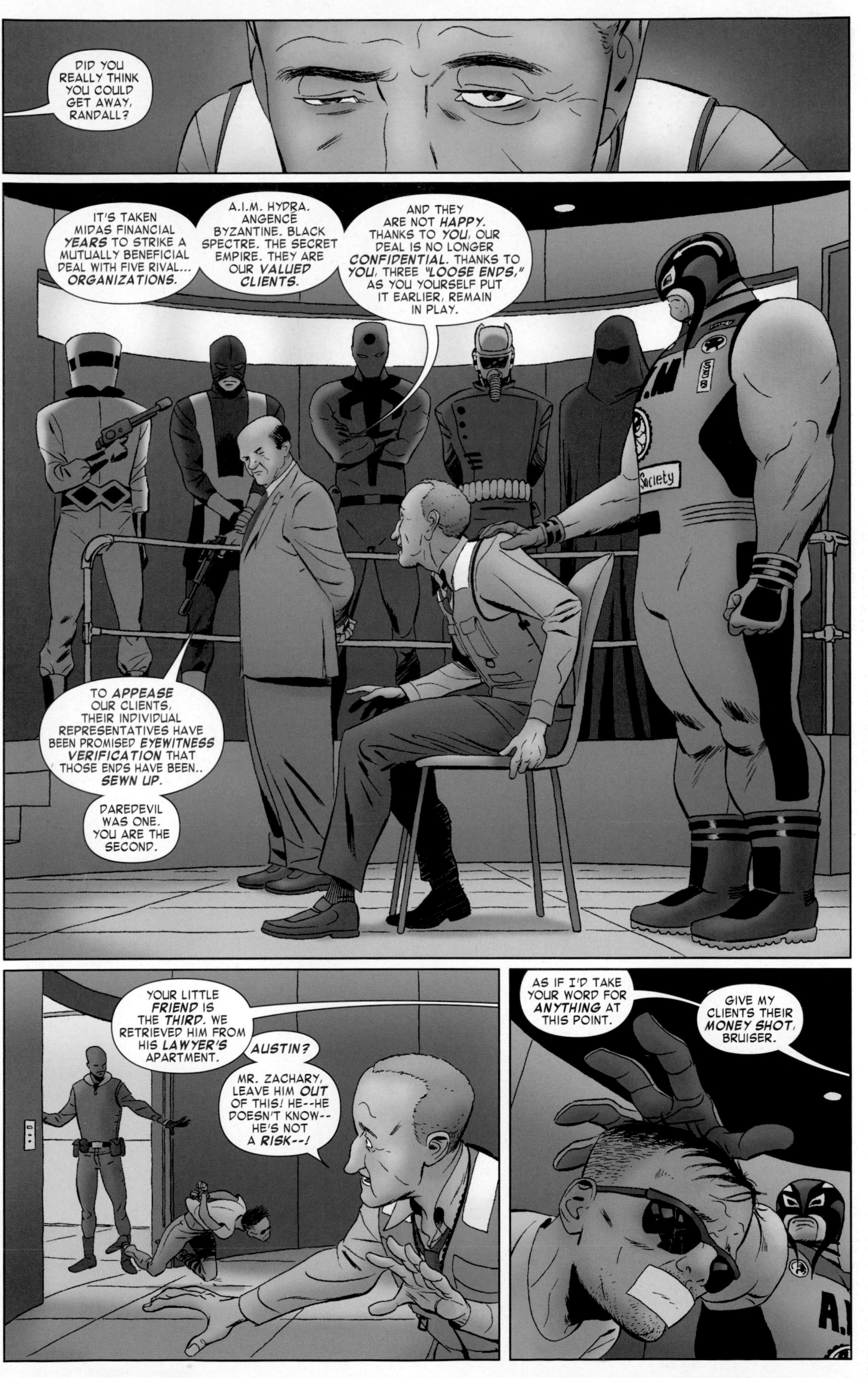
DID YOU REALLY THINK YOU COULD GET AWAY, RANDALL?
IT'S TAKEN MIDAS FINANCIAL YEARS TO STRIKE A MUTUALLY BENEFICIAL DEAL WITH FIVE RIVAL... ORGANIZATIONS.
A.I.M. HYDRA. ANGENCE BYZANTINE. BLACK SPECTRE. THE SECRET EMPIRE. THEY ARE OUR VALUED CLIENTS.
AND THEY ARE NOT HAPPY. THANKS TO YOU, OUR DEAL IS NO LONGER CONFIDENTIAL. THANKS TO YOU, THREE "LOOSE ENDS," AS YOU YOURSELF PUT IT EARLIER, REMAIN IN PLAY.
TO APPEASE OUR CLIENTS, THEIR INDIVIDUAL REPRESENTATIVES HAVE BEEN PROMISED EYEWITNESS VERIFICATION THAT THOSE ENDS HAVE BEEN.. SEWN UP.
DAREDEVIL WAS ONE. YOU ARE THE SECOND.
Society
YOUR LITTLE FRIEND IS THE THIRD. WE RETRIEVED HIM FROM HIS LAWYER'S APARTMENT.
AUSTIN?
MR. ZACHARY, LEAVE HIM OUT OF THIS! HE--HE DOESN'T KNOW-- HE'S NOT A RISK--!
AS IF I'D TAKE YOUR WORD FOR ANYTHING AT THIS POINT.
GIVE MY CLIENTS THEIR MONEY SHOT, BRUISER.

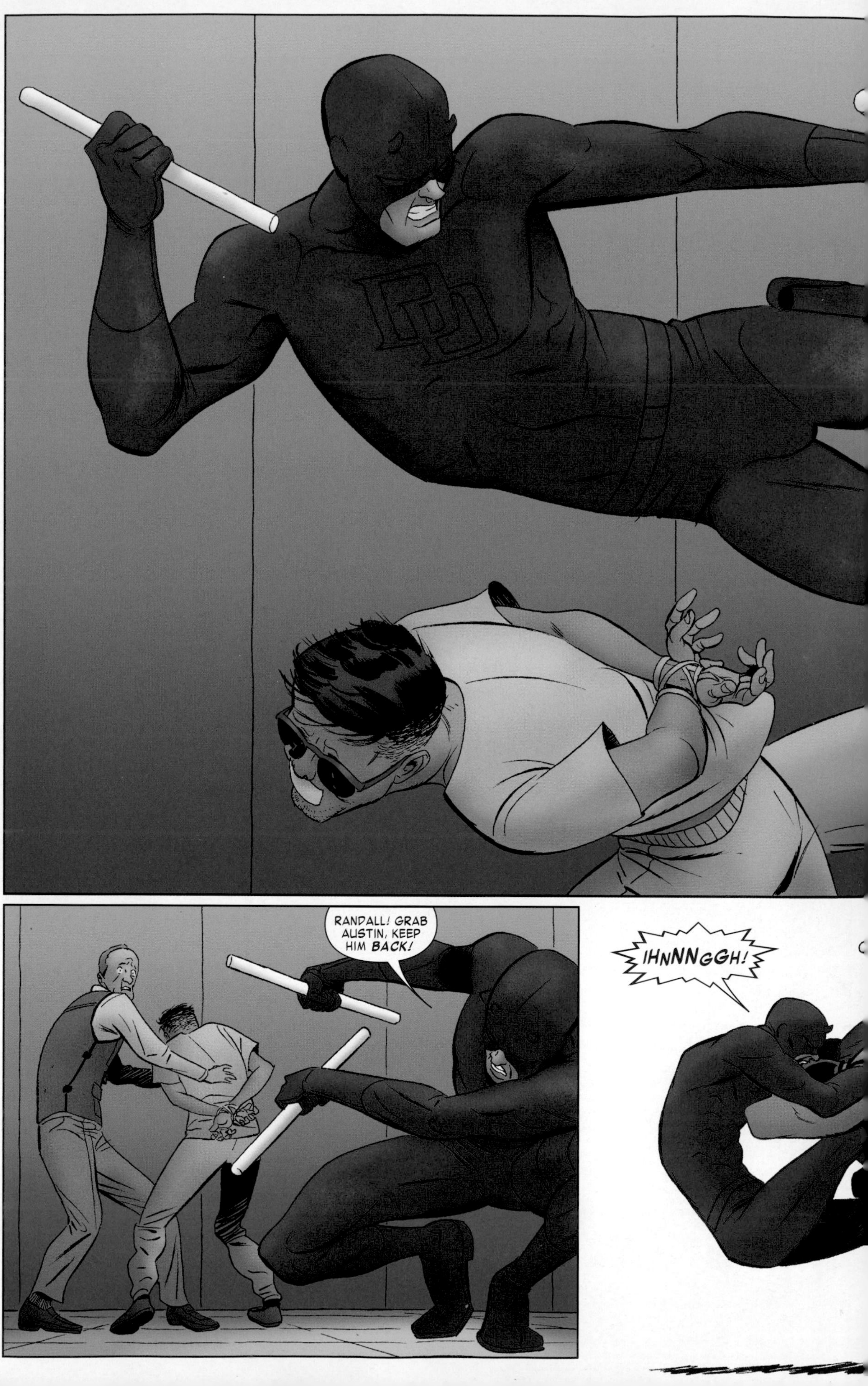
RANDALL! GRAB AUSTIN, KEEP HIM BACK!
IHNNNGGH!

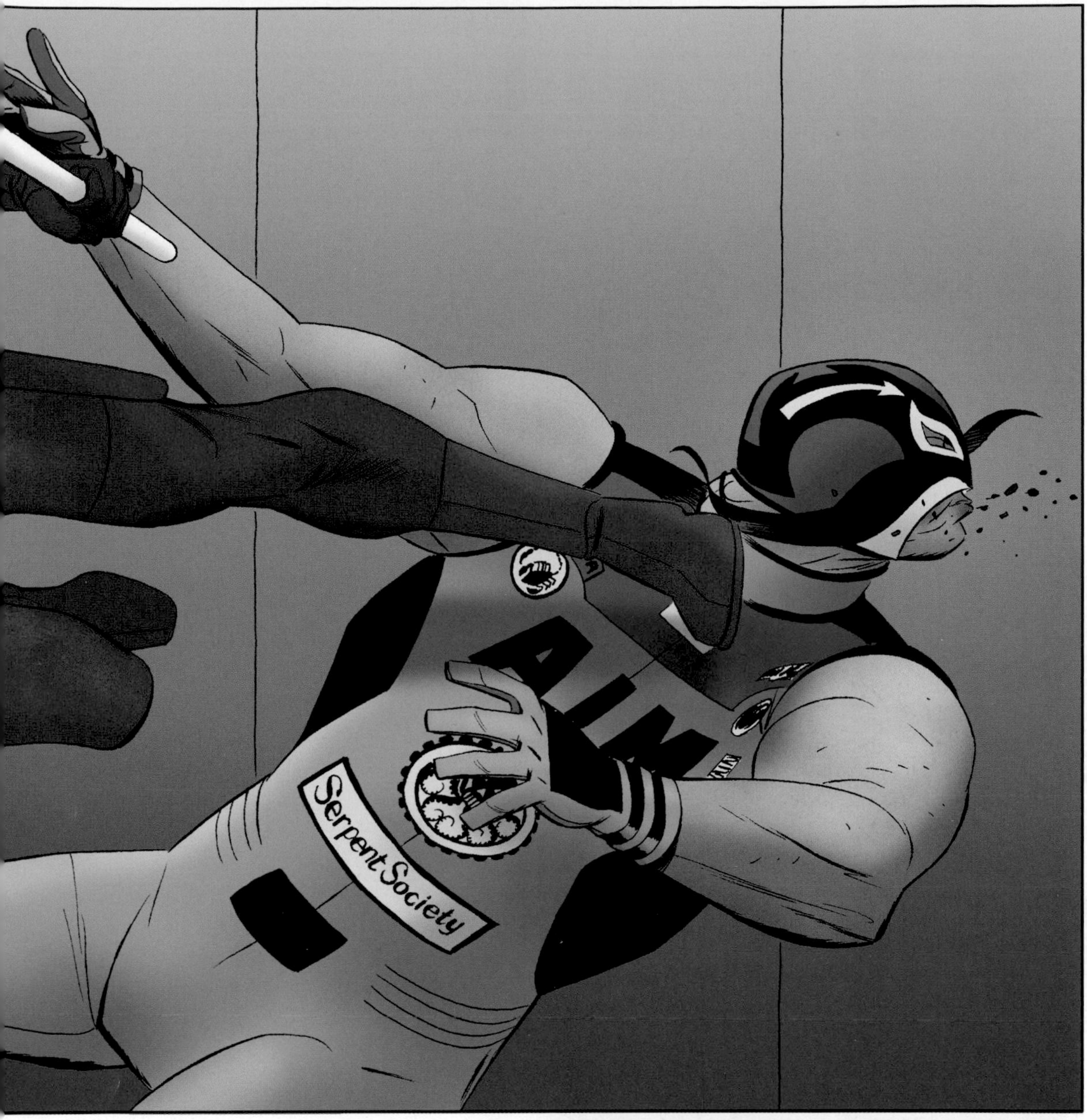
AIM
Serpent Society

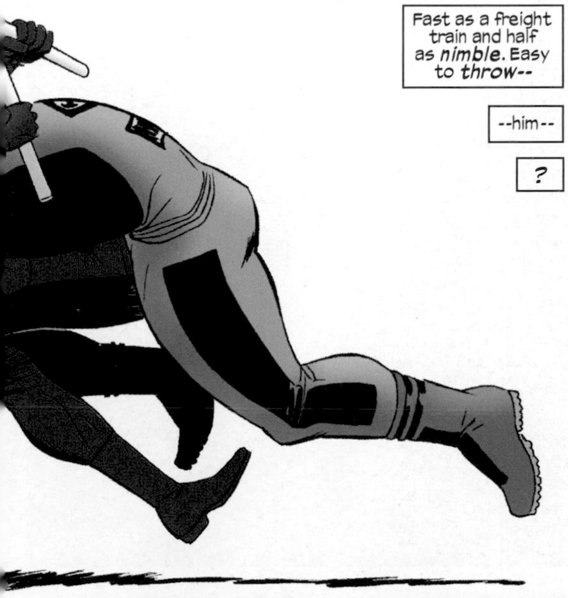
Fast as a freight train and half as *nimble*. Easy to *throw*--
--him--
?

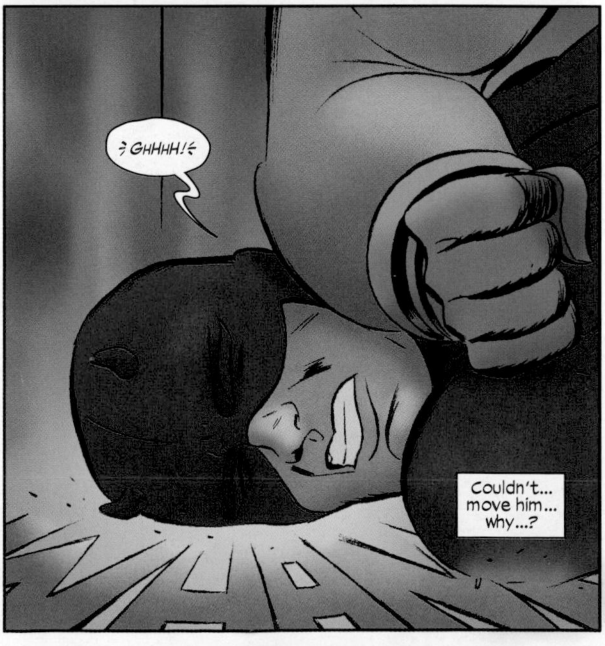
GHHHH!
Couldn't... move him... why...?

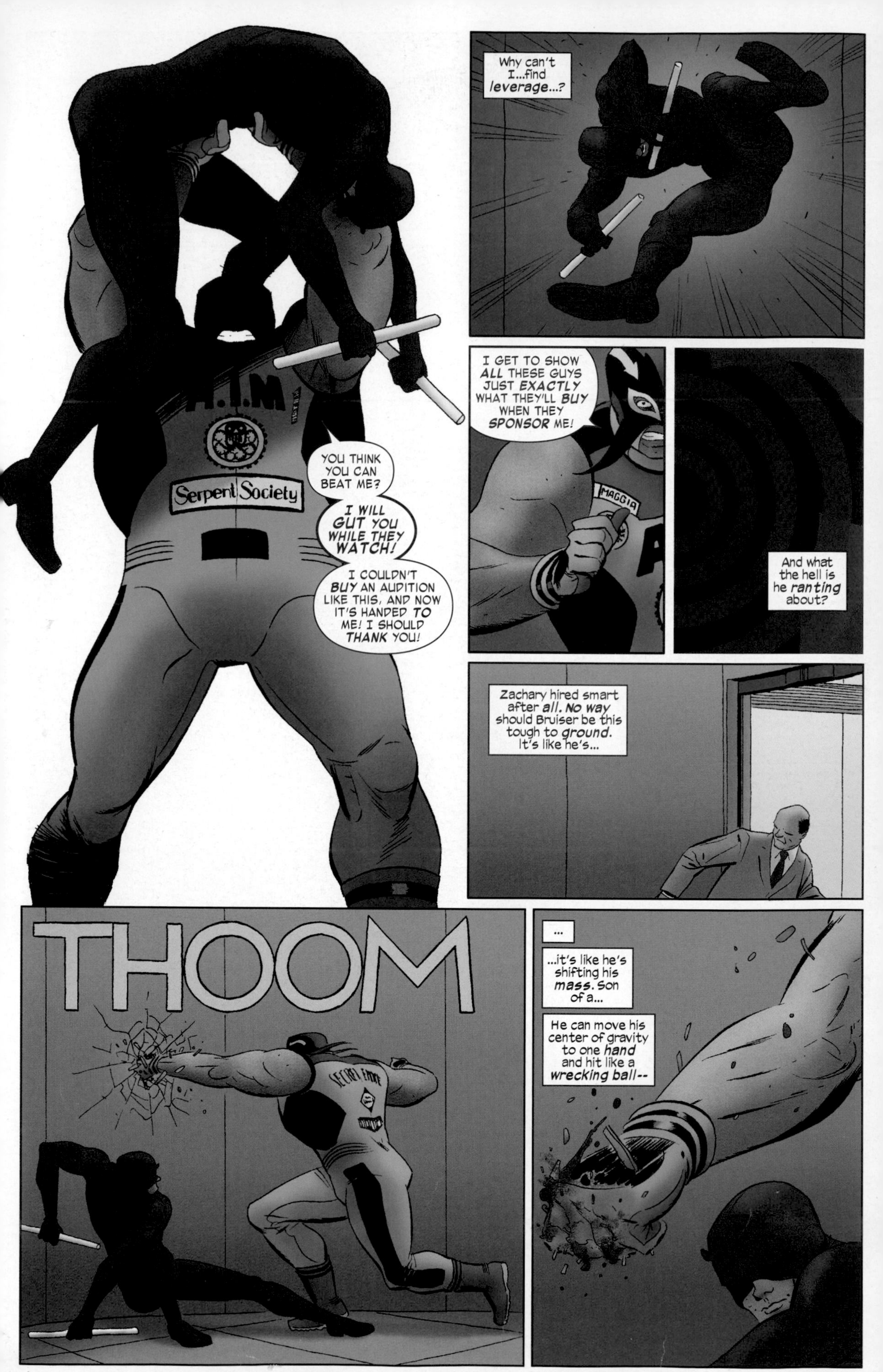
Why can't I...find leverage...?
I GET TO SHOW ALL THESE GUYS JUST EXACTLY WHAT THEY'LL BUY WHEN THEY SPONSOR ME!
MAGGIA
And what the hell is he ranting about?
Serpent Society
YOU THINK YOU CAN BEAT ME?
I WILL GUT YOU WHILE THEY WATCH!
I COULDN'T BUY AN AUDITION LIKE THIS, AND NOW IT'S HANDED TO ME! I SHOULD THANK YOU!
Zachary hired smart after all. No way should Bruiser be this tough to ground. It's like he's...
THOOM
...
...it's like he's shifting his mass. Son of a...
He can move his center of gravity to one hand and hit like a wrecking ball--

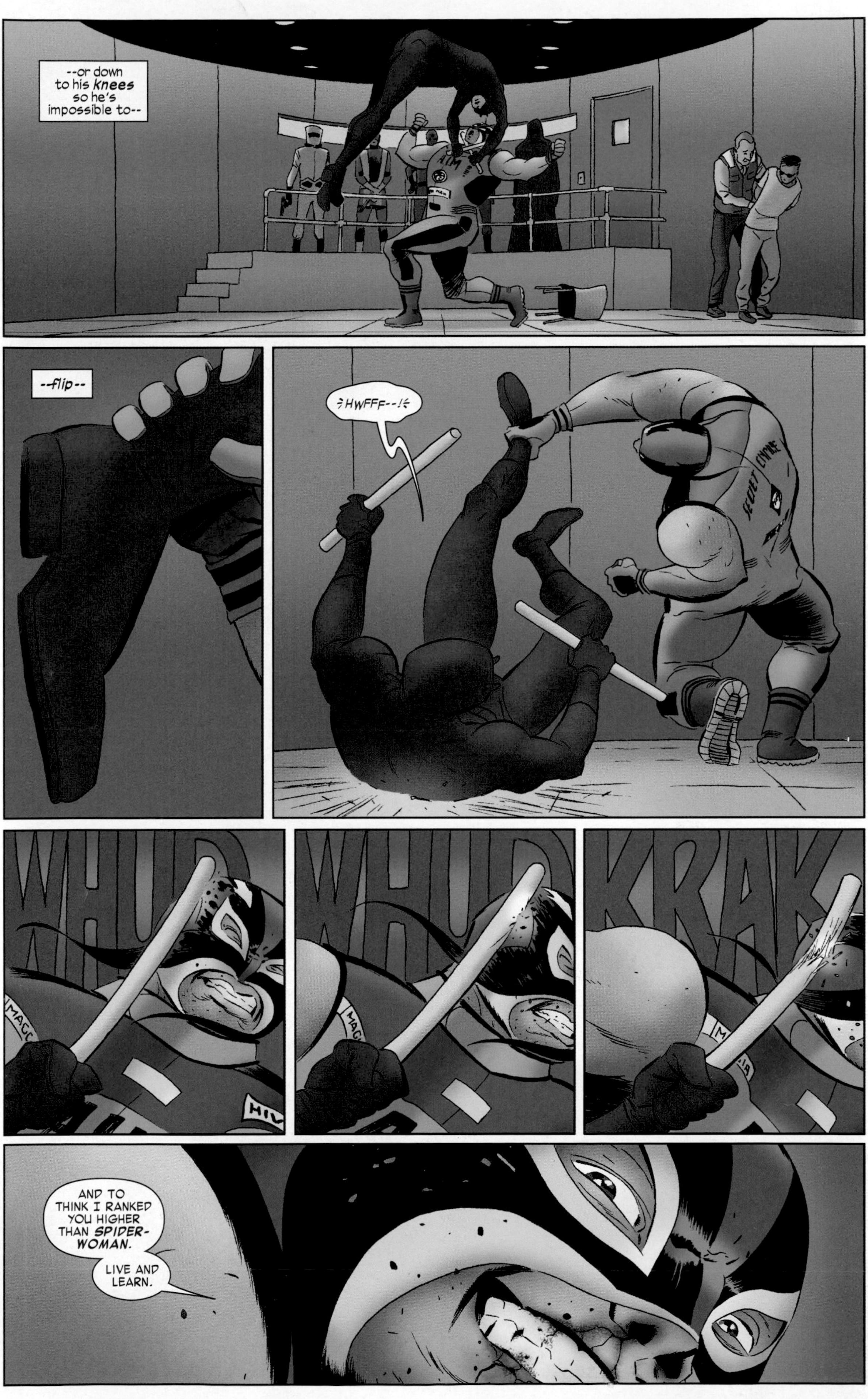
--or down to his *knees* so he's impossible to--
--flip--
HWFFF--!
WHUD
WHUD
KRAK
AND TO THINK I RANKED YOU HIGHER THAN *SPIDER-WOMAN*.
LIVE AND LEARN.

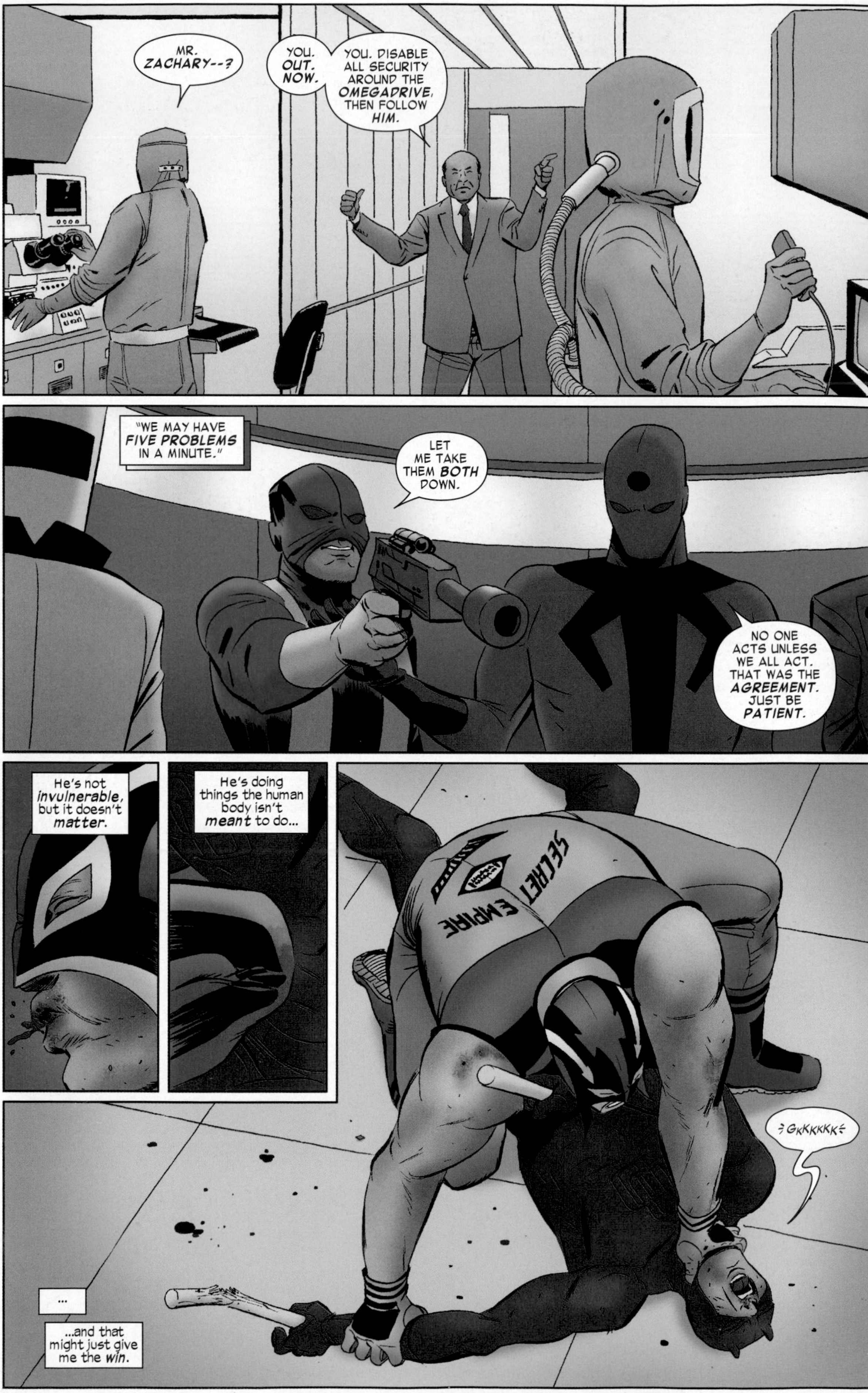
MR. ZACHARY--?
YOU. OUT. NOW.
YOU. DISABLE ALL SECURITY AROUND THE OMEGADRIVE, THEN FOLLOW HIM.
"WE MAY HAVE FIVE PROBLEMS IN A MINUTE."
LET ME TAKE THEM BOTH DOWN.
NO ONE ACTS UNLESS WE ALL ACT. THAT WAS THE AGREEMENT. JUST BE PATIENT.
He's not invulnerable, but it doesn't matter.
He's doing things the human body isn't meant to do...
SECRET EMPIRE
GKKKKKK
...
...and that might just give me the win.

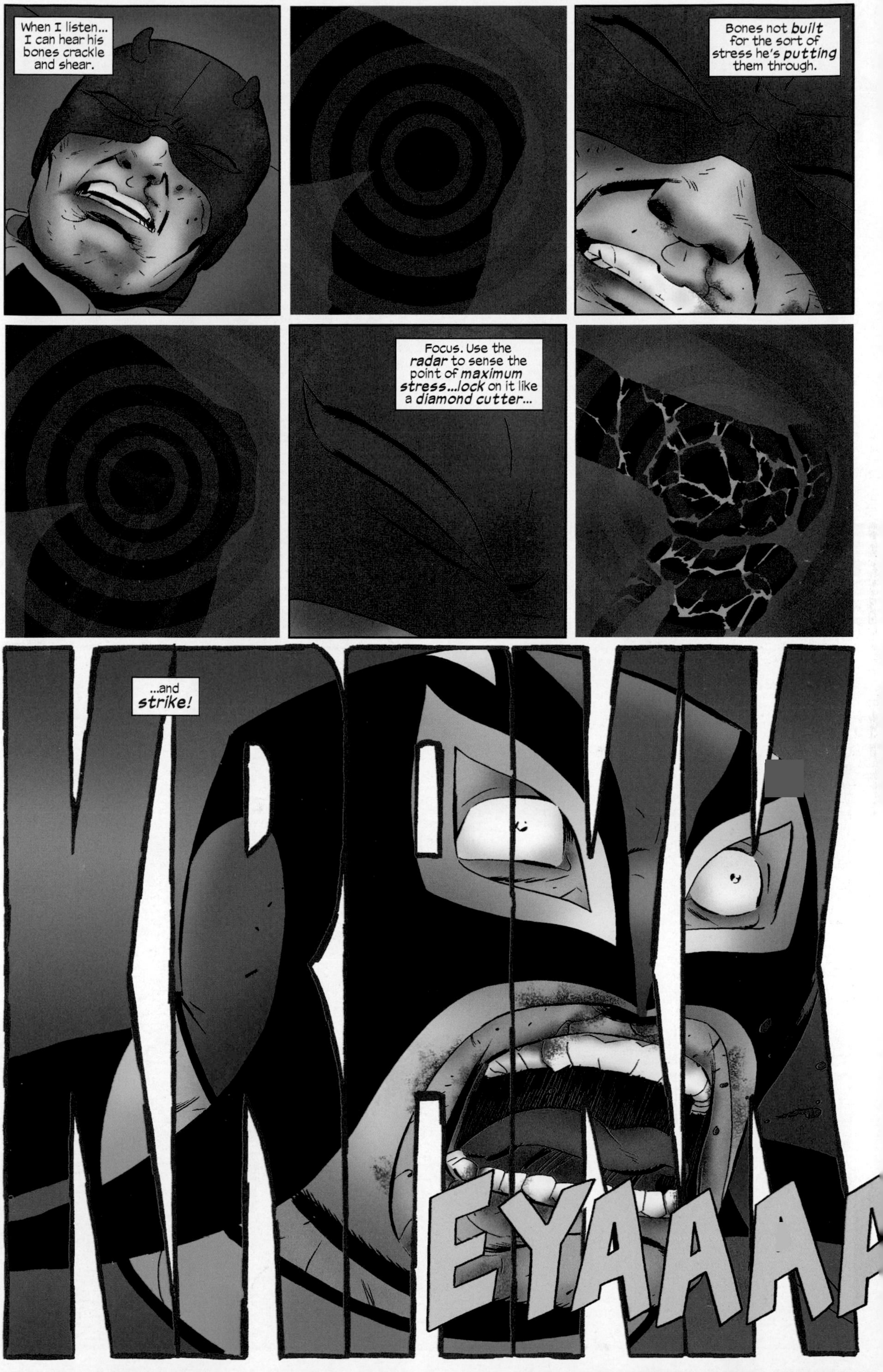
When I listen... I can hear his bones crackle and shear.
Bones not *built* for the sort of stress he's *putting* them through.
Focus. Use the *radar* to sense the point of *maximum stress...lock* on it like a *diamond cutter*...
...and *strike!*
EYAAAA

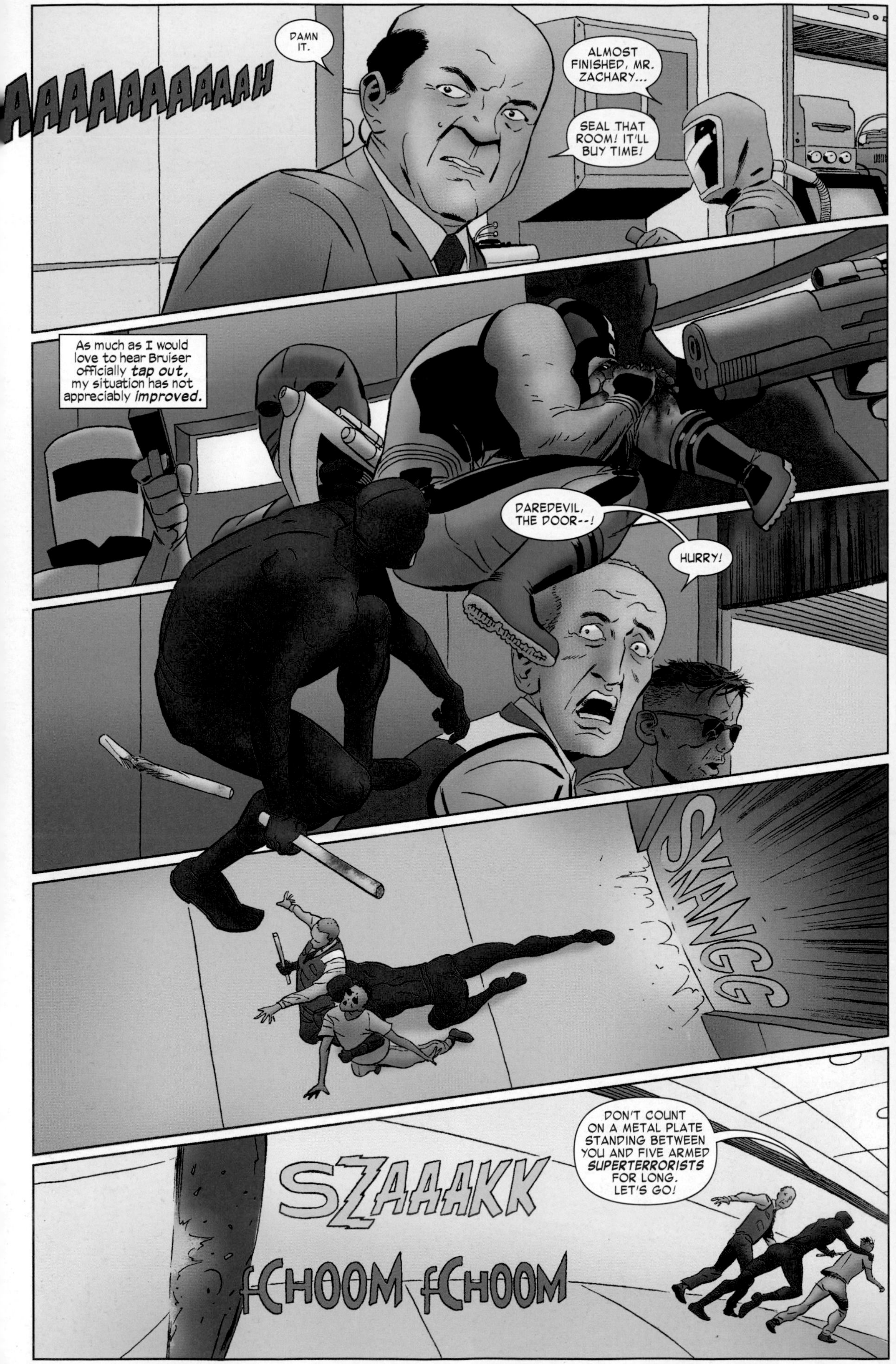
AAAAAAAAAAAH
DAMN IT.
ALMOST FINISHED, MR. ZACHARY...
SEAL THAT ROOM! IT'LL BUY TIME!
As much as I would love to hear Bruiser officially *tap out,* my situation has not appreciably *improved.*
DAREDEVIL, THE DOOR--!
HURRY!
SKANGG
SZAAAKK
DON'T COUNT ON A METAL PLATE STANDING BETWEEN YOU AND FIVE ARMED *SUPERTERRORISTS* FOR LONG. LET'S GO!
fCHOOM fCHOOM

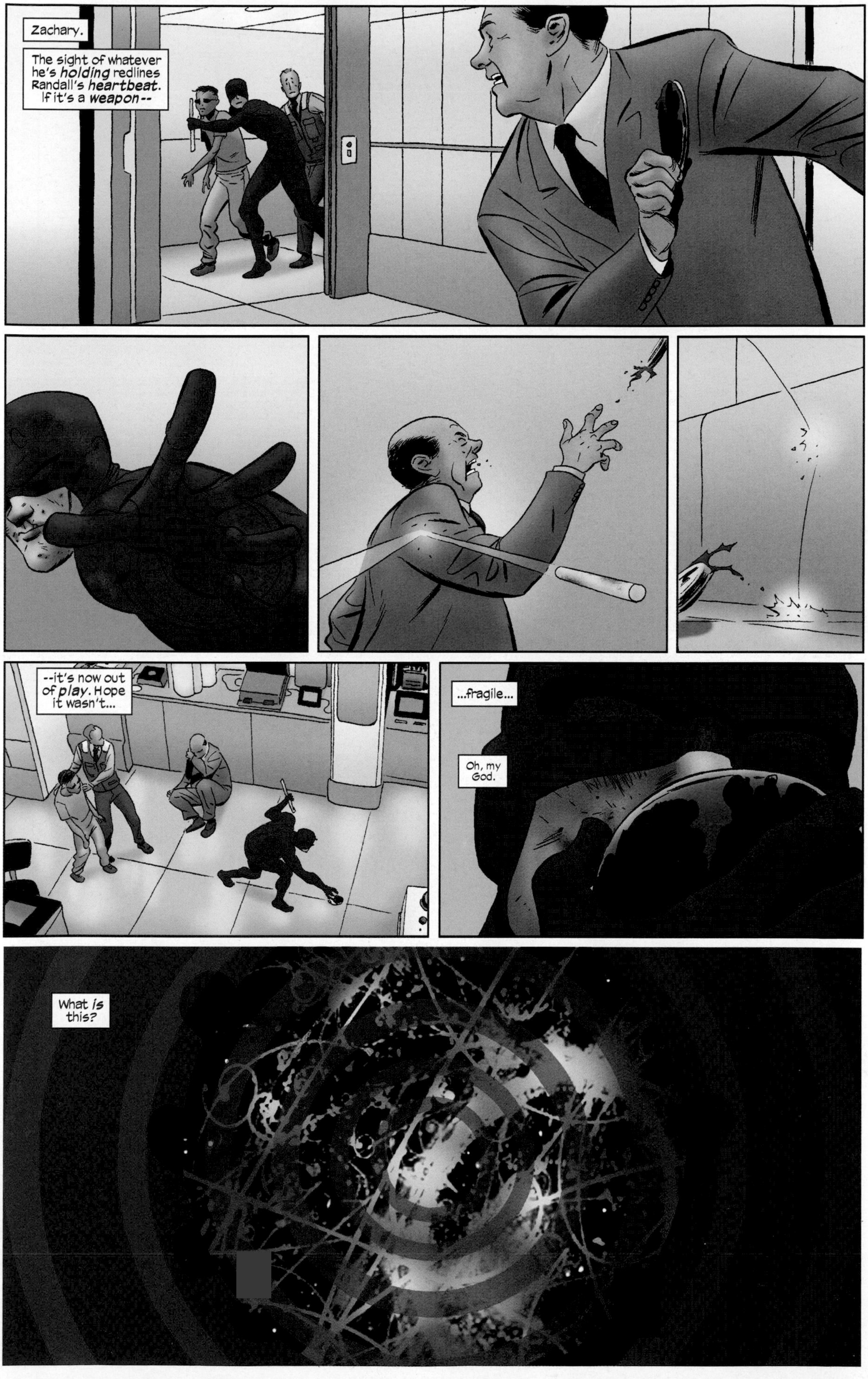

Zachary.
The sight of whatever he's *holding* redlines Randall's *heartbeat*. If it's a *weapon*--
--it's now out of *play*. Hope it wasn't...
...fragile...
Oh, my God.
What *is* this?

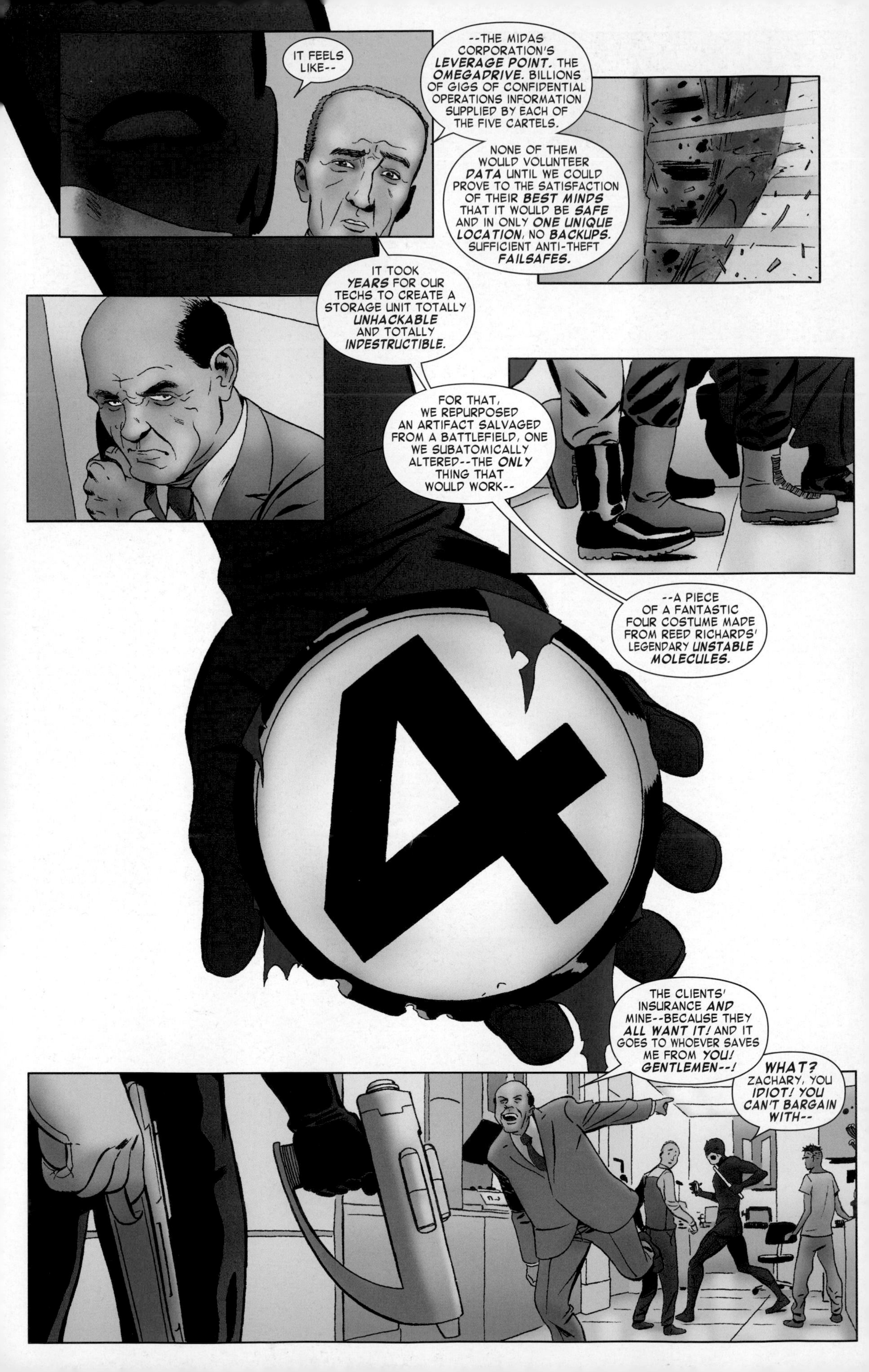
IT FEELS LIKE--
--THE MIDAS CORPORATION'S LEVERAGE POINT. THE OMEGADRIVE. BILLIONS OF GIGS OF CONFIDENTIAL OPERATIONS INFORMATION SUPPLIED BY EACH OF THE FIVE CARTELS.
NONE OF THEM WOULD VOLUNTEER DATA UNTIL WE COULD PROVE TO THE SATISFACTION OF THEIR BEST MINDS THAT IT WOULD BE SAFE AND IN ONLY ONE UNIQUE LOCATION, NO BACKUPS. SUFFICIENT ANTI-THEFT FAILSAFES.
IT TOOK YEARS FOR OUR TECHS TO CREATE A STORAGE UNIT TOTALLY UNHACKABLE AND TOTALLY INDESTRUCTIBLE.
FOR THAT, WE REPURPOSED AN ARTIFACT SALVAGED FROM A BATTLEFIELD, ONE WE SUBATOMICALLY ALTERED--THE ONLY THING THAT WOULD WORK--
--A PIECE OF A FANTASTIC FOUR COSTUME MADE FROM REED RICHARDS' LEGENDARY UNSTABLE MOLECULES.
THE CLIENTS' INSURANCE AND MINE--BECAUSE THEY ALL WANT IT! AND IT GOES TO WHOEVER SAVES ME FROM YOU! GENTLEMEN--!
WHAT? ZACHARY, YOU IDIOT! YOU CAN'T BARGAIN WITH--

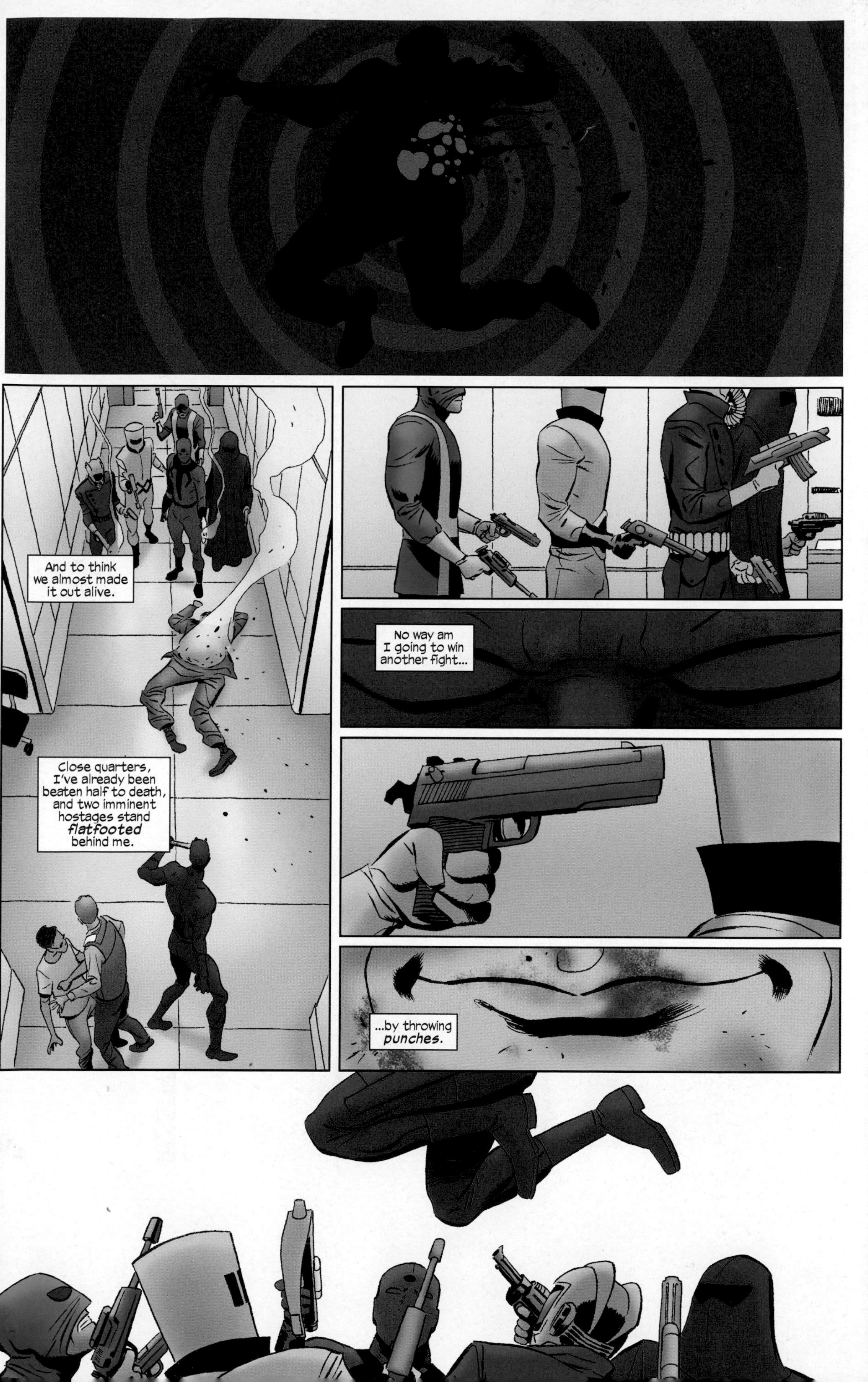
And to think we almost made it out alive.
Close quarters, I've already been beaten half to death, and two imminent hostages stand *flatfooted* behind me.
No way am I going to win another fight...
...by throwing *punches*.

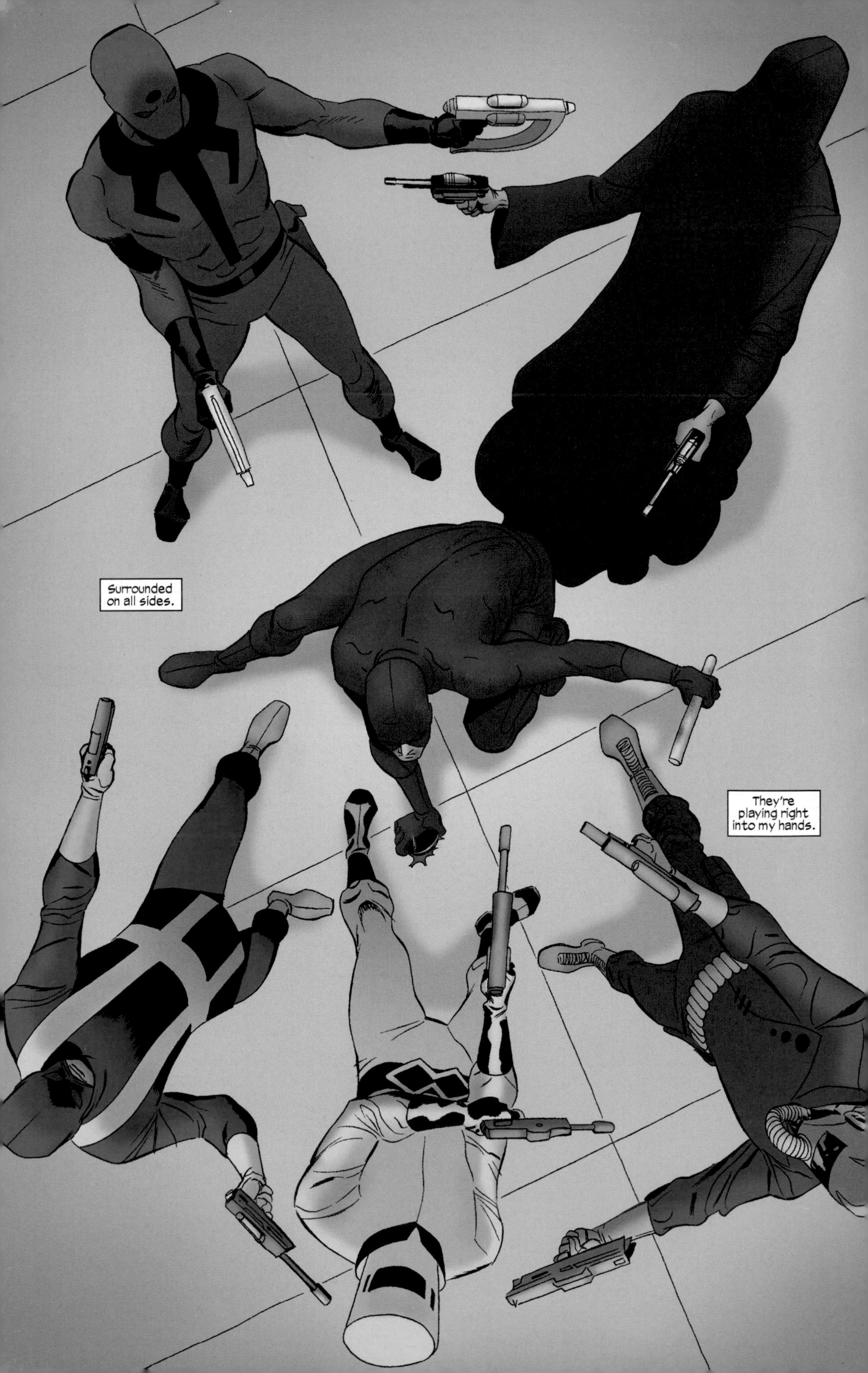
Surrounded on all sides.
They're playing right into my hands.

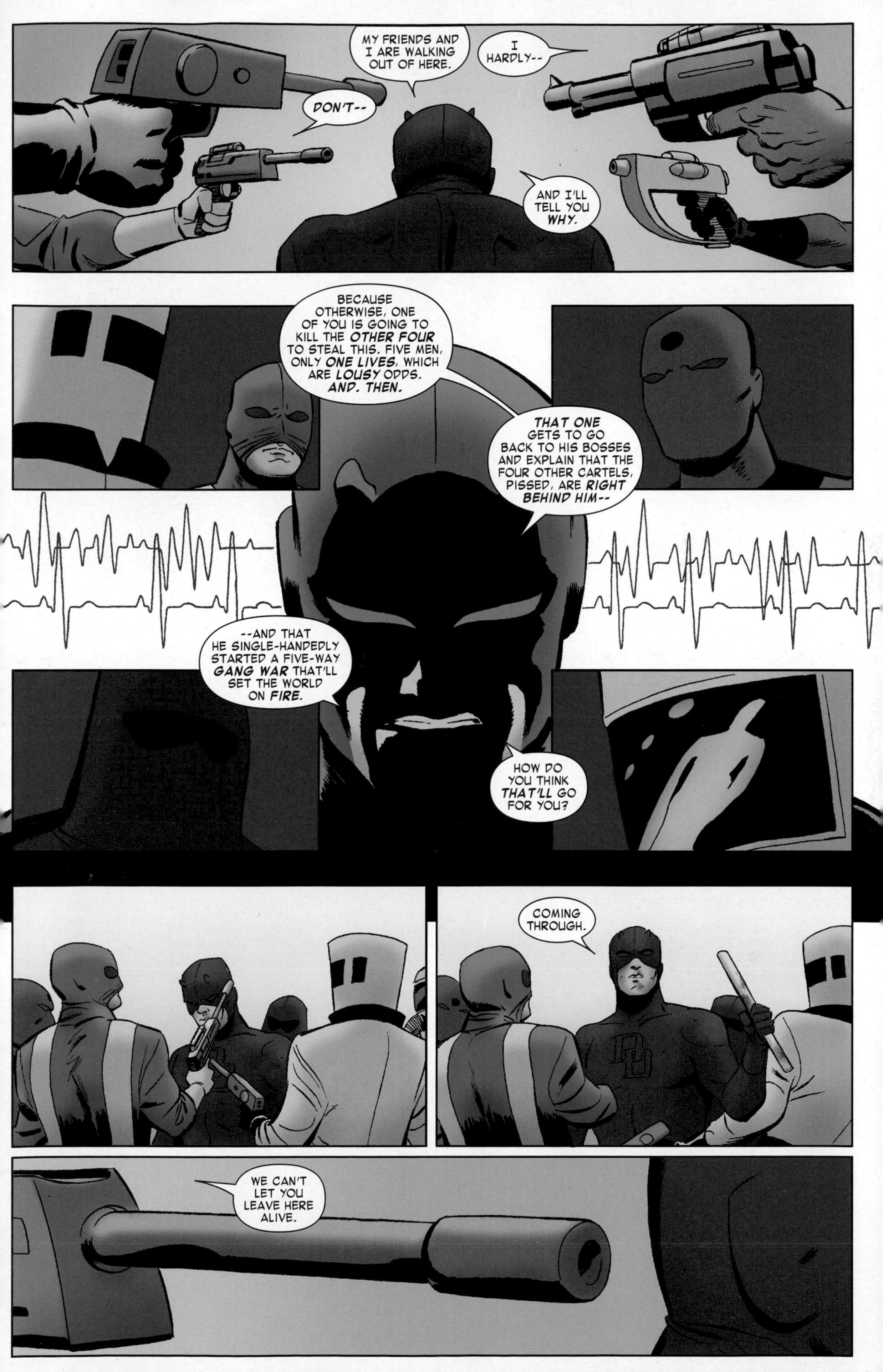
MY FRIENDS AND I ARE WALKING OUT OF HERE.
DON'T--
I HARDLY--
AND I'LL TELL YOU WHY.
BECAUSE OTHERWISE, ONE OF YOU IS GOING TO KILL THE OTHER FOUR TO STEAL THIS. FIVE MEN, ONLY ONE LIVES, WHICH ARE LOUSY ODDS. AND. THEN.
THAT ONE GETS TO GO BACK TO HIS BOSSES AND EXPLAIN THAT THE FOUR OTHER CARTELS, PISSED, ARE RIGHT BEHIND HIM--
--AND THAT HE SINGLE-HANDEDLY STARTED A FIVE-WAY GANG WAR THAT'LL SET THE WORLD ON FIRE.
HOW DO YOU THINK THAT'LL GO FOR YOU?
COMING THROUGH.
WE CAN'T LET YOU LEAVE HERE ALIVE.

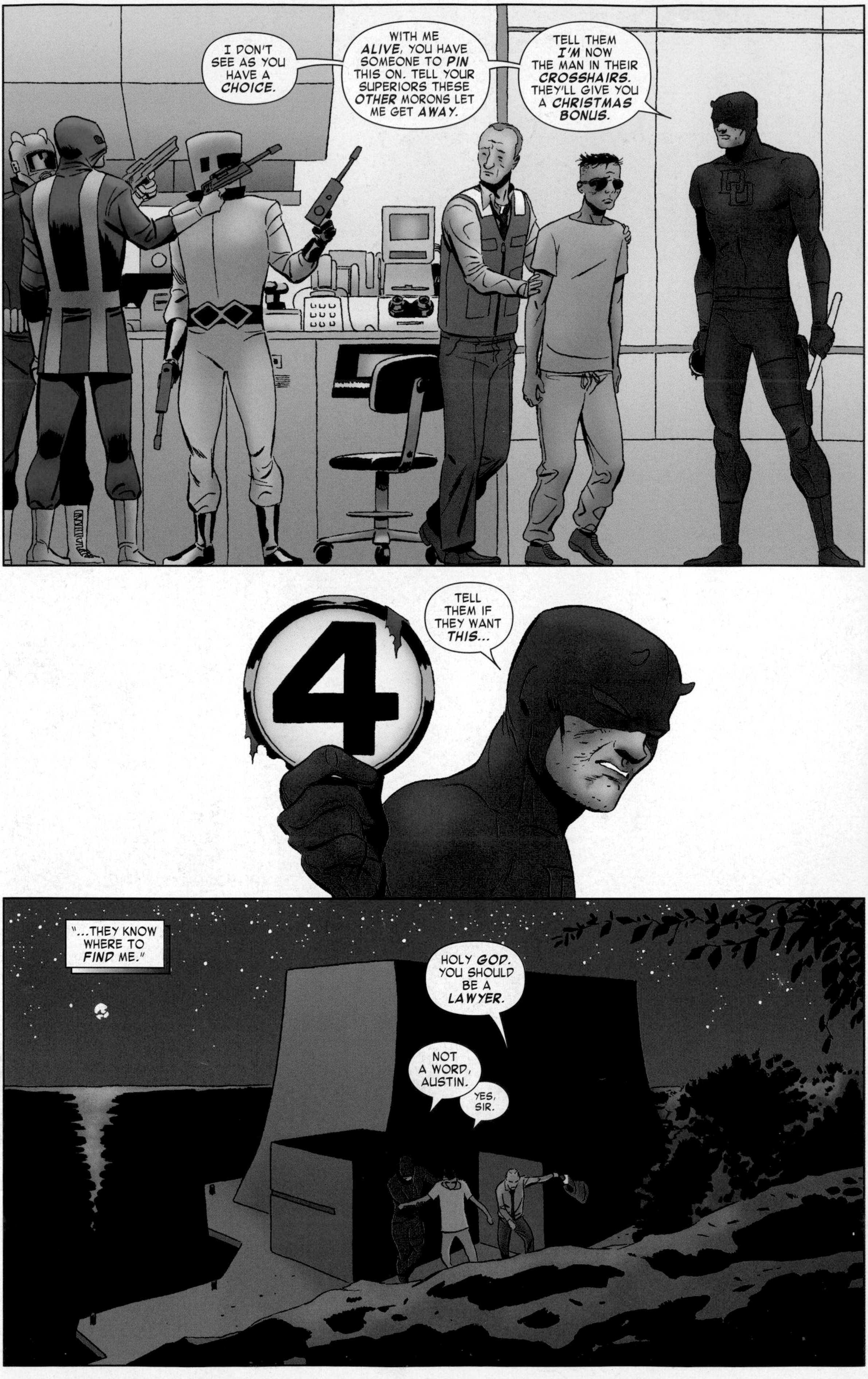
I DON'T SEE AS YOU HAVE A CHOICE.
WITH ME ALIVE, YOU HAVE SOMEONE TO PIN THIS ON. TELL YOUR SUPERIORS THESE OTHER MORONS LET ME GET AWAY.
TELL THEM I'M NOW THE MAN IN THEIR CROSSHAIRS. THEY'LL GIVE YOU A CHRISTMAS BONUS.
4
TELL THEM IF THEY WANT THIS...
"...THEY KNOW WHERE TO FIND ME."
HOLY GOD. YOU SHOULD BE A LAWYER.
NOT A WORD, AUSTIN.
YES, SIR.

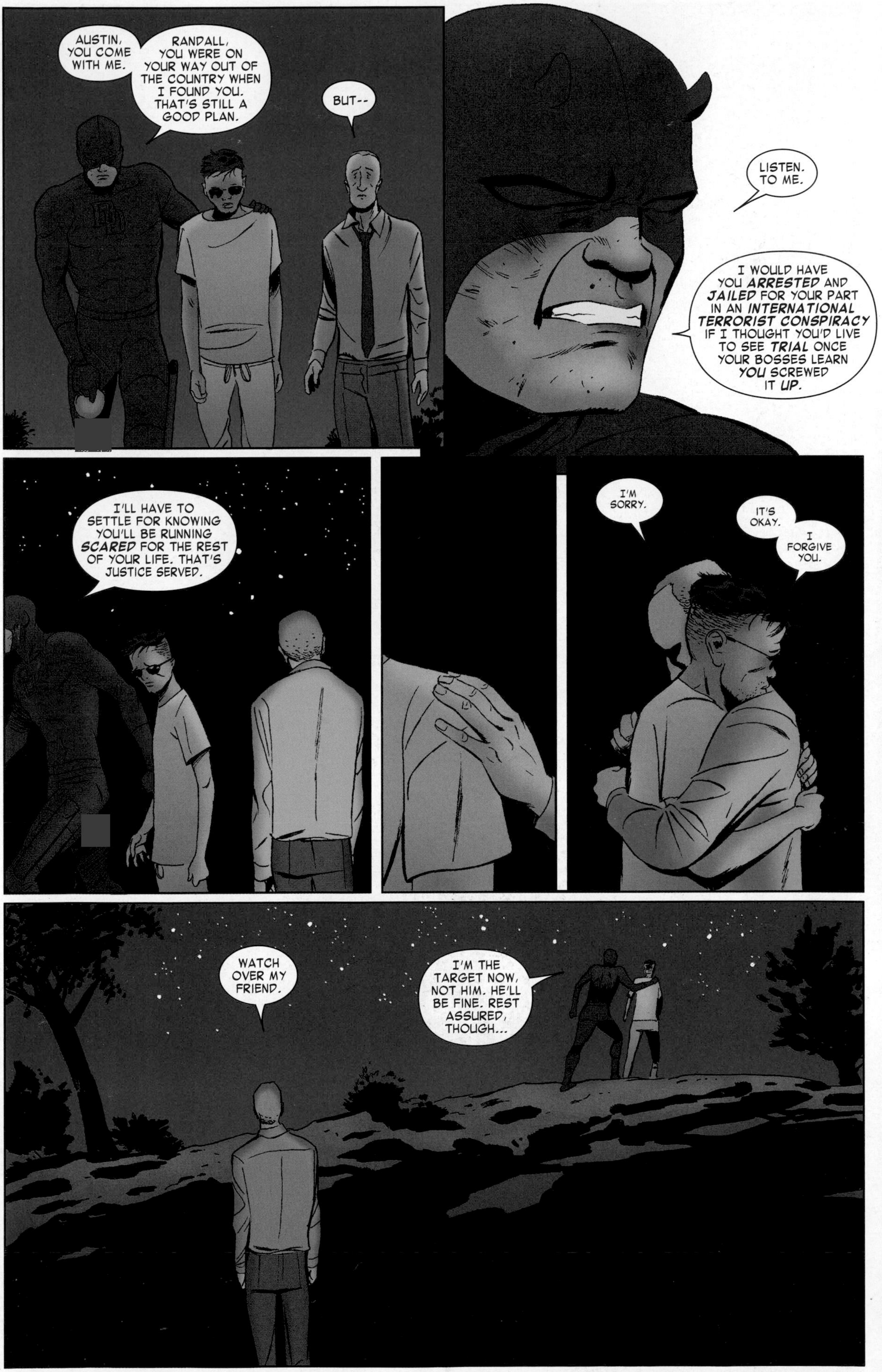
AUSTIN, YOU COME WITH ME.
RANDALL, YOU WERE ON YOUR WAY OUT OF THE COUNTRY WHEN I FOUND YOU. THAT'S STILL A GOOD PLAN.
BUT--
LISTEN. TO ME.
I WOULD HAVE YOU ARRESTED AND JAILED FOR YOUR PART IN AN INTERNATIONAL TERRORIST CONSPIRACY IF I THOUGHT YOU'D LIVE TO SEE TRIAL ONCE YOUR BOSSES LEARN YOU SCREWED IT UP.
I'LL HAVE TO SETTLE FOR KNOWING YOU'LL BE RUNNING SCARED FOR THE REST OF YOUR LIFE. THAT'S JUSTICE SERVED.
I'M SORRY.
IT'S OKAY.
I FORGIVE YOU.
WATCH OVER MY FRIEND.
I'M THE TARGET NOW, NOT HIM. HE'LL BE FINE. REST ASSURED, THOUGH...

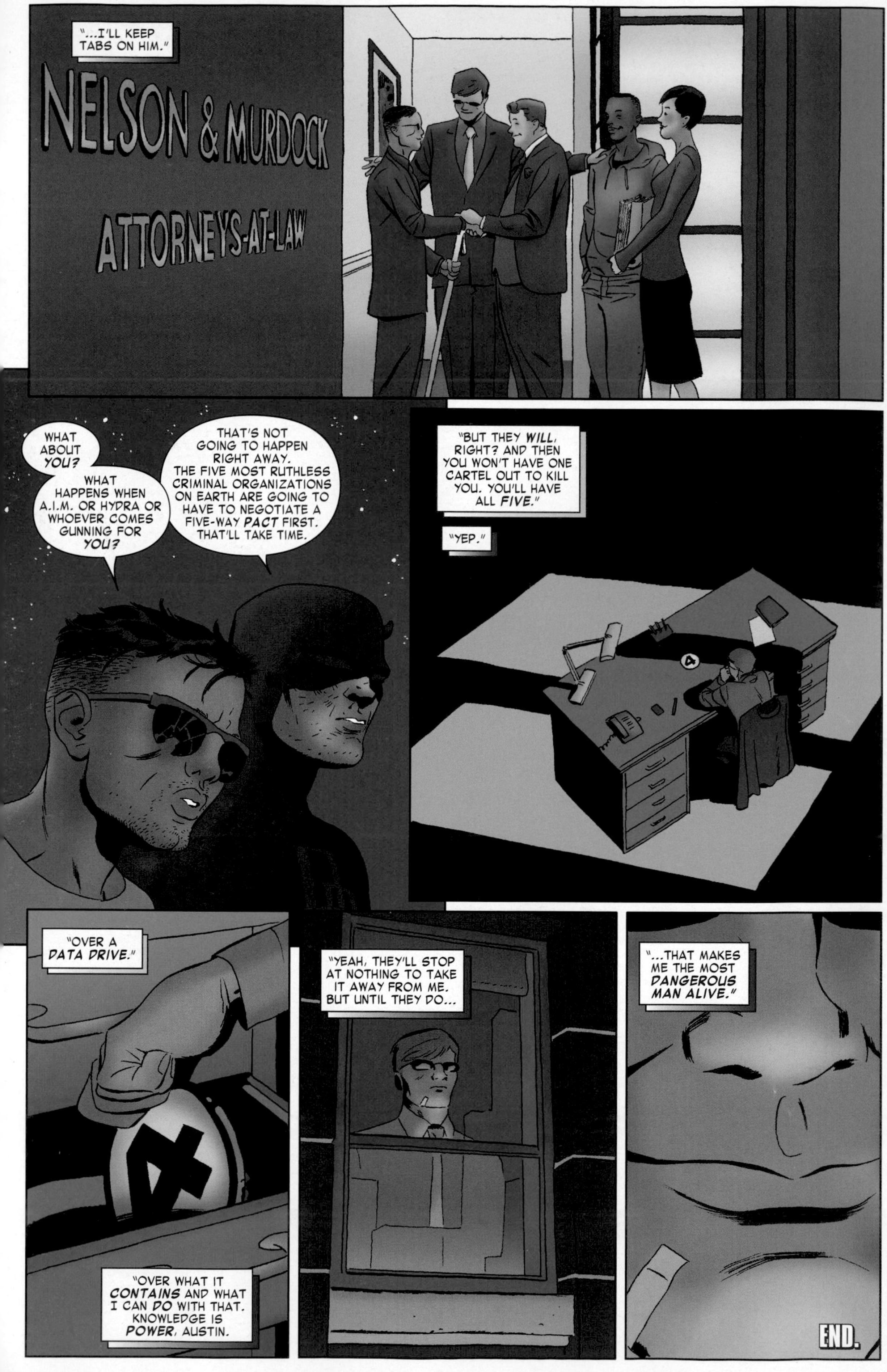
"...I'LL KEEP TABS ON HIM."
NELSON & MURDOCK
ATTORNEYS-AT-LAW
WHAT ABOUT *YOU?* WHAT HAPPENS WHEN A.I.M. OR HYDRA OR WHOEVER COMES GUNNING FOR *YOU?*
THAT'S NOT GOING TO HAPPEN RIGHT AWAY. THE FIVE MOST RUTHLESS CRIMINAL ORGANIZATIONS ON EARTH ARE GOING TO HAVE TO NEGOTIATE A FIVE-WAY *PACT* FIRST. THAT'LL TAKE TIME.
"BUT THEY *WILL*, RIGHT? AND THEN YOU WON'T HAVE ONE CARTEL OUT TO KILL YOU. YOU'LL HAVE ALL *FIVE*."
"YEP."
"OVER A *DATA DRIVE*."
"OVER WHAT IT *CONTAINS* AND WHAT I CAN *DO* WITH THAT. KNOWLEDGE IS *POWER*, AUSTIN.
"YEAH, THEY'LL STOP AT NOTHING TO TAKE IT AWAY FROM ME. BUT UNTIL THEY DO...
"...THAT MAKES ME THE MOST *DANGEROUS MAN ALIVE*."
END.

WRITER **MARK WAID** JOINS THE DEVIL-MAY-CARE DUO OF **MARCOS MARTIN** AND **PAOLO RIVERA** FOR AN EXCITING NEW TAKE ON DD!

BY DUGAN TRODGLEN
DESIGN BY RODOLFO MURAGUCHI

E ver since the 1998 Marvel Knights relaunch of the title, *Daredevil* has attracted some of the most talented writers in the comic-book business (including Kevin Smith, Brian Michael Bendis, Ed Brubaker, and Andy Diggle). And there's no other way to say it: They put Matt Murdock through hell. It started with him witnessing his girlfriend Karen Page being killed by Bullseye and ended with him becoming the demon-possessed leader of the Hand. Nowhere to go but up, right? That's where Mark Waid comes in.

It's hard to believe now, but despite Frank Miller's definitively gritty reimagining of the character — and the decades-long influence Miller has had — Daredevil hasn't always been a brooding, brutal hero of the night. It looks like the time is right for the Daredevil pendulum to swing from darkness back to derring-do, and Mark Waid — he of masterful runs on *Fantastic Four* and *Captain America*, not to mention stellar recent contributions to *Amazing Spider-Man* — appears to be the right man for the job. As you'll surmise from the following conversation with Mark, the man is eager and knows what he wants his *Daredevil* book to be.

IN A TIGHT SPOT! DAREDEVIL SQUARES OFF AGAINST THE REALITY-BENDING BAD GUY THE SPOT! (ART FROM *DD #1* BY PAOLO RIVERA.)

SPOTLIGHT: When we talked recently about Captain America, you said that although you grew up a DC fan, the two Marvel characters you liked most were Cap and Daredevil. Little did I know at the time that you were days away from being announced as the new *Daredevil* writer!

MARK: That's right!

SPOTLIGHT: You talked about Cap's appeal, but what about Daredevil? What made him stand out to you?

MARK: There were a few things. I loved the contrast between his secret identity as a lawyer and his "nighttime job" as a costumed vigilante. But mostly I liked the fact that Matt Murdock seemed more like a grownup than a lot of the other Marvel heroes when I was a kid. He seemed to take a more mature approach to his problems, and he didn't mope or whine. Instead, whenever he got frustrated by something, he would just bound off into the night and kick somebody in the face. I loved that as a kid.

And I have to say I just loved that billy club! (*Laughter.*)

SPOTLIGHT: What aspects of the early years of *Daredevil*, some of which have been left behind for decades, do you hope to bring back to the book?

MARK: One thing I wanted to do that hasn't been done for a while — and for good reason; I understand why everyone went in the darker direction — is give Matt a more sardonic voice and make him, at least in tone, a little funnier. Not Spider-Man funny, but just less grim.

Also, I want to show that Matt is a bit of a swashbuckling adventurer. He's a guy who is constantly leading with his face. It's like the old line, "If he could see half the things he's facing, he'd be scared to death." We're trying really hard to have at least one scene in every issue where Daredevil is doing something that would make Green Lantern wet his pants. (*Laughter.*) That any other ostensibly "fearless" hero in the Marvel Universe would say, "Well, I'm not gonna do *that*!"

SPOTLIGHT: I'm glad you used the word "swashbuckling" because I was going to if you didn't. That's exactly how I would describe the scripts for the first two issues.

MARK: Yeah, good, good.

WRITER MARK WAID.

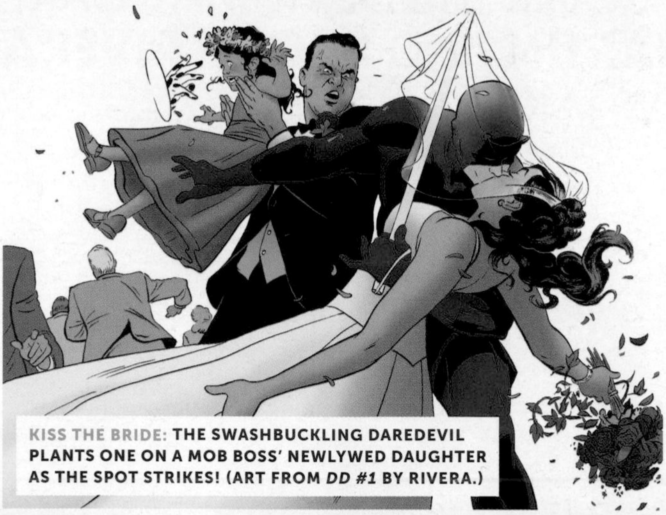

KISS THE BRIDE: **THE SWASHBUCKLING DAREDEVIL PLANTS ONE ON A MOB BOSS' NEWLYWED DAUGHTER AS THE SPOT STRIKES! (ART FROM *DD #1* BY RIVERA.)**

lot of what's happened, but it did become this relentless hammering of Matt Murdock to the point where there was nothing else you could do to make him even darker. So I really want to give him a victory every once in a while. Not all the time, just every once in a while. (*Laughter.*)

SPOTLIGHT: Tom Brevoort recently tweeted after seeing your first issue that *Daredevil* was going to have the most stylish art of any Marvel book in years — and having seen the few pages I've seen, I'd have to agree. Marcos Martin and Paolo Rivera are as good as it gets as far as I'm concerned. Did you know going in that their distinctive artwork would be part of the book's sell?

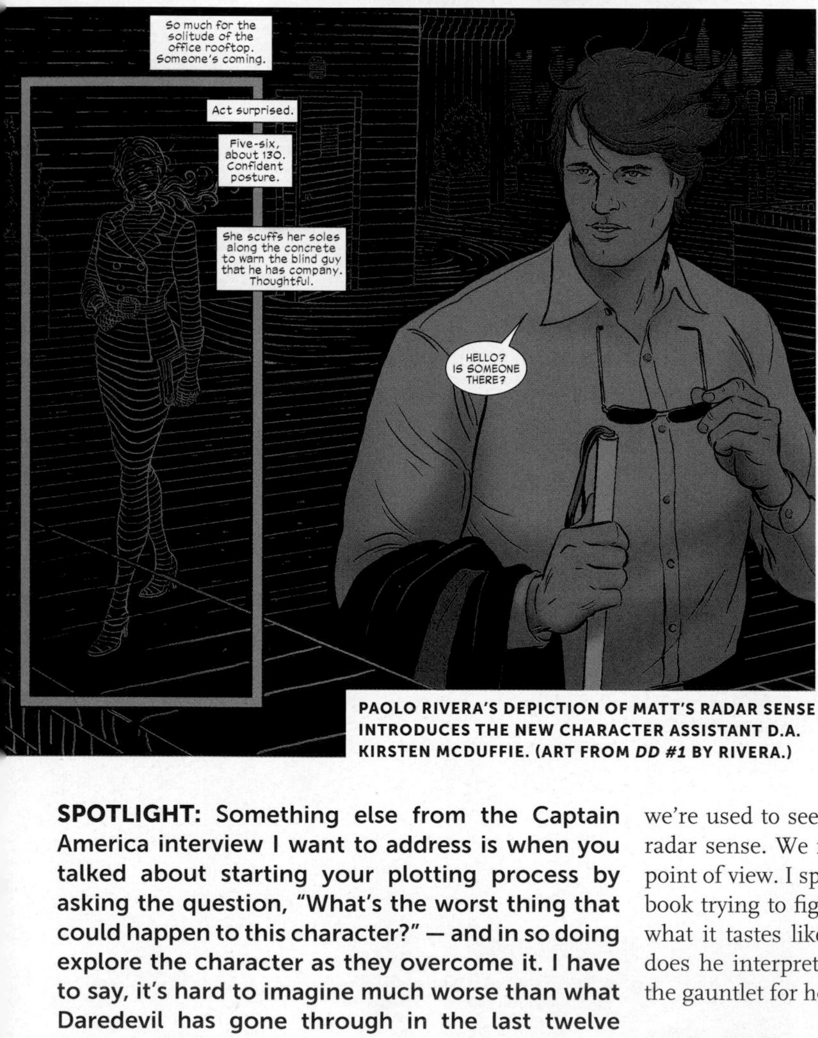
So much for the solitude of the office rooftop. Someone's coming.
Act surprised.
Five-six, about 130. Confident posture.
She scuffs her soles along the concrete to warn the blind guy that he has company. Thoughtful.
HELLO? IS SOMEONE THERE?

PAOLO RIVERA'S DEPICTION OF MATT'S RADAR SENSE INTRODUCES THE NEW CHARACTER ASSISTANT D.A. KIRSTEN MCDUFFIE. (ART FROM *DD #1* BY RIVERA.)

MARK: Yeah, I knew going in that it was a big part of it. It made it easy to say yes to doing the book. I mean, I was inclined to anyway, but anyone would have to be crazy not to want to work with these guys. I worked with Marcos on a Spider-Man story before. [*See* Amazing Spider-Man #578-579, *found in the highly recommended* Spider-Man: Death and Dating TPB — *Ed.]*

SPOTLIGHT: I loved that story.

MARK: Well, thanks. That's mostly because Marcos is a genius. I'd never worked with Paolo before, but really loved his work. He did some great *Daredevil* covers over the last year or so. I remember there was one set in a ski chalet with Daredevil bouncing around in the snow, and it was just beautiful.

What I love is that both of these guys are committed to finding a new visual shorthand for a lot of what we're used to seeing in a Daredevil book, especially the radar sense. We really want to show more from Matt's point of view. I spend a lot of time when I'm writing this book trying to figure out how Matt perceives the world: what it tastes like or sounds like or "looks" like. How does he interpret the world? These guys are taking up the gauntlet for how we portray that visually.

SPOTLIGHT: Something else from the Captain America interview I want to address is when you talked about starting your plotting process by asking the question, "What's the worst thing that could happen to this character?" — and in so doing explore the character as they overcome it. I have to say, it's hard to imagine much worse than what Daredevil has gone through in the last twelve years or so! (*Laughter.*)

MARK: Yeah, I may not be taking that approach with Matt Murdock! First of all, again, the stories from the last ten, twelve years have been great. I remember after Kevin Smith's run was over, I ran into him at a restaurant and went over to his table to tell him I quit comics. His whole run was so good, I didn't feel like I could even sit at a keyboard anytime soon. So I like a

SPOTLIGHT: Going into your script, I was wondering how you would approach working with artists with such a creative flair. It looked pretty standard from that perspective. You seemed to just know that they, or Paolo specifically in these issues, would take your cues and run with it.

MARK: I told both these guys that I know this is a collaborative medium. What I put down in the script is just a starting point in terms of the visuals. If they have better ideas, then we should talk about it, bounce ideas off each other. A lot of good stuff has come out of that.

SPOTLIGHT: When it comes to Marvel characters, I think the two whose alter egos are just as important to the plots as their costumed identities are Iron Man and Daredevil. In your approach to the book, do you intend to give Matt Murdock equal airtime?

MARK: Oh, definitely. Probably more, really. But one thing (editor) Steve Wacker and I talked about was that we didn't want to go too heavy on Matt as a lawyer, because there are few things in comics that are duller than extended courtroom scenes. So the question arose: "How do we have Matt practice his profession in a way that's not visually dull?" And I can't give away what happens in *Daredevil #3*, but we have found a new way for Matt to approach his job in a way that totally makes sense for the character, and I don't think we've seen in a comic book before.

....

"WE HAVE FOUND A NEW WAY FOR MATT TO APPROACH HIS JOB IN A WAY THAT TOTALLY MAKES SENSE FOR THE CHARACTER, AND I DON'T THINK WE'VE SEEN IN A COMIC BOOK BEFORE."

....

SPOTLIGHT: What about the supporting cast? You can't have Daredevil without Foggy. It looks like you're bringing in at least one new key cast member. What is your approach to the cast?

MARK: In books with big supporting casts, rather than hitting you over the head with everyone at once, I want to get comfortable with each one. I did the same thing with *Flash* several years ago. I stripped the cast down to a couple of characters and built it up from there. So at first, it's Matt and Foggy with a new assistant D.A., Kirsten McDuffie. Kirsten is now my editor's favorite character, so I've had to promise to include her as often as possible. (*Laughter*.)

Her whole thing is that she has a real disdain for Matt Murdock because Matt doesn't seem to get the fact that just by being in a courtroom trying to represent an ordinary citizen, he's creating a media frenzy from the fact that

COVER TO *RUSE #1* BY BUTCH GUICE, MIKE PERKINS AND LAURA MARTIN.

MARK WAID/**RUSE**

Our story opens in 2000 in Tampa, Florida, with new comic-book publisher CrossGen. Among the many talented creators the company lured to Tampa: Mark Waid. Among the many genres CrossGen ambitiously attempted: Victorian mystery. *Ruse*, particularly the Waid-penned issues, was among CrossGen's most well-received titles. Now, years after the publisher went bankrupt and was purchased by Disney, *Ruse* is back — Marvel's purchase by Disney having provided the opportunity to resurrect several long-dormant CrossGen titles. And with Mark Waid writing for Marvel — well, it doesn't take a brilliant detective to deduce what happened next. The recently completed *Ruse* limited series, soon to be collected in trade paperback, afforded fans a new entrée into the world of genius detective Simon Archard and his assistant — or partner, depending on who you ask — Emma Bishop. Mark chatted with us about his return to *Ruse*.

I can't imagine you ever pictured yourself with the opportunity to return to the world of *Ruse*.

It never crossed my mind that I would be returning to these characters. I just thought that was a done deal; that those characters had wrapped up with the end of CrossGen. Then, Steve Wacker called some time back and said, "Listen, if I could get the rights to that book would you be interested?" Knowing it was an impossible task I said, "Sure, I'd be interested." But then Disney buys Marvel, and Disney owns the *Ruse* property as part of CrossGen, and Steve calls back and says, "Ha ha, I got you!"

But it certainly was no hardship. It was fun. It felt natural to return to these characters, and they're very easy for me to write.

Was it a different experience to write them from your home than it was punching the clock at CrossGen?

Yeah, from the CrossGen compound? (*Laughter*.) Yes it was!

Did you go back and check out your original run for reference?

I did. I read the first ten issues or so, which is what I wrote of the first series. I didn't really need to read the rest because Marvel's idea was not to make it seem like issue 28 of the original series. They wanted us to make it seem new. But at the same time, I didn't really need to change anything from my first run in order to make it new.

It's sort of like a series of mystery novels, where each book has its own new beginning, even with the same characters.

That's exactly how I approached it.

What is the appeal of the genre to you?

Well, first of all, I looove mystery stories. I love puzzle stories, and I love to be challenged to stay one step ahead of the reader and ultimately make the pieces come together. I'll admit that plotting *Ruse* is a challenge. It's virtually impossible to write a detective story that hasn't already been done. That well has been drawn on a lot. But once I had the pieces in place, once I had the villain set — I'd like to say it came together, but there were times when I was making it up as I went along. It all ended up working out at the end, thankfully!

....

That it did! Look for the Ruse: A Victorian Guide to Murder TPB *wherever fine Victorian-era comic books are sold. (By that, we mean your local comic shop!)* – DT

“WE’RE TRYING REALLY HARD TO HAVE AT LEAST ONE SCENE IN EVERY ISSUE WHERE DAREDEVIL IS DOING SOMETHING THAT WOULD MAKE GREEN LANTERN WET HIS PANTS.”

some people still think he’s Daredevil. As an assistant D.A., she thinks, “I’m trying to get justice for as many people as possible as quickly as possible through the process of law, and you’re gumming up the works with your antics.” So she’s not thrilled with him. And add to that the fact that she is sure he is Daredevil. Of course, she’s right, and Matt knows it, but he denies it. Not because he’s trying to hide his secret identity, but just because it winds her up. It’s not Lois Lane following Clark Kent around with a pair of scissors trying to prove he’s Superman by clipping his hair. It’s foreplay for them, and Matt just enjoys making her apoplectic over it. It’s funny to him.

SPOTLIGHT: This question is a little out of left field: A couple of people I know, when they found out you were going to be writing *Daredevil* and what your approach was going to be, eagerly speculated that we might see Matt’s phony-brother pseudonym Mike Murdock again. [*Who? Me? — Ed.*] What are the chances?

MARK: (*Laughs.*) Sadly, no. I still believe — and will until the day I die — that there is something in the Mike Murdock concept that is brilliant beyond belief. The idea that a blind guy is tricking his friends into thinking he’s not blind is funny, but there’s no way to make it work now.

I do love that early stuff — but as I’ve said in other interviews before, it’s like the Beatles. I love the Beatles, but that doesn’t mean I think everyone in 2011 should sound like the Beatles. When it comes to these classic comic-book characters, the trick is not to replicate what you enjoyed as a kid. It’s to find the core of the things you liked and filter out the stuff that just doesn’t ring true in the 21st century. That said, there is a brief tip of the hat to Mike Murdock in *Daredevil #2*. You may have to squint.

Hear that, folks? A chance to play “Where’s Mike Murdock” is just one of many reasons to pick up the new Daredevil *book — the others being Mark Waid, Paolo Rivera and Marcos Martin, of course!* ■

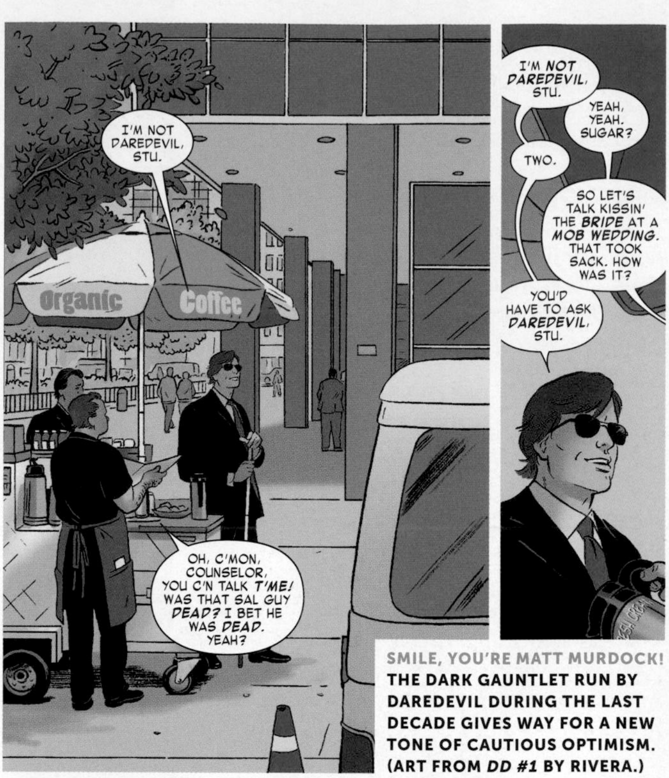
I'M NOT DAREDEVIL, STU.
Organic
Coffee
OH, C'MON, COUNSELOR, YOU C'N TALK *T'ME!* WAS THAT SAL GUY *DEAD?* I BET HE WAS *DEAD.* YEAH?
I'M *NOT* DAREDEVIL, STU.
YEAH, YEAH. SUGAR?
TWO.
SO LET'S TALK KISSIN' THE *BRIDE* AT A *MOB WEDDING.* THAT TOOK SACK. HOW WAS IT?
YOU'D HAVE TO ASK *DAREDEVIL,* STU.

SMILE, YOU’RE MATT MURDOCK! THE DARK GAUNTLET RUN BY DAREDEVIL DURING THE LAST DECADE GIVES WAY FOR A NEW TONE OF CAUTIOUS OPTIMISM. (ART FROM *DD #1* BY RIVERA.)

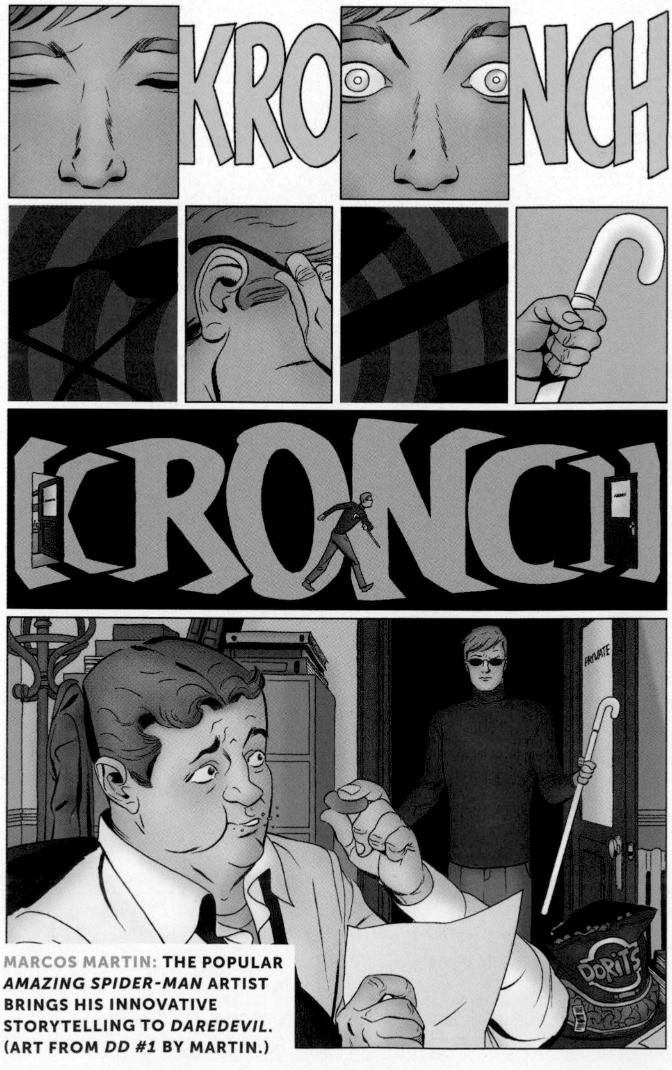
KRO
NCH
KRONCH

MARCOS MARTIN: THE POPULAR *AMAZING SPIDER-MAN* ARTIST BRINGS HIS INNOVATIVE STORYTELLING TO *DAREDEVIL*. (ART FROM *DD #1* BY MARTIN.)

OPENING THE SKETCHBOOK

DAREDEVIL'S PAOLO RIVERA

BY DUGAN TRODGLEN
DESIGN BY RODOLFO MURAGUCHI

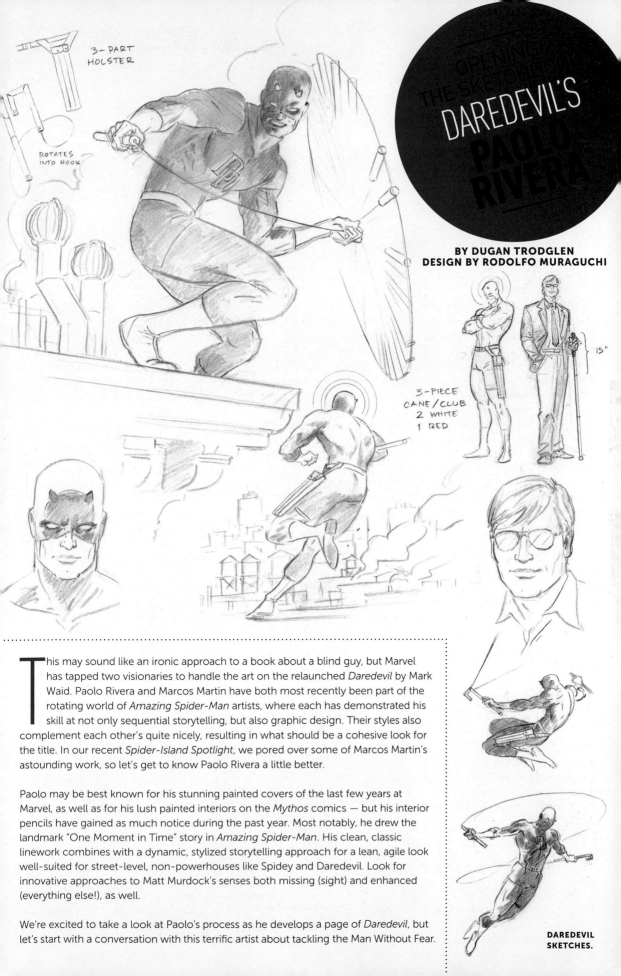

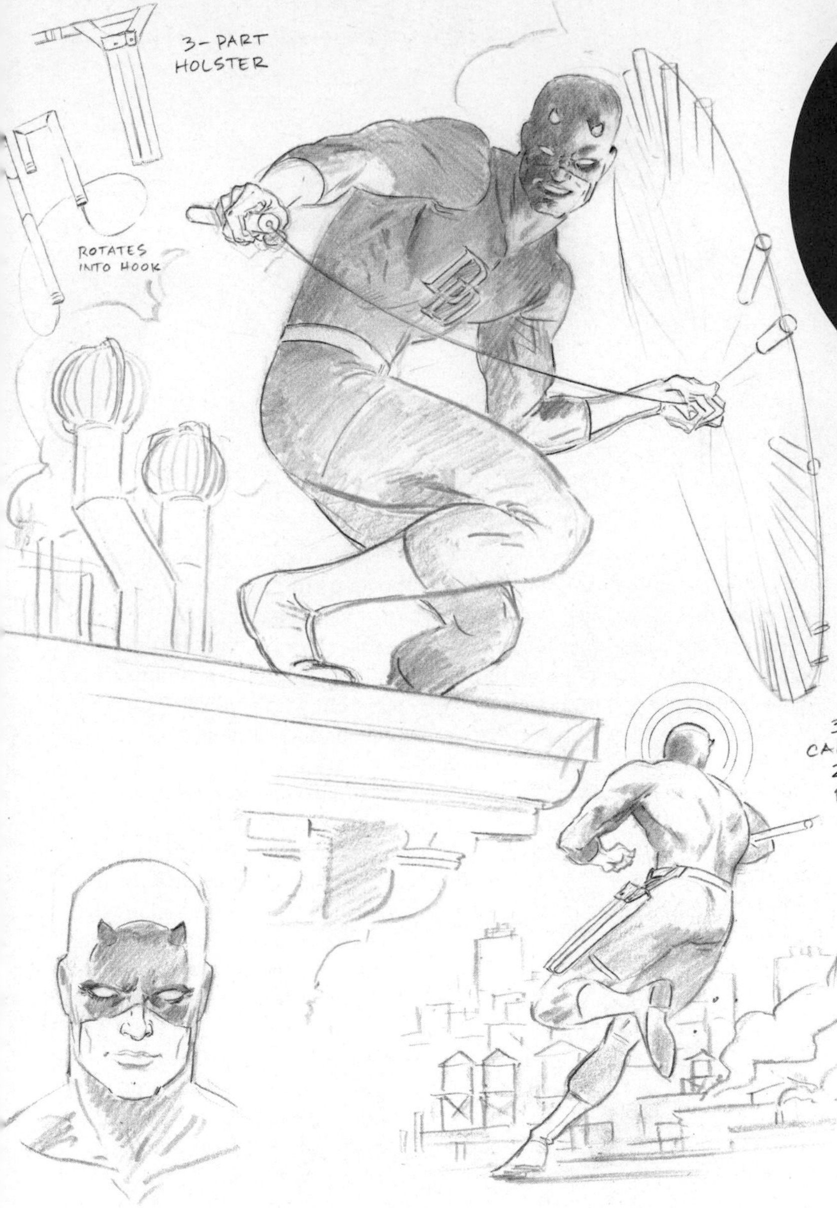
3-PART HOLSTER
ROTATES INTO HOOK

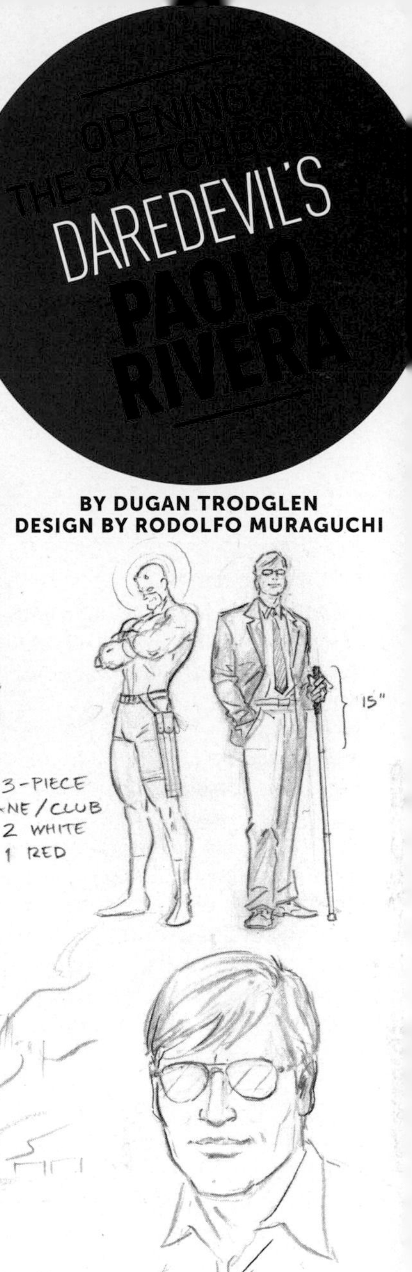
3-PIECE CANE / CLUB 2 WHITE 1 RED
15"

This may sound like an ironic approach to a book about a blind guy, but Marvel has tapped two visionaries to handle the art on the relaunched *Daredevil* by Mark Waid. Paolo Rivera and Marcos Martin have both most recently been part of the rotating world of *Amazing Spider-Man* artists, where each has demonstrated his skill at not only sequential storytelling, but also graphic design. Their styles also complement each other's quite nicely, resulting in what should be a cohesive look for the title. In our recent *Spider-Island Spotlight*, we pored over some of Marcos Martin's astounding work, so let's get to know Paolo Rivera a little better.

Paolo may be best known for his stunning painted covers of the last few years at Marvel, as well as for his lush painted interiors on the *Mythos* comics — but his interior pencils have gained as much notice during the past year. Most notably, he drew the landmark "One Moment in Time" story in *Amazing Spider-Man*. His clean, classic linework combines with a dynamic, stylized storytelling approach for a lean, agile look well-suited for street-level, non-powerhouses like Spidey and Daredevil. Look for innovative approaches to Matt Murdock's senses both missing (sight) and enhanced (everything else!), as well.

We're excited to take a look at Paolo's process as he develops a page of *Daredevil*, but let's start with a conversation with this terrific artist about tackling the Man Without Fear.

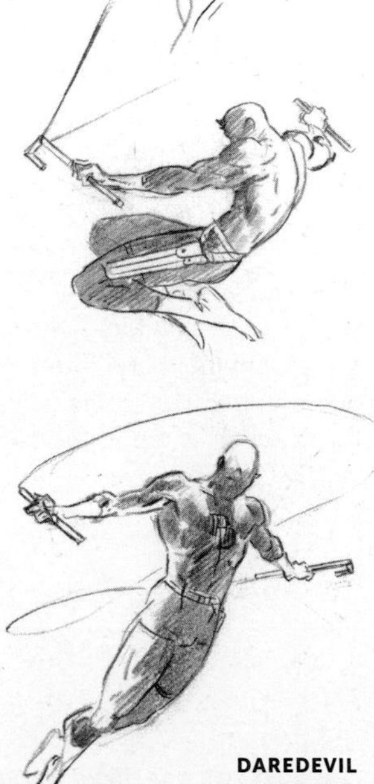

DAREDEVIL SKETCHES.

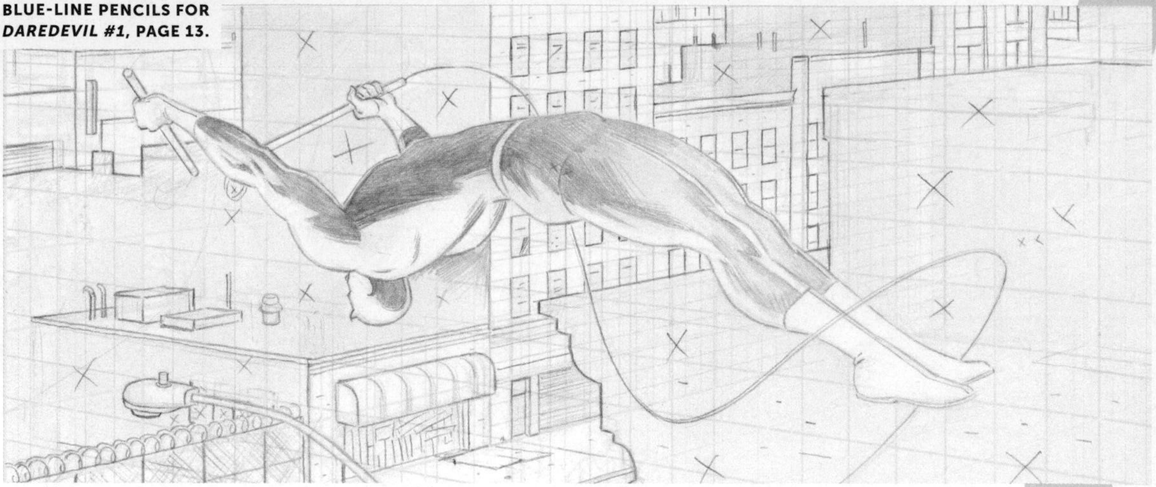

BLUE-LINE PENCILS FOR *DAREDEVIL #1*, PAGE 13.

You balance graphic design with your storytelling so well. Is there a lot of trial and error that goes with that?

Most definitely. That's the heart of the process. Each page represents a fixed area of real estate that can be divided and rearranged, but not exceeded. Every panel plunders space from its roommates, so the goal is to achieve some kind of optimum balance that allows each to shine in its own way. Sometimes it's a breeze, and other times it's a fight to the death. Either way, I'm the referee who has to avoid getting punched.

Practically speaking, the method involves a host of tiny thumbnail sketches that are indecipherable to anyone but me. Once a particular composition and point of view is resolved for each panel, then the entire collection is composed into a coherent whole. It's sort of a divide-and-conquer strategy.

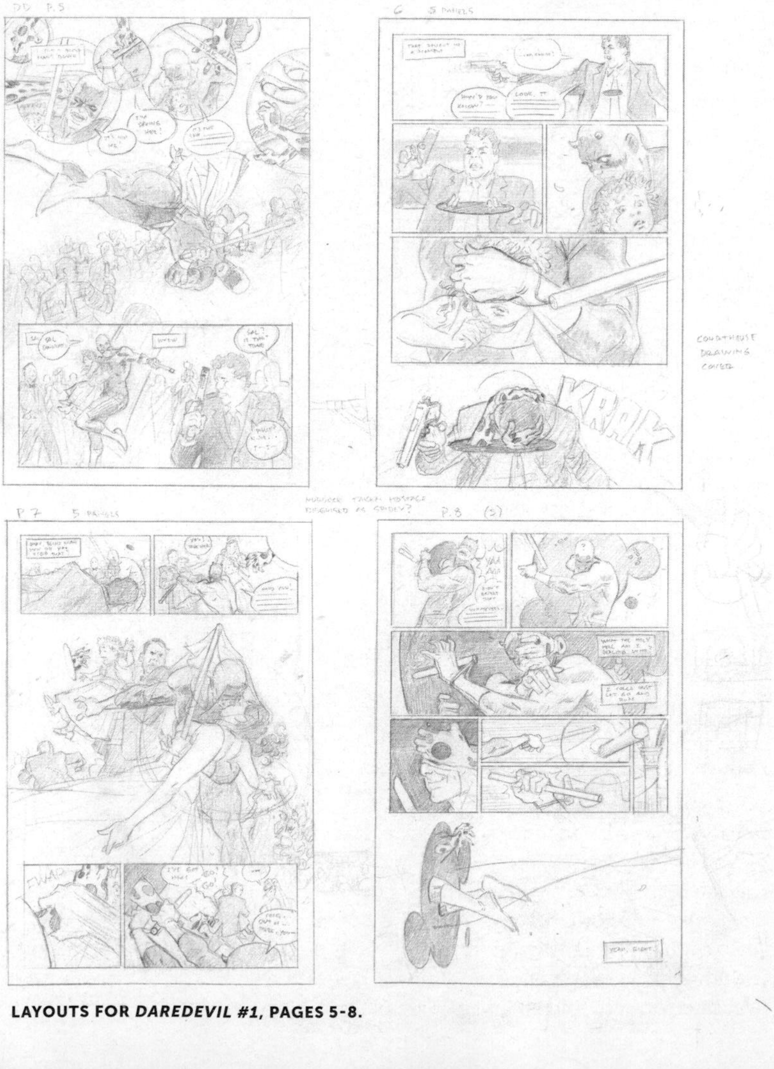

LAYOUTS FOR *DAREDEVIL #1*, PAGES 5-8.

You, Marcos and Mark have embraced the challenge of visually representing Matt Murdock's perception of the world, from how you present his radar sense to capturing his other enhanced senses. Is that one of the things that attracted you to the book?

Aside from the cover, I hadn't given it much thought prior to receiving the first script. Mark, on the other hand, wanted Matt's senses to be a prime focus of both the narrative and, as a result, the artwork. He challenged us to discover new ways to reveal what a blind man can see. We've come up with a couple different methods of representing his world, but hopefully more things will occur to us as we progress through the series.

What is your favorite example of this?

So far, I'd have to say page 6 from the first issue. It was a great example, morbid as it may be, of the collaboration that makes comics such a great medium. Mark had written a scene in which the Spot snaps the neck of a mobster by coming out of a portal on his chest. My first draft wasn't really what Mark had imagined, and he replied with a more specific explanation. This, in turn, spurred me to an

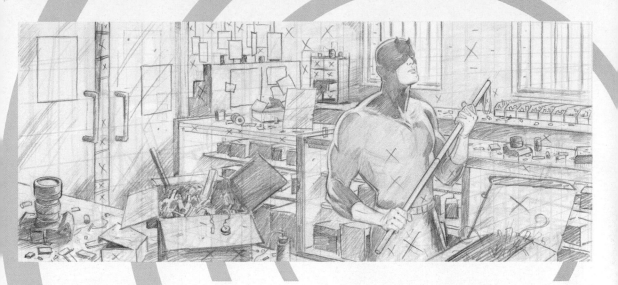

even more gruesome idea in which a second portal is formed on the mobster's back, making it look as though the Spot is clawing his way out of the body. Daredevil, helpless to save the doomed mobster, does what he can by shielding the eyes of the innocent child in his arms. By drawing this panel in "radar-vision," I hoped to drive home the point that Matt — unlike those of us blessed with vision — can't "close his eyes" to any horror.

You've done a lot of covers and painted interiors. How is your approach different doing a monthly, penciled comic?

Although the pace is frantic, the results are much more satisfying. Before, I would work for a week or more on a single page, whereas now I'm pumping out four pages a week — not a great deal by industry standards, but practically light speed for me. It's very satisfying because the progress is so tangible. And this is all before it's even been published. I'm looking forward to being part of a book that is on the stands on a regular basis.

We hear you have a one-of-a-kind inker these days. Tell us about him and how he got recruited.

My inker is Joe Rivera, my old man! I finally get to tell him what to do. How cool is that? But seriously, I couldn't be more proud of him.

While he's painted custom motorcycles for years, this is his first professional work in comics. We've been mulling this over for about a year, during which time I've

LAYOUTS FOR *DAREDEVIL #1*, PAGES 13-16.

been sending him practice pages of my inks in blue-line for him to ink over. As *Daredevil* — and its deadlines — became a reality, I realized that I literally couldn't do it without him, especially for the first three issues. And so I went

home to Florida for a month to train him and establish a good digital workflow, everything from printing and scanning to FTP uploads. He picked it all up immediately and hit the ground running. I owe that man a lot already — and now there's this.

PROCESS: DAREDEVIL

Paolo Rivera walks us through page 18 of Daredevil #1.

SO WHAT MAKES
IS HE A TARGET OF SOME SORT?
BECAUSE IF HE'S, WE HAVE THAT IN COMMON
SOMEONE'S —
TOO FAR AWAY

1 LAYOUT
"This is a 4 x 6" comprehensive sketch that I show to my editors and collaborators for approval. Captions are included to ensure the page reads fluidly."

4 BLUE-LINE PRINT
"My dad prints this out and inks directly over it. Borders and any finalized elements are printed in black."

5 FINISHED INKS
"He scans it and sends it back to me."

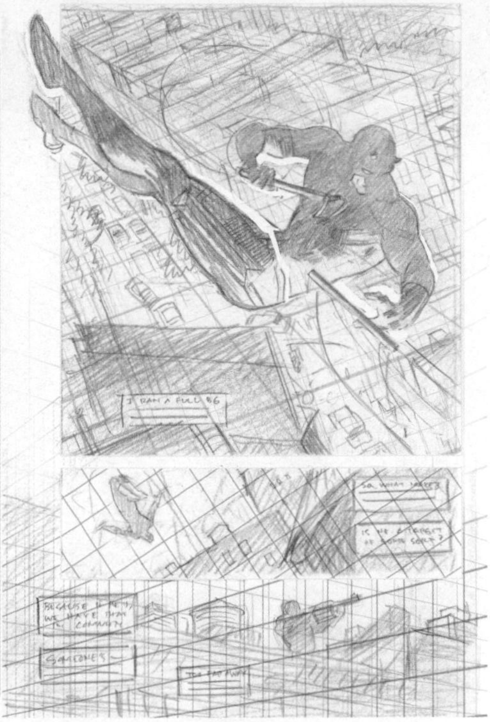

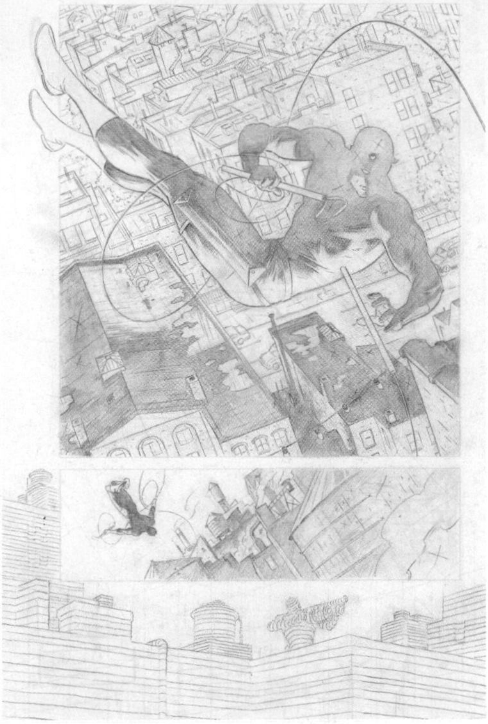

2 DIGITAL COMPOSITE
"Here I copy and paste the layout into my digital template and rearrange elements as needed. I then superimpose perspective guidelines to help with backgrounds and architecture. Borders are drawn in digitally to streamline the process."

3 PENCILS
"All the elements are fully rendered, Xs indicating solid black to the inker."

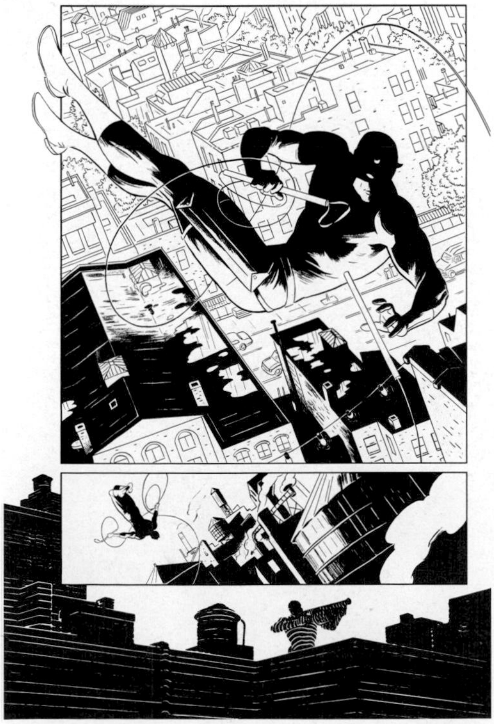

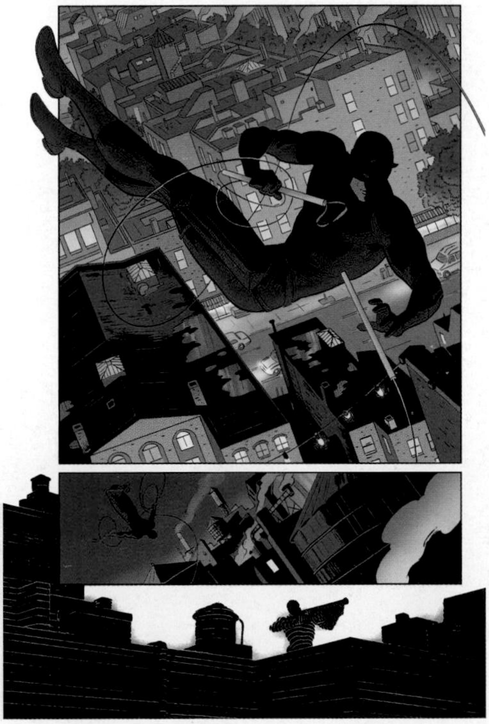

6 FINAL PRODUCT
"I make any final edits, including post-production transformations like the negative image in the last panel. This is turned in to my editor, who passes it on to the colorist."

7 PUBLISHED PAGE
Page 18 of *Daredevil #1!*

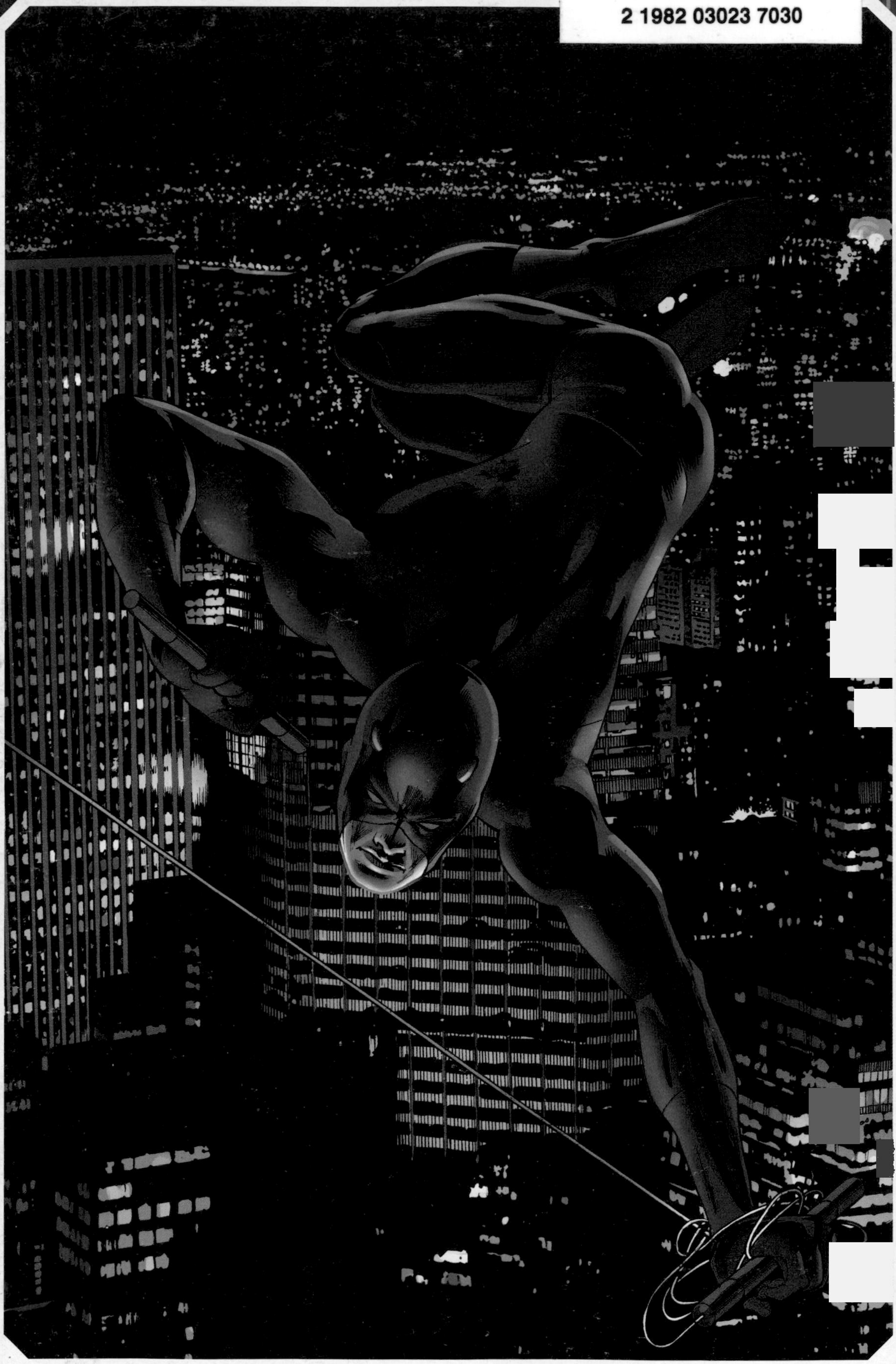

ISSUE #4 *VARIANT BY BRYAN HITCH, PAUL NEARY & PAUL MOUNTS*